Realism and Consensus in the English Novel

Realism and Consensus
in the English Novel

Elizabeth Deeds Ermarth

PRINCETON UNIVERSITY PRESS
PRINCETON, NEW JERSEY

Library of Congress Cataloging in Publication Data will be
found on the last printed page of this book

Publication of this book has been aided by a grant from
The Andrew W. Mellon Foundation

This book has been composed in Linotron Goudy
Clothbound editions of Princeton University Press books
are printed on acid-free paper, and binding materials are
chosen for strength and durability

Printed in the United States of America by
Princeton University Press, Princeton, New Jersey

FOR
Thomas Vargish

CONTENTS

CONTENTS

PREFACE

My discussion of realism focuses primarily on the realistic novel, but it extends beyond the nineteenth century, the period in which the realistic novel flourished, and even beyond the scope of purely literary considerations. I assume that aesthetic forms reveal certain premises about human experience that are not exclusive to literature or even to art but common to a variety of modes and to a variety of disciplines. For example, the conception of time and space as common, neutral media is essential to empirical science as well as to verisimilitude in art. To establish the premises of realism, then, I resort to analogies with painting and to illustrations from geometry because the space intuitions evident in these arts provide suggestive new approaches to temporal realism in literature. By contrasting realistic with typological forms of art and by comparing different forms of realism I intend to locate the premises that are implied by realistic conventions.

In making such comparisons, I necessarily leap over centuries. I assume that premise and convention can best be illustrated by contrast, and that changes in premise and convention involve homeostatic cultural shifts that cannot be perceived except on a large scale. So, for example, while there are important differences between quattrocento painting and nineteenth-century literature, they are less significant for my purposes than what unites them. The informative contrast lies between medieval and post-Renaissance art rather than between two forms of realism, however widely separated in time. By looking at literary realism in such a context and by using necessarily generalized terms, I wish to locate the realistic novel in relation to a wider historical and intellectual tradition.

To summarize my theoretical discussion, I argue that fictional realism is an aesthetic form of consensus, its touchstone being the agreement between the various viewpoints made available by a text. To the extent that all points of view summoned by the text agree, to the extent that they converge upon the "same" world, that text maintains the consensus of realism; to the extent that such agreement remains unsupported or becomes impossible, to that extent the realistic effect is compromised. It is not only the presence of points of view that confers verisimilitude; it is their consensus alone that homogenizes the medium of experience and thus objectifies a common world.

Considered as a form of consensus, realism belongs to the mainstream of humanistic tradition since the Renaissance. Part One of this book (Chapters One, Two, and Three) takes up the dominant modern idea of time as it has developed since the Renaissance, and specifies its implications for an entire view of consciousness. The subsequent discussion (Chapters Four through Seven and the Epilogue) traces changes in realistic conventions using six major English novelists: Defoe, Richardson, Austen, Dickens, George Eliot and James. My purpose in each chapter is to clarify both the special powers of realistic conventions and also their particular limitations. I use *realistic* as a descriptive term, not an evaluative one, and I do not suggest that the changes in realism from Defoe to James represent some teleological development. These interpretive chapters dispel, I hope, any lingering superstition that realistic conventions are impoverished. One of my central themes, stated most succinctly in Chapter Three ("The Narrator as Nobody") concerns the increasing importance of the narrator as mediating consciousness in the realistic economy.

In explaining and extending my theoretical argument I do not intend to define realism absolutely, to impose prescriptive terms, or even to find a purely realistic novel. In exploring the relation between form and value, what interest me are questions of emphasis and degree, and of the way changes in degree become actual and even radical changes in kind of thought. Eventually I want to determine the extent to which any novel subscribes to realist premises by using realist techniques, and to what extent any novel qualifies those techniques and so limits those premises. Some novels and narratives (*Paradise Lost, Pilgrim's Progress, Tris-*

tram *Shandy*, *Finnegans Wake*, *Hopscotch*, *Ada*, *The Faerie Queene*, the *Iliad*, to name a few) go about their business without depending on realistic conventions at all, or doing so parodically. In seeking to define the powers of realistic conventions I assume that realism is one convention, but not the only one.

In approaching such a vexed matter as the meaning of *realism* I naturally encounter problems of usage. Even though recent debate about realism has focused on the connection between convention and value, this new clarity has not dispelled a profound terminological confusion. Usage of *realism* differs widely depending upon what qualities a writer, often casually, isolates as essential to realism. Some familiar qualities of fictional realism, for example, are chronology, particularity, interiority, viewpoint, and everyday subject matter. While these usages do all partially describe realism, what they have in common has remained unclear. Furthermore, different discussions also create an odd fluidity between *realism* and other terms like *mimesis*, *narrative*, and *novel*. Sometimes *novel* and *narrative* include all fiction, at other times they exclude the likes of *Finnegans Wake* or *Ada*. Sometimes *narrative* generalizes what seems a more limited definition of realistic narrative.

Those recent studies that introduce new terminology in an attempt to sophisticate the mechanical language of point-of-view criticism sometimes create new problems of association and recall. Admittedly *omniscient narrator* and *distance* are inadequate terms, but the mind quails before such substitutions as *heterodiegetic*. Why *analeptic* instead of *flashback* or *proleptic* instead of *anticipation*? Does *narrativity* describe anything? These problems arise partly from translation, partly from the need to avoid the language of empiricism. But the enterprise, presumably, is to restore capacity to language and not so to reflect its arbitrariness as to become incomprehensible. Structural and semiotic criticism has been especially responsible for a proliferation of linguistic paradigms and terminologies echoing each other inharmoniously, not to say dumbfoundingly, without seeming to take each other into account.

Apart from terminology, the major difficulty with many systematic approaches to literary realism is that they ignore history and, in so doing, tend toward a taxonomy that reduces the importance of linear succession. This is true regardless of allegiance to structural or semiotic theory. Seymour Chatman's *Story and Discourse* and Wayne Booth's *Rhetoric of Fiction* both search for the units of narrative or for the positions of the narrator relative to character and reader. These searches achieve interesting and useful results, but only at a penalty—the penalty of necessarily speaking in terms of discrete states and architectonic combinations. The taxonomic approaches draw emphasis away from the treatment of linear time, which I consider the central problem of realistic fiction. Among the relatively few historical discussions of realism, Ian Watt's exemplary *The Rise of the Novel* stands out for its combination of theoretical and historical problems. Discussions of the novel like Lukács' *Theory of the Novel* and *Realism in Our Time* (despite their historical schematism), and more recently George Levine's *The Realistic Imagination* and Michael Holquist and Caryl Emerson's translation of Bakhtin's *Dialogic Imagination*, are discussions that accommodate the diachronic qualities of literary realism better than does criticism derived from structuralist and semiotic categories.

The concern of semiotic criticism with "codes" and with modes of "discourse" clearly has value for a form like realistic fiction that makes so much of the plurality of worlds. But where semiotics reduces the continuous to the discrete, the realistic novel reverses that direction, moving against discreteness and toward the reconciliation of divergent codes. My discussion is thus doubly diachronic, involving historically based definitions concerning literary convention and also privileging the temporal dimension of fiction. My own methodology thus reflects the assumptions I discuss, and deliberately so, in order to allow the realistic convention to speak in its own voice as much as possible. I have learned from various critical approaches—history of ideas, phenomenological and reader-response criticism, formalism, semiotics, and structuralism—but neither my method nor my vocabulary belongs exclusively to any of these.

The term *realism* inevitably raises questions about referentiality and about the status of language. Realism, along with the values it presupposes, has entered the age of suspicion, and with this passage it has lost the linguistic innocence it may once have claimed (although, as George Levine suggests, *naive realism* is largely a critical fiction). The language that appears referential, innocently pointing toward an objective world beyond it, can now be seen as opaque, self-reflexive, gesturing toward its own principles of operation. The referential word is a means; the reflexive word is an end. It will be clear from my discussion that I find both referential and reflexive functions at work in realism. This is an old problem, the reality of the word, and the current debate does humanists serious disservice when it urges separation of these two functions. Competition in critical discourse between referential and reflexive functions generates false problems of interpretation and masks a deeper problem, the one that stems from the tendency to universalize and naturalize one or the other as a norm for literature. It is not enough that a norm of reference (or reflexion) temporarily be assumed; it must be made absolute. Thus we have *realisms* of various types, such as *allegorical realism*. Realism becomes the property of all great art. It follows that nonrealistic art cannot be great. The same result occurs when self-reflexiveness becomes the valuable property. Used in this way either aesthetic norm becomes for the critic what the market seems to be for some economists: a means for naturalizing what would otherwise appear artificial and value-laden.

Realistic fiction is not the only kind, any more than representational politics is the only kind. But the difference between one kind of convention and others is no neutral matter. The values implied by realistic conventions are not immutable, eternal, grounded in the nature of things and beyond human responsibility or choice. They are grounded in collective assertion and are limited historically. By considering the premises of realism I intend to denaturalize them, to unhinge them from absolutes, and thus to restore them to their historical element.

ACKNOWLEDGMENTS

From the generative stages of this study down to the final publication I have benefited from the work of many people, especially those whose own high standards for scholarship and intellectual accountability have been so fortifying an influence. I owe to Owen Jenkins, Stanley Fish, and Sara Klarén some intangible but essential debts for helping, either by teaching or by talk, to formulate the basic problem; and a similar debt to publications by Leo Bersani and the late William J. Ivins, Jr. For valuable comments and references, and for reading parts of the manuscript in various drafts, I am grateful to Jonathan Culler, Hoyt Duggan, Avrom Fleishman, Gordon S. Haight, Katherine Hayles, and Charles Wood.

Several people read the entire manuscript and helped shape the final result. Robert Caserio, John P. Farrell, and George Levine read with generous comprehension and pitiless red pencils, and I am indebted to them for many improvements. Patricia Spacks has been unfailingly munificent with definitive suggestions and timely encouragement. Thomas Vargish has thought through this book with me, has shared his knowledge and his time, and has been tough-minded and considerate through one draft after another.

A condensed version of the first two chapters appeared in *Critical Inquiry* and parts of Chapter Seven appeared in *Nineteenth-Century Fiction* and *Victorian Newsletter*; the editors of these journals kindly gave permission to use this copyrighted material. The National Endowment for the Humanities provided support for writing during the summer of 1980. Elizabeth Carroll, Katherine Raab, and the University of Maryland, Baltimore County, supplied invaluable assistance with the manuscript. My editors at Princeton University Press, Jerry Sherwood and Joanna Hitchcock, have been expert and resourceful, and I am grateful to them for their careful work and many kindnesses.

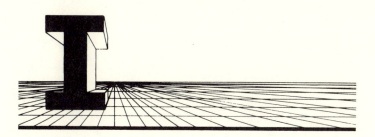

PERSPECTIVE
AND CONSENSUS

CHAPTER ONE

The Premises of Realism

Realistic conventions belong to a cultural tradition that took its direction from Renaissance humanism. Today the changing fortunes of realism are registering seismic cultural activity. Harry Levin puts the case succinctly: "Historically, as in other ways, the realistic approach has been exceptional and there have been hints at many levels that its epoch, which began with the Renaissance, will soon have receded into the past." The ideological import of such change has not been lost on critics who perceive the connection between realistic conventions on the one hand and, on the other, certain liberal and humanist traditions which still have enormous practical importance. and with which realism shares fundamental assumptions.[1] In Part One, I explore the connections between realism

[1] Harry Levin, *The Gates of Horn: A Study of Five French Realists* (New York: Oxford University Press, 1963), p. 468. Even critics like Robbe-Grillet and Lukács, who disagree on so much else, agree perfectly on this connection between realism and humanism. See Alain Robbe-Grillet, *Essays for a New Novel*, trans. Richard Howard (New York: Grove Press, 1965), especially the chapter on "Nature, Humanism, Tragedy," pp. 49-76; Georg Lukács, *Realism in Our Time*, trans. John and Necke Mander (New York: Harper and Row, 1971), especially "The Ideology of Modernism," pp. 17-46. Robert Scholes writes of the "ideological watershed" ending the epoch of realism and humanism in "On Realism and Genre," *Novel*, 2, no. 3 (Spring 1969), 269. Milan Kundera in the *New York Times Book Review* (8 January 1978) associates "the novel" with traditions of tolerance. W. J. Harvey, describing the liberal connections of "the novel," calls

3

and its *episteme* in order to discover, without lobbying for or against realism, what the powers and limitations of this aesthetic convention actually are.

My first three chapters provide an extended answer to the question: what does depth in fiction have in common with pictorial depth? We know what it means to speak of depth in space, but what, if anything, does that have to do with depth of character? We know what it means to speak of "depth perception" (meaning visual power) and "depth of perception" (meaning mental power) but what, if anything, do these ordinary locations have to do with depth in realism? How is such depth possible in the temporal medium of literature? What does the narrator's controlling perspective have to do with the illusion of depth? And, most importantly, what values does the art of depth presuppose and confirm? In answering these questions I will begin by contrasting the realistic conventions evident in Renaissance art with earlier typological models, and then I will consider the use of perspective in time and the consequences of such a usage for individual consciousness.

The consensus of realism, I will argue, produces in literature a rationalization of consciousness analogous to the rationalization of sight evident in realistic painting.[2] When quattrocento painters began to use the single vanishing point to organize their pictures,

---

it "the distinct art form of liberalism," meaning "not a political view or even a mode of social and economic organization but rather a state of mind" (*Character and the Novel* [Ithaca: Cornell University Press, 1965], p. 24; see also p. 133). Robert Alter, like Levin, sees nineteenth-century realism as exceptional in the history of the novel (*Partial Magic: The Novel as a Self-Conscious Genre* [Berkeley and London: University of California Press, 1975]). Most useful essays on the connection between technique and value are Robbe-Grillet, *Essays for a New Novel* and Leo Bersani's two essays, "Realism and the Fear of Desire," *A Future for Astyanax: Character and Desire in Literature* (Boston and Toronto: Little, Brown & Co., 1969), and "The Subject of Power," *Diacritics* (September 1977), pp. 2-21.

[2] The "rationalization of sight" is William Ivins Jr.'s phrase. In formulating my basic thesis about realism I am thoroughly indebted to his two charming and irreverent studies: *On the Rationalization of Sight, with an Examination of Three Renaissance Texts on Perspective*, Paper no. 8 (New York: Metropolitan Museum of Art, 1938; rpt. Da Capo, New York, 1973); and *Art and Geometry: A Study in Space Intuitions* (1946; rpt. New York: Dover Publications, Inc., 1964).

they made their chief formal principle the point of view of a single, fixed spectator: a graphic illustration long before Descartes of that primacy of individual experience over received truths that characterizes realism and that has its philosophical analogues in Cartesian epistemology. While quattrocento realism belongs in significant ways to an early Renaissance, intelligible more in terms of the twelfth century than the nineteenth, nevertheless the fifteenth-century appearance of depth in painting testifies to the presence of a cultural change with important implications for realistic fiction. Both forms of realism attempt comparable kinds of verisimilitude. Even the critical terminology proper to Renaissance realism—point of view, distance, horizon, depth—applies as well to realistic novels.

My thesis in this chapter can be stated briefly as follows: in realism, identity becomes series-dependent, which is to say that it becomes abstract, removed from direct apprehension to a hidden dimension of depth. In speaking of realistic identity I use the term *identity* to mean the oneness or the invariant structure by which we recognize a thing, by which we judge it under varying conditions to be the same.[3] This conception of identity, with all it implies about the regularity of nature and the possibilities of knowledge, belongs to an empirical epistemology that was relatively unimportant to the Middle Ages and is being radically modified today; but it was current through the otherwise diverse period from the Renaissance through the nineteenth century. It is a conception of identity so obvious to us that we have ceased to see it as the convention it is, but it was not obvious in the Renaissance, and it took a long time to become common sense.

[3] In classical mathematics two forms that were congruent achieved "identity." In modern mathematics identity in this sense cannot properly be said to exist at all, since the invariant qualities that constitute identity cannot be perceived except in a whole series of different aspects, and so the form of a thing thus "identified" is not congruent with any particular instance in the series that produced it. Properly speaking, perhaps, "identity" should always wear quotes in the era of humanistic and realistic premises to signal its problematic nature. I will avoid this typographical awkwardness, but in speaking of the modern period, and of novels in particular, I use the term "identity" in its new sense, as referring to something that is series-dependent and incongruent with any particular instance.

5

Discontinuity in Medieval Art

The unities of field and of identity that we have learned to take for granted and that are assumed in certain kinds of artistic, mathematical, or historical formulation have no significant role in medieval historiography, mathematics, and art. In those medieval disciplines, for example, time and space were conceived as discontinuous. A medieval historian treated time as one single field of influences that was without significant chronological organization.[4] He saw in the record of events no unity of flow, no continuity of series, no inner dynamic that would give meaning to distinctions between past, present, and future. Within this static and discontinuous historical field the historian could draw interpretive generalizations from typological paradigms which would reveal congruences between events widely separated in time, without regard for what we would call their historical context. The successful French king, for example, was one who approximated the condition of Charlemagne in every detail of his legendary achievement, however remote Charlemagne's immediate concerns might have been from those of his successor.[5] The unifying principles

[4] See Gabrielle Spiegel, "Political Utility in Medieval Historiography: A Sketch," *History and Theory*, 14, no. 3 (1975), 322.

There were many developments in the Middle Ages that resemble the historical awakening during the Renaissance, enough in fact to make the term *renaissance* a locus of debate. Father Chenu writes of a new awareness of "universalism" in time, "a sense of continuity; the definition of constant causes this side of transcendent providence" (*Nature, Man and Society in the Twelfth Century* [Chicago: University of Chicago Press, 1968], p. 178), and Eugene Vance points to a new "consciousness of structure" in the twelfth century and in twelfth-century narrative, a development he associates with the resurgence of Aristotle and of logic ("Pas de Trois: Narrative, Hermeneutics and Structure in Medieval Poetics," in Mario Valdes and Owen Miller, eds., *Interpretation of Narrative* [Toronto: University of Toronto Press, 1965], p. 128). But logic was still not temporal logic, and the "law of continuity" formulated by Aristotle did not, as Lovejoy notes, assert "that the qualitative difference of things must similarly constitute linear or continuous series . . . still less that they constitute a single continuous series" (*The Great Chain of Being* [New York: Harper and Bros., 1960], pp. 55-56).

[5] Gabrielle Spiegel, "The Reditus Regni ad Stirpem Karoli Magni: A New Look," *French Historical Studies*, 7, no. 2 (Fall 1971), 169-70. This is what Auerbach calls "medieval realism" (i.e., the medieval break with the Platonic doctrine of levels, which produced "completely different results" from the parallel

of history were past patterns that repeated themselves in the arena provided by time, and the interpretation of even the most trivial action could only be sought in some typological pattern. Hence the mystic, Henry Suso, carefully eats three-quarters of an apple for each person of the Trinity and one-quarter for the love of Mary, who gave her son an apple.[6] The difference between a quarter of an apple and a person of the Trinity is irrelevant to the simple numerical congruence between them.

This is not at all to say that medieval historians were too naive to perceive time as sequential, although many historians were perhaps less sophisticated than St. Augustine; rather, it is to say that they had good reasons for perceiving time as discontinuous. Even Augustine's reflections on time and memory emphasize the paltry and perishable nature of temporal things. His awareness that measuring time means measuring mental impressions (*Confessions*, XI, xxvii) does not elevate those impressions to the status we give them. In fact, he says, "we can affirm that time *is* only in that it tends towards not-being" (*Confessions*, XI, xiv, p. 271). He emphasizes the paradoxical nature of time and memory. "Thus it seems to me that time is certainly extendedness—but I do not know what it is extendedness of: probably of the mind itself" (XI, xxvi, p. 281).[7] This intimacy between time and consciousness, given a positive value, becomes primary in realistic narrative; Augustine, however, gives it a negative value. His investigation of time and consciousness is "a study in contingency, finiteness, creatureliness, dependency, incompleteness, imperfec-

---

Renaissance break). In this medieval conception "an occurrence on earth signifies not only itself but at the same time another, which it predicts or confirms, without prejudice to the power of its concrete reality here and now. The connection between occurrences is not regarded as primarily a chronological or causal development·but as a oneness within the divine plan, of which all occurrences are parts and reflections. Their direct earthly connection is of secondary importance, and often their interpretation can altogether dispense with any knowledge of it" (*Mimesis: The Representation of Reality in Western Literature*, trans. Willard Trask [Princeton, N.J.: Princeton University Press, 1953], p. 490).

[6] Johan Huizinga, *The Waning of the Middle Ages*, trans. F. Hopman (London: Edward Arnold and Co., 1937), pp. 136-37.

[7] *The Confessions of St. Augustine*, trans. F. J. Sheed (New York: Sheed and Ward, 1943), pp. 283, 271. All references are to this edition.

tion—a study of the limitation of being that characterizes *any* finite entity, that entity which *is*, but which is not He Who Is."[8] The *discontinuity* of earthly life has positive value for Augustine because it throws the mind, with its need for relation and completion, on the superhuman Creator.

Discontinuous time cannot support modern conceptions of personality. The medieval writer, according to Gabrielle Spiegel, treated personality as "a collection of attributes with more or less independent status."[9] When Henry Suso renders homage to a beggar woman because she is a type of the Virgin, he is making an identification, not a similitude, and he does this by selecting one attribute of the beggar and one of the Virgin. Only that one attribute is explained by the typological reference. The fact that the woman is a beggar may be capable of some other typological reading but is irrelevant to the typological identification between her and the Virgin that is made on the basis of their sex and is absolute. Instead of forcing on the beggar woman a demand for consistency that would purchase unity by reduction, he considers her womanliness quite apart from her beggarliness. With the beggar woman as with the whole historical field, discrepancies between proximate instances were no cause for alarm because proximity held no value. One detail might be referred to one prototype and the next detail to another without any sense of contradiction, and this could be done because the valid references were vertical, intersecting the field of human experience at every turn and separating it into discrete instances that had no interesting relations to each other.[10]

---

[8] Robert Jordan, "Time and Contingency in St. Augustine," in R. A. Markus, ed., *Augustine: A Collection of Critical Essays* (Garden City, N.Y.: Doubleday and Co., Inc., 1972), p. 257.

[9] Spiegel, "Political Utility," 319-21.

[10] In a modern instance, Seymour Chatman argues for redefining the conception of "character" in fiction "as a paradigm of traits, using 'trait' in the sense of 'relatively stable or abiding personal quality.' " His reasoning is that "the functional or *actaniel* theory is inadequate" (*Story and Discourse: Narrative Structure in Fiction and Film* [Ithaca: Cornell University Press, 1978], pp. 126, 131). See also Michel Foucault's discussion of "similitude" or "resemblance" as opposed to "representation" (in my terms, "congruence" as opposed to "similitude") in *The*

8

The great literary exemplar of typological thinking is Don Quixote, who as the Knight of the Sad Countenance strives in every gesture to live up to some type of the knight-errant such as the well-known Amadis of Gaul. The fact that this type had little to do with Don Quixote's immediate context is the basis for the endless series of jokes at his expense, jokes that only seem funny to someone more committed to the chronological than to the typological habit of mind. Don Quixote is wonderful partly because he is, in Lukács's term, "distanceless,"[11] out of synchrony with his time and its set of meanings. Such typological thinking in historiography does not by any means disappear with the Renaissance, but it does yield priority to linear, chronological thinking. The more humanism proved to be a solvent for scholasticism, the more typological thinking lost its primacy.

Like medieval historiography, medieval painting emphasizes discrete, discontinuous forms, and it devalues continuity or relationship between proximate instances. In medieval paintings there is a near-absolute discontinuity between the figures and the tripartite or patterned backgrounds, even those backgrounds that have some resemblance to the natural environment.[12] The elements in the pictorial foreground are treated separately, often with attention to detail, and the artist pays "little attention to anything in the way of a systematic spatial relation between ob-

---

Order of Things: An Archaeology of the Human Sciences (translation of *Les Mots et Les Choses*) (New York: Random House Vintage Book, 1973), p. 28. For a suggestion of ways in which even duration can be made discontinuous and hierarchical, see Georges Poulet's discussion of "the architecture of medieval duration" (*Studies in Human Time*, trans. Elliott Coleman [New York: Harper and Row, 1959], p. 7).

[11] Lukács, *The Theory of the Novel*, trans. Anna Bostock (Cambridge, Mass.: M.I.T. Press, 1971), pp. 101-104.

[12] See Miriam Bunim, *Space in Medieval Painting and the Forerunners of Perspective* (New York: Columbia University Press, 1940), especially her discussion of the heritage from classical painting of a disunified spatial field, p. 178. Even Roman painting, despite its suggestion of depth by convergence and diminution, was nevertheless dominated by "planes parallel to the picture plane and by isolated objects and groups of objects," an effect uncongenial to perspective painting, where the represented planes intersect the picture plane.

9

jects."[13] This spatial discontinuity radically undermines the importance of the spectator. "If an object is to be represented so as to be optically recognisable, it must be represented from somewhere. We therefore cannot eliminate the spectator entirely." But the spectator is of little importance. There is "no countenance to the idea that is the essence and foundation of converging European perspective—the idea that we are more distant from one part than from another." We get a minimum of subjectivity and of optical form and a maximum of essential qualities. "A square thing is square, a round thing is round; no further concession is made to the spectator." Any implied spectator in fact has a fractured existence, somewhat like the personality described by Huizinga: "there is no point of view at which the spectator is supposed to stand," and so the viewer must be imagined as stationed in front of whatever surface is presented, i.e., simultaneously in several different places.[14] The arrangements depend upon conventions that have informative value or ornamental value, more like a tryptich than like the spatial continuities of realistic painting.

This spatial discontinuity gives primary value to detail. If you must know a thing not through measuring its relationships to neighboring things or to similar things but by referring it to various appropriate prototypes, then you pay close attention to its discrete features. The habit "of accentuating every detail, of developing every thought and every image to the end, of giving concrete form to every concept of the mind"[15] belonged to a general habit of mind intent more upon congruence than upon continuity. Even spaces were considered objects in themselves, and each space was thought to end at the edge of a neighboring object.

[13] Samuel Y. Edgerton, Jr., *The Renaissance Rediscovery of Linear Perspective* (New York: Basic Books, Inc., 1975), p. 21.

[14] The passages cited here apply substantially to medieval painting but they are quoted from Wilfrid H. Wells's instructive book on *Perspective in Early Chinese Painting* (London: Edward Goldstone, Ltd., 1935), pp. 18-21. This excellent little book reaches frequently to consider the premises of art, and suggests some interesting comparisons between Chinese painting and that of medieval Europe.

[15] Huizinga, *Waning*, pp. 255-56.

Such spatial intuitions allowed little opportunity for the modern idea of space as a homogeneous medium populated by mobile objects whose identifying structures are independent of location. In the world of "watertight categories and discontinuities" which the Middle Ages inherited from the Greeks, every object has its discrete form in its discrete location.[16] Form and position are not relative, as they are implicitly in realism, but absolute.

Turning from the temporal discontinuities of history and the spatial discontinuities of painting, we find in the temporal medium of medieval narrative a similar absence of systematic relationships. The interlaced narrative structure is full of action, full of incident, and without slack time. Its episodes remain discrete, unconfined and uncoordinated by systematic temporal or spatial relationships. It has "a richness and multiplicity of form, a musical technique which has nothing to do with organic unity."[17] Even when time is thematically important, it has no formal importance and is largely ritual time rather than chronological or historical time. The *Morte d'Arthur* or the *Song of Roland* baffles modern readers, who assume that a narrative of events is a *temporal* sequence without recognizing that there are other kinds of sequence, such as rhetorical ones.[18]

This absence of temporal continuity, as Stanley Fish says, is no mere "incompatibility of aesthetics," but rather the difference between one epistemological framework and another.

A Christian plot, in the sense that there is one, is haphazard, random in its order, heedless of visible cause and effect, episodic, inconclusive, consisting of events that are both reversible and interchangeable. This is more, however, than an incompatibility of aesthetics; for the logic of narrative, of sequential causality, is the logic of human freedom and choice: the free-

---

[16] Ivins, *Art and Geometry*, p. 79.

[17] Pamela Gradon, *Form and Style in Early English Literature* (London: Methuen & Co., Ltd., 1971), pp. 150-51. She also touches on the importance of congruence in distinguishing medieval from mimetic narrative (pp. 30-31).

[18] Eugene Vinaver makes a similar point about the baffling way that the *Song of Roland* "triumphantly" discards the "twin principles of rational and temporal motivation" (*The Rise of Romance* [Oxford: The Clarendon Press, 1971]), p. 10.

11

dom to take a step that is determining and the choice to be a character in an action that is either fortunate or unfortunate. Within a Christian framework, however, the plot is fortunate by divine fiat, and one reaches a point not because he chooses, but because he has been chosen, that is, redeemed.[19]

Such figural and rhetorical organization dominates medieval narrative time, competing at all levels with the chronological, linear, or historical possibilities of the sequence. When the paradigmatic place of anything has this kind of ontological importance, change and mobility have limited or even negative value.

Chaucer plays masterfully in the *Canterbury Tales* with the tension between these two competing imperatives. His pilgrims are moving along the road to Canterbury, but even that motion has typological significance; they do get out of line, in the sense of that proper hierarchical arrangement according to social place which is implied in the General Prologue, but that disorderliness is only amusing when it is tightly contained. The altercation between the Pardoner and the Host threatens disaster, especially since the Host is the democratically elected arbiter for the journey, and disorder is only averted by the intervention of the Knight, whose authority implicitly depends on his social place. In the *Canterbury Tales* each pilgrim is framed off from the others, each concrete, irreducible, faithful to type. To the extent that any one character exhibits the contradictory characteristics we would consider realistic, the character reveals irreligious and antisocial qualities that signify a disorder in the proper hierarchy of the soul. This is only part of a full response to the *Tales*, but a part important to a tension that is not merely "dramatic."

[19] "Sequence and Meaning," *To Tell A Story: Narrative Theory and Practice* (Los Angeles: William Andrews Clark Memorial Library, 1973), p. 74. The lived sequence of reading a sermon of Lancelot Andrews proceeds "from point to point, but in a progression that is not generating meaning but merely creating new spaces into which the meaning that is already there expands; the syntagmatic axis, in all of its manifestations—in discourse, in history, in time itself—is simply a succession of areas in which the paradigmatic equivalences are made manifest. Sequence is not causal "but additive" (pp. 67-72). See also Fish's critique of the "transgression" of sequential discourse in Roland Barthes (p. 60).

In Boccaccio and in More's *Utopia* there are kinds of dialogue that represent the realist impulse, but it is by no means clearly dominant. It is worth passing notice that the *Utopia* separates two functions that eventually appear united in realistic fiction: point of view and social structure. In Book I the introductory conversation at Cardinal Morton's house treats the ironies of viewpoint and the moral nuance of speech with utmost sophistication; in Book II Raphael's narrative treats a complete social structure, one that exists no place but in the mind. The practical fragment and the ideal of completeness remain pointedly separate. The temporal, historical world in Book I exists side by side with the timeless, idealized world of Book II, and the question of a bridge remains open. The obviously realistic elements in More's work are like fragments in search of a context, and the context offered is decidedly not an historical one. The case of *Utopia* is a fascinating example of a work that both uses and qualifies the new historical spirit, both uses and abandons techniques proper to realism. Despite such explorations, the prevailing medieval tendency in literature, as in painting and historiography, was "to isolate each thing as a special entity" with its own special relation to "the eternal verities"; things had their proper places "not in relation to each other, but to the center of the universe."[20]

Medieval art thus reflects intuitions about identity and relationship that Europe had inherited from the Greeks practically unmodified and that had received their mathematical statement in Euclidean geometry.[21] Where modern geometry would develop one proof for a series of different but similar figures, Greek geometry would develop a different proof for each discrete figure. Differences in the appearances of figures were considered unmediatable:

[20] Huizinga, *Waning*, p. 212; Edgerton, *Rediscovery*, p. 159.

[21] These intuitions, according to William Ivins, Jr., have the powers and limitations of their origins in tactile-muscular intuitions rather than in visual ones. For example, parallel lines converge to sight but not to touch. The fact that the Greeks had almost no descriptive theorems is testimony to their independence of visual intuitions (*Art and Geometry*).

By Euclidean geometry I mean the unmodified version as it existed before the Renaissance and not the modified versions taught today.

13

Every difference in the arrangement of the given and sought lines of a problem presents a new problem in regard to the proof; to every difference in the total appearance of a figure corresponds a difference in interpretation and deduction. A problem which modern synthetic geometry solves by a single construction, was analysed by Apollonius into more than eighty cases, differing only in position. The unity of the constructive principles of geometry is hidden by the specialization of its particular forms, of which each one is conceived as irreducible.[22]

Where the modern geometer thinks of discrete forms mainly in terms of their mutual relationships, the early Euclidean geometers, with their watertight categories and discontinuities, conceived a world without relation in which differences in the appearance of forms were absolute. This mathematical symbolization of Greek space intuitions reflects the view of a static, discontinuous universe that remained essentially unmodifed until the Renaissance.

In Homer's *Iliad*, a particularly good literary example of these intuitions, all explanations of human action refer eventually to *moira*, destiny, the way things are. The Erynes, or Spinners, have predetermined all things, human and natural things alike, in specific detail, and however much Achilles might delay his final appointment with Hektor, it would take place in exactly the way it was determined and no other. Achilles, Hektor, Diomedes, Ajax, each had their separate thread from the original spindle, and no change could be wrought on this *moira*, not even by the gods. Because each single figure in the *Iliad* has this separate destiny, its separate thread running back to the original center,

[22] Ernst Cassirer, *Substance and Function*, trans. Marie Swabey and William Swabey (New York: Dover Publications, Inc., 1953), p. 70 (published together with *Einstein's Theory of Relativity*). Ivins quotes this passage in *Art and Geometry*, p. 101. Cassirer credits to Descartes the insight that, for rational knowledge, no cognitive member can be "introduced as an entirely new element, but each must issue step by step from the earlier members according to a certain rule." This insight was, he says, the essential beginning of the "transformation of geometry in modern times."

14

no action by one character can essentially influence that of another. The great battle scenes present epic description first of one hero fighting, then of his opponent fighting and falling; we do not see the fight between them. That relationship, the "unity of the group in flow," which has become "the essential aspect of the world for modern eyes," is a relationship "to which the Greeks were blind."[23] For the Greek hero the most one could do in this life was to achieve the fullest possible momentary expression of one's whole being, as the warriors do in battle. Since he has no control over his destiny, the Greek hero has no reason to withhold his power, to save it up for some future time. Everything urges him to be fully manifest, and nothing brings out his full energy more brilliantly than mortal combat.

Though the field of Western art before the Renaissance is various and heterogeneous, its creations consistently give expression to this static and discontinuous world. So long as the gaps between different discrete instances cannot be mediated by similitude, as they are in realism, the emphasis in art remains on detail and concreteness. The gap between two similar appearances is a total difference; it is not even an abyss, as we might call it in our vocabulary of humanist nostalgia for unity, but rather a discrete manifestation with certain definition. No unity of field makes possible the conception of inner coherence necessary to the idea of self or, for that matter, to the presumption of uniformity in nature upon which modern science depends.

The Greek and medieval emphasis on discontinuity does not mean that they had no conception of unity, any more than our skeptical interest in particulars means that we have no universals. The medieval artist assumed a unified, finite, providential universe and then, wholeness being assumed, proceeded to make distinctions with ever-increasing refinement and nicety. In the scholastic method, whenever one met with an irreconcilable difference, one made another distinction, permitting it by making room for it with a new category.[24] The proper goal of any gen-

---

[23] Ivins, *Art and Geometry*, p. 15.

[24] For further discussion of medieval methods and medieval perceptual modes

eralization or theory was to save the appearances, to accommodate all particulars, with ever-new categories if need be, rather than to subsume different particulars into one category. By referring discontinuous particulars to typological paradigms, the medieval artist found the meaning of particulars *sub specie aeternitatis*, and any contradictions between species were left to the refinements of learned disputation.

The Rationalization of Sight

The realistic artist finds continuities where the medieval found absolute distinction. In realism the identity—and hence the meaning—of particulars is discovered horizontally, that is, through the similitudes discovered by comparing particular cases to each other. Objects that in medieval art presented themselves in the fullest possible detail and with few concessions to the logic of spectator awareness present themselves in realism as incomplete, in aspect, as they appear from one vantage point. Form and position are relative in realism, not absolute, so that invariant identity of anything cannot be discovered at once, but only eventually, through a series where similitudes or recurrent elements can be distinguished among the differences. The details that formerly were understood as discrete cases now come to be understood as partial expressions of hidden wholes: wholes, or identities, which are independent of any particular form of visual apprehension or, as in the novel, of apprehension by a single consciousness in a single moment. The identity of anything— that is, its rational, structured, formal quality—can only be discovered in relationship, and so, in realism, discrete forms are replaced by continuities, stasis is replaced by implied motion, and hierarchy is replaced by horizon. The *veritas* of medieval art is

see C. S. Lewis, *The Discarded Image* (Cambridge: Cambridge University Press, 1964), Owen Barfield, *Saving the Appearances* (New York: Harcourt, Brace and World, Inc., n. d.), and William Brandt, *The Shape of Medieval History: A Study in Modes of Perception* (New Haven: Yale University Press, 1966).

16

succeeded by the verisimilitude of realism, the truth found in similarity.

These new features in art reflect nothing less than a shift in human consciousness about the nature of experience in the physical world, a shift of which we have aesthetic evidence in the linear realism of quattrocento painting. Whatever the causes for the revolution in consciousness, and however slowly it found full expression, this shift introduced two premises that are fundamental not only to the logic of realism in art but also to the scientific and humanistic thinking of Western culture since the Renaissance. The two premises are these: that space and time are homogeneous; and that nature is uniform.[25]

In the discontinuous universe of medieval art one could not make generalizations based on a series of cases, because the differences between cases were absolute; each change in position presented a new problem of explanation because conditions were discrete and in no way the same in one time or place as in another. This discontinuity in the conditions of events prevented the medieval artist and scientist alike from conceiving uniformity in nature, because it was impossible to compare a series of positions of the same object.[26] However, when time and space are conceived as homogeneous—that is, the same universally—then it becomes possible to chart both the differences and similarities in nature which give rise to those generalizations in science and art

[25] "Either the exterior relations of objects, such as their forms for visual awareness, change with their shifts in location, or else their interior relations do. If the latter were the case there could be neither homogeneity of space nor uniformity of nature, and science and technology as now conceived would necessarily cease to exist. Thus perspective, because of its logical recognition of internal invariances through all the transformations produced by changes in spatial location, may be regarded as the application to pictorial purposes of the two basic assumptions underlying all the great scientific generalizations, or laws of nature" (Ivins, *Rationalization*, pp. 9-10).

[26] The search for uniformities in nature was not wholly absent before the Renaissance. Both the Pre-Socratics and the medieval alchemists sought to reduce matter to common elements or essences, so my general characterization of Greek and medieval attitudes should be qualified by the recognition that such efforts were made long before the Renaissance. I am indebted to Katherine Hayles for suggesting this qualification.

17

that we call laws. In formulating such laws no attempt is made to save the appearances. In fact, we might say that in reducing the welter of particulars to some abstract regularity, scientific and realistic generalizations represent an attempt to save the essences. As continuous, homogeneous, neutral media, space and time are populated by objects that exhibit certain consistencies of behavior, regardless of changes in position, which enable us to recognize them as the same. Neither people nor objects are any longer merely collections of attributes, each with independent status; instead, they reveal uniformities that constitute identity. Both the identities of things and the conditions in which they appear have a consistency and a constancy that permit them to be measured and reproduced. In painting, a series of aspects will produce a better idea of the object than one aspect only, because changes in appearance are inessential, implying no change in the object itself, and because the inner identity can only be revealed through the similitudes that appear in comparative instances.

Spectators of Raphael's *The School at Athens*, for example, do not explicitly see that the blocks in the parquet floor are square, as they might in a medieval or Chinese painting. The squares are represented in one aspect only, and so have a trapezoid visual form. There is no assertion made that the squares *are* trapezoids, but merely that they seem so from a certain visual angle. However, the squareness that cannot be seen directly, except from some improbable position in the air, can be inferred from the governing set of relationships in the picture. Even though the visual form presented is trapezoid, viewers clearly apprehend the squareness of the parquet sections because they understand that the actual form of something emerges from a series of vantage-points implicit in the painting. What looks trapezoid from here, so the convention goes, would look square from somewhere else, or rhomboid from some third perspective. The squareness of the sections, which is their identity, can only be gathered from a series of implied viewpoints and can be fully grasped only as an abstraction from immediate experience. What remains constant or similar in the accumulated series of aspects points to identity; what changes merely points to the inevitable limitation of the viewer.

18

The importance to the realistic effect of multiple viewpoints and their proper management was explained, long before Henry James, by Leon Battista Alberti, who in his influential treatise *Della Pittura* (1435) provided rules for achieving the kind of verisimilitude already being accomplished by artists like Masolino and Masaccio. The painter was to project onto the picture plane not one but two intersecting visual cones in order to achieve consistency within a single visual horizon. Constructed by aid of one central view only (Figure 1) the realistic illusion would be incomplete, and there would be no guide for the painter in presenting other than frontal aspects of the objects viewed. It is only the intersection of visual cones, their consensus, that produces the realistic system of relationships (Figure 2), and so unifies the field.

Figure 1

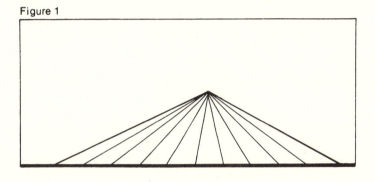

Figure 2

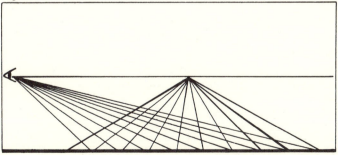

By this projective method the artist establishes "an abstract, uniform system of linear coordinates" that can be seen from any position, so long as it is single,[27] and that implicitly reflects objective laws of relationship that do not change, even though the position of the viewer does. Furthermore, the fact that the objects in the field remain the same even though their aspects and relationships change implies that they have an identity not available to direct perception, an interiority that cannot be grasped at first or even second sight.

The implications of this new perceptual model will appear in my discussion gradually, but four deserve special mention. The first is the presence of depth. The idea of depth dematerializes the surfaces of things. When the real or essential qualities lie hidden, then what appears is factitious in some way, a mere façade hiding reality. What we have in experience, then, in the fields of visual and (in fiction) conscious apprehension are counters, signs, mere concretia that owe their significance to the invisible inner reality they register. All action in the field may thus be an exchange of counters.

The second implication of this new perceptual model is the importance of the spectator, particularly the fixity and arbitrariness of its position. The implied presence that controls the arrangement of the representational field in realism has an importance that is impossible in medieval painting. At the same time, however, the arbitrariness of the controlling viewpoint suggests the arbitrariness of its privilege. The spectator's position could be moved without altering the essential relations in the scene pictured—relations that are, after all, only apparent ones.

Third, that arbitrariness suggests a potential equality among viewpoints. Because the realistic medium of experience is neutral, the same everywhere, there is a potential continuity between the vision of the spectator and the vision of all possible spectators in the same horizon. Any position would reveal the "same" world with as much validity; and any person could take up the position

[27] Edgerton, *Rediscovery*, p. 7. Edgerton reconstructs the way Brunelleschi first "managed to work out the complex geometry of realistic painting," formulating principles that Masaccio and others followed and that Alberti probably had in mind (p. 5).

20

of the implied spectator. The implied spectator's privilege, that is, depends not upon qualitative distinctions between "better" and "worse" points of view, but rather upon quantitative distinctions, between more and less distance. It is a privilege available to anyone who is willing to travel.

The generalizing power of perspective, by homogenizing the media of experience and inviting the projective extension of its laws universally, thus supports generic conceptions like "man" and "human nature," ideas that are not simple referential terms but, as Michel Foucault has suggested, reflexive parts of an *episteme* that has developed historically.[28] I will have more to say in Chapters Two and Three about the generalizing power of consciousness and the implicit species identification in the narrators of fiction.

Fourth, and most important, this consensus among possible views homogenizes the medium of perception and unifies the field perceived; it literally creates a common horizon. This realist consensus is in some ways a profoundly self-reflexive device, because it calls attention to the act of rationalization itself rather than to the objects used to specify that act.

Because consensus thus establishes that the same conditions hold everywhere in space, and because objects have an invariant structure that does not change with position, the realistic artist can project from a limited number of cases to general laws of relationship or sequence. Implicit in the very idea of horizon, for example, is the faith that what cannot be seen will be much like what can, in terms of the fundamental laws of operation. The vanishing point and infinity in realistic art are, by convention, arbitrary limitations on a system of relationships that has universal extension and validity. These projective methods of the painters owed much to the Ptolemaic method for projecting the globe, recently revived in fifteenth-century Europe, which made it possible to reduce "the traditional heterogeneity of the world's surface to a complete geometrical uniformity"; by using a grid system of

---

[28] See Foucault, *Order of Things*, p. 71. Foucault draws the conclusion "that man is only a recent invention, a figure not yet two centuries old, a new wrinkle in our knowledge, and that he will disappear again as soon as that knowledge has discovered a new form" (xxiii).

invariant relationships, the cartographer conceptualized space and therefore could project from the charted relationships of the known world (*oikumene*) by extension to the uncharted world.[29] This projection gave theoretical support and encouragement to those who believed that an organized world existed beyond the known horizons that was continuous with and similar to the charted world. The method implies a certain confidence in the orderliness, the rationality, of the world perceived at a certain level of generalization. No matter what particular situations may be revealed over the horizon, the basic grid is agreed upon, and so a whole world can be projected in which there will be no absolute discontinuities, no disturbing anomalies that cannot, at this general level, be rationalized.

The full mathematical statement of these space intuitions did not appear until the 1630s when the French mathematician Gérard Desargues produced the modified version of Euclidean geometry in which he developed proofs for the relationships between figures rather than for discrete figures themselves.[30] For example, where medieval geometers developed a different proof for every different conic, Desargues saw "the descriptive qualities that ran invariantly through the whole series of conics."[31] If, for example, one slices a cone into sections cutting each section at a different angle, the individual forms that result can still be described in terms of a single figure. Individual forms became merely cases of the more abstract forms perceptible in the invariances that ran through any series. Thus Desargues could develop a mathematical proof that the arc of the widest circle is a straight line, something

[29] Edgerton, *Rediscovery*, pp. 113, 122.

[30] The space intuitions of the first realist painters thus anticipated by two centuries the first mathematical statement of those intuitions, and it was another two centuries before this projective geometry was formulated independently (Desargues' major work having been lost in the interim) and came into its own in the late eighteenth and early nineteenth centuries because of its use to developing technology. "It is hardly too much to say that without the development of perspective into descriptive geometry by Monge and into perspective geometry by Poncelet and his successors modern engineering and especially modern machinery could not exist" (Ivins, *Rationalization*, p. 12).

[31] Ivins, *Art and Geometry*, p. 92.

that would have made no sense to the ancients. In antiquity, according to Alfred North Whitehead,

> mathematics was the science of a static universe. Any transition was conceived of as a transition of static forms. Today we conceive of forms of transition. The modern concept of an infinite series is the concept of a form of transition, namely, the character of the series of the whole is such a form.

For the modern mathematician there are "no longer unbridgeable gaps between the different kinds of lines."[32] Discrete forms, whether in realistic art or in mathematical theory, are but symbols of an abstract system and, as such, they can only be understood in terms of their relationships within that system.

> The various sensuously possible cases of a figure are not, as in Greek geometry, individually conceived and investigated, but *all interest is concentrated on the manner in which they mutually proceed from each other*. In so far as an individual form is considered, *it never stands for itself alone but as a symbol of the system to which it belongs* and as an expression for the totality of forms into which it can be transformed under certain rules of transformation.[33] (Italics mine.)

Any figure is a sign that points beyond itself; it is not apprehensible in itself, but only as a symbol of a reality hidden in the series of apparent forms and coordinating them invisibly.

[32] A. N. Whitehead, *Modes of Thought* (New York: Macmillan, 1938), p. 112; quoted by Ivins, *Art and Geometry*, p. 101.

[33] Cassirer, *Substance and Function*, p. 78; quoted by Ivins, *Art and Geometry*, p. 101. Cassirer recurs to the comparison between ancient and modern methods: "the effect of the ancient method consists in that they neglect this fundamental logical instrument [these ideal correlations] and thus consider only magnitude of an absolute and quasi-physical existence. The new view is obliged to break with this procedure, since from the beginning it defines as the real object of geometrical investigation not the individual form in its sensuous existence, but the various species of dependency that can subsist between forms" (*Substance and Function*, p. 83). A form, then, can be a process and, in mathematics at least, "to belong to a concept does not depend on any generic similarities of the particulars, but merely presupposes a certain principle of transformation, which is maintained as identical" (ibid., p. 82). For a discussion of the serial basis of representation see Foucault, *Order of Things*, pp. 53 ff.

23

This importance of the series for establishing identity holds not only for a mathematical series but for a spatial series in realistic painting or for a temporal series in realistic fiction. The invariant qualities, those that reveal themselves as similitudes and permit us to identify an object or a character, can only be perceived in a series of cases. No single expression of identity can ever be more than partial, and it cannot be interpreted except by comparison with other similar expressions. What can be seen is always an aspect, what is essentially there has receded to an abstract realm of conceptualization that we might call depth and that is inaccessible to direct experience at the same time as it entirely informs it. Thus realistic technique introduces a distinction between the secondary properties and the essential properties of objects or persons. What appears is merely a promissory note that can be collected only through a series of viewpoints. Any detail must be interpreted in terms of the form that emerges from a whole series, so the continuous relationships between discrete instances are the object of focus. Things that are wholly alike, that is, congruent, or things that are wholly different and discontinuous have no interest for realists because continuity and consistency require that comparable things must be both alike and different. In the Viator's phrase, "Les quantitez / et les distances / Ont concordables differences."[34] The realist needs differences that are concordable. Still, when the arc of a circle can be seen together with a straight line as different cases of the same form, the generalizing power of the system is so increased that the question is always open as to whether two forms that appear to differ absolutely may not actually have a hidden connection, a buried affinity.

Adiaphora

The consensus that unifies space and rationalizes sight in Renaissance painting has similar effects in realistic fiction where con-

---

[34] From the end of the French text of the *De Artificiali Perspectiva* (Toul, 1509). See the last pages of Ivins, *Rationalization of Sight*.

sensus unifies time and rationalizes consciousness. This temporal rationalization appears, long before nineteenth-century fiction, in the Renaissance redefinition of history, a redefinition that owed much to humanism. The discontinuities of medieval historiography and narrative imply a view of time in which the meaningful distinctions depend upon the contrast between time and eternity and not upon the contrast between past and present. By recognizing the difference between past and present, Renaissance historians homogenized the temporal medium by finding past and present mutually informative. The later, fictional formulations of this new idea of time have important links with this insight of Renaissance humanism.

Alberti stressed the historical value in realism as being central to its moral function. For him realistic technique fulfilled its moral purpose best by representing the high moments of historical achievement, and his treatise on perspective, *Della Pittura*, deals not only with the procedures for achieving verisimilitude but also with the purpose of art as *istoria*.[35] The generalizing power that made possible realist technique, he thought, could produce simultaneously in one image the significant forms that history had expressed sequentially and in bits.

A narrative interest is evident even in early realistic painting because of its adherence to the importance of series. Though such narrative interest often remained implicit in the Renaissance, the narrative painting of the nineteenth century eventually demonstrated how explicitly this narrative potential could be realized. Well-known examples like Millais' *The Blind Girl* or Holman Hunt's *Light of the World* and *The Awakening Conscience* provide salutary reminders of the abstractness possible within the realistic convention. In these pictures the inner lesson or implied story is what unifies the scene, so that the consistency of horizon merely reinforces the impression that the accidents of daily life contain meanings, what Courbet called "l'allegorie réele." Although nar-

---

[35] See William Ivins Jr.'s reconstruction of Alberti's experiments and conclusions in *Rationalization of Sight*. Part One of Alberti's treatise deals with the techniques for achieving perspective, Part Two with *istoria*, and Part Three with the moral development of the artist. See Edgerton, *Rediscovery*, p. 41.

rative painting sometimes appeared serially in the manner of Hogarth, generally the narrative interest was confined to one canvas. There the visible details of the painting are but the tips of an historical iceberg; the canvas is a field of intersection not merely of various visual angles but (implicitly) of various lived sequences as well, and has depth that is temporal as well as spatial.[36]

Alberti's still-synoptic view of historical time seems very different from the lived sequences implied by later narrative painting, and more different yet from the sequences of consciousness important to narrative realism. But these differences should not obscure the shared premises about time characteristic of both these realistic forms, premises that both the early and the later realists owed chiefly to the humanists. The gap of several centuries between the pictorial realism of the Renaissance and the fictional realism of the novelists signals in part the magnitude of those perceptual changes initiated by the humanist view of time.

For my purposes, the key to defining realism, like the key to understanding humanism and liberal traditions, is history. Etienne Gilson's comparison of medieval and Renaissance humanism puts the case succinctly.

> It is often said, and it is in a sense fair to say, that the Middle Ages remained almost completely a stranger to history, at least in the way the Renaissance understood it and as we still understand it today. Its humanism is very different from the historical humanism which characterizes the Renaissance; it is a humanism of the present, or, if you prefer, of the timeless.

By comparison with medieval humanism, humanism "chez Érasme" features "a passion for historical difference" ("le goût passioné de la différence historique").[37] Gilson's point is con-

---

[36] See Raymond Lister, *Victorian Narrative Paintings* (London: Museum Press, Ltd., 1966). How fully a canvas can yield narrative meaning is evident in Ford Maddox Brown's description of his own painting, *Last of England* (1855), included in Linda Nochlin, ed., *Realism and Tradition in Art 1848-1900: Sources and Documents* (Englewood Cliffs, N.J.: Prentice Hall Inc., 1966).

[37] "Le Moyen Age et le naturalisme antique," *Archives d'histoire doctrinale et littéraire du Moyen Age*, 7 (1932), 35-36 (translation mine). "On a dit souvent,

firmed in different terms by Panofsky, writing about the difference between the Renaissance and various prior renascences. The Renaissance, he says, entombed the classics in history.

> The Middle Ages had left antiquity unburied and alternately galvanized and exorcised its corpse. The Renaissance stood weeping at its grave and tried to resurrect its soul. And in one fatally auspicious moment it succeeded. This is why the medieval concept of the Antique was so concrete and at the same time so incomplete and distorted; whereas the modern one, gradually developed during the last three or four hundred years is comprehensive and consistent but, if I may say so, abstract. And this is why the medieval renascences were transitory; whereas the Renaissance was permanent.

This passage has importance not only for its suggestion, confirming Gilson, that history makes the difference, but also for its recognition of the abstractness of post-Renaissance conventions, including those of realism. As I will show in a moment, realism in no way signals a death of abstraction; realism relocates abstractions, but depends upon them as much as if not more than ever. The shift in historical sensibility that made all this possible Panofsky calls the "real Renaissance" of the fifteenth century, "in contrast to the various mediaeval 'renascences' "; it was a "mutational" not an evolutionary change—"a change both sudden and permanent."[38]

---

et il est en un sens vrai de dire, que le moyen âge est resté presque complètement étranger à l'histoire, du moins telle que la Renaissance allait l'entendre et que nous l'entendons encore aujourd'hui. Son humanisme est très différent de l'humanisme historique du passé qui caractérise la Renaissance; c'est un humanisme du présent, ou, si l'on préfère, de l'intemporel." For a discussion of the connections between changes in literary convention and changes in sensibility see Peter Demetz, "Defenses of Dutch Painting and the Theory of Realism," *Comparative Literature*, 15, no. 2 (Spring 1963), 102.

[38] Erwin Panofsky, *Renaissance and Renascences in Western Art*, 2 vols. (Stockholm: Almquist and Wiskell, 1960), pp. 113, 162, 102. See Bakhtin's discussion of the Renaissance interanimation of languages succeeding the polyglossia of the Middle Ages and leading to the critical monoglossia of modern times (*The Dialogic Imagination*, trans. Michael Holquist and Caryl Emerson [Austin: University of Texas Press, 1981], esp. pp. 68, 351).

Questions about when this shift in historical awareness took place inevitably produce disagreement, a disagreement sometimes enhanced by differences in the material under discussion. Critical consensus puts the period of efflorescence into the seventeenth century, a judgment I do not dispute; the analogies between quattrocento painting and later forms of realism, however, should act as a reminder that the seventeenth century saw a culmination of trends that had been developing for several centuries, and in various forms besides aesthetic ones. I agree with those who find the modern sense of history present in the sixteenth century, a period of intense humanist activity: in England the period in the early sixteenth century when humanists were contributing to the establishment of a new social order.[39]

[39] Peter Burke, for example, argues that this sense of history, so much a part of Western culture "since about 1800 . . . began to develop during the Renaissance (the fifteenth century in Italy, the sixteenth and early seventeenth centuries elsewhere), and that it was lacking in the Middle Ages" (*The Renaissance Sense of the Past* [New York: St. Martin's Press, 1969], p. 1); he names three factors crucial to this sense of history—the sense of anachronism, the awareness of evidence, and the interest in causation. George Huppert in his study of French historiography finds "historical mindedness—historicism if you will—solidly established in the mental habits of a handful of scholars in the sixteenth century. Neither Locke's psychology nor the scientific revolution seem to have been prerequisites for the growth of a sense of history as we understand it. This state of mind existed in all its essentials before 1600" (*The Idea of Perfect History* [Urbana: University of Illinois Press, 1970], p. 166). Frank Kermode calls this historical time of the Renaissance, Aevum, or temporality belonging neither to clock time nor to eternity (*Sense of an Ending: Studies in the Theory of Fiction* [New York: Oxford University Press, 1967], pp. 46-80, esp. pp. 55-56, 72). Erwin Panofsky discusses Kairos and Aion in the Renaissance iconology of time, *Studies in Iconology: Humanistic Themes in the Art of the Renaissance* (New York: Harper and Row, 1962), esp. pp. 71-72.

For important discussions treating the seventeenth century as the watershed for modern history see Herbert Butterfield, *Man on His Past: The Study of the History of Historical Scholarship* (Cambridge: Cambridge University Press, 1969), esp. pp. 130, 135-36; A. O. Lovejoy, "Temporalizing the Great Chain of Being" in *The Great Chain of Being* (New York: Harper and Row, 1960); and Michel Foucault, *Order of Things*, esp. pp. 52-65, and his discussion of the "mutation of Order into History," pp. 217-220. For arguments that the shift towards valuing continuity appears before the sixteenth century see Erwin Panofsky's discussion of the "comprehensive 'picture space' " of late gothic architecture and sculpture,

28

In speaking of English humanism I mean transalpine humanism, and specifically the Erasmian humanism that left so deep a mark on English institutions and attitudes. Its influence was in-

Gothic Architecture and Scholasticism (Cleveland and New York: World Publishing Co., 1957), esp. p. 17; Peter Burke's discussion of the influence of literacy on the developing sense of history, "Towards a Sociology of Historiography," *The Renaissance Sense of the Past*, p. 149; Peter Laslett, *The World We Have Lost* (New York: Charles Scribner's Sons, 1965, esp. ch. 8, "The Pattern of Authority and our Political Heritage: Literacy, Social Mobility, and the Rule of an Elite"; and Pere Chenu, on the influence of political and demographic changes in medieval Europe, *Nature, Man and Society*, pp. 187-94: "When a man went beyond the ocean frontier, history as well as geography changed; the medieval period was over." Douglas Bush emphasizes the conservatism of the Renaissance and its medieval links in *The Renaissance and English Humanism* (Toronto: University of Toronto Press, 1939), esp. p. 30; and Hiram Hayden's still useful discussion focuses on the tension between conservative and progressive humanism, what he calls the Renaissance and the Counter-Renaissance, in *The Counter-Renaissance* (New York: Harcourt, Brace and World, 1950). For arguments supporting the persistence of medieval methods well past the seventeenth century see Leo Braudy's discussion of the "exemplary view of history," which, however subtle it may be, "when pressed always reveals a past that is only a discontinuous collection of discrete incidents," and for which "the past is a grab-bag of unrelated parts," *Narrative Form in History and Fiction: Hume, Fielding, and Gibbon* (Princeton: Princeton University Press, 1970), p. 28; Martin Price's discussion of the competition between hierarchical views of order on the one hand and the individualism and emphasis on generic humanity on the other, *To the Palace of Wisdom: Studies in Order and Energy from Dryden to Blake* (New York: Doubleday, 1964), esp. pp. 7-10; Earl Miner's edition *Literary Uses of Typology: From the Late Middle Ages to the Present* (Princeton: Princeton University Press, 1977), which testifies that typology was not dead in 1500; and, finally, Leo Spitzer's discussion of the persistence of Pythagorean notions of harmony, in which he finds the "great caesura in occidental history" beginning in the seventeenth century and not ending until the eighteenth, *Classical and Christian Ideas of World Harmony* (Baltimore: The Johns Hopkins University Press, 1963), pp. 75-76; see also p. 138.

For developments in music analogous to those I am describing in painting and literature, Leo Spitzer's *Classical and Christian Ideas of World Harmony*, especially his discussion of the progressive "independence of the voices" in tonal music, the development of "a supravocal principle," and the gradual giving way of polyphony to symphony, pp. 39-44. For Charles Rosen the development of the sonata represents an "attack upon the tendency to isolate" and an increasing emphasis on "imbalance" as a basis for "tension and resolution" in music. See *The Classical Style: Haydn, Mozart, Beethoven* (New York: Viking Press, 1971), esp. pp. 23-29.

calculably diffuse, affecting not only art and scholarship but also an entire social and political system; and this diffusion multiplied the influences in England that began to popularize the new sense of history.[40] Scholars proposed to recover from the corruptions of time the true Greek and Latin scripture. In order to find the true Word they had to compare and to clarify the differences and similarities between texts—in short, to evaluate historical difference in order to salvage from it the single truth. These humanists sought unity among differences, and, instead of merely selecting from the available versions, they sought the common denominator that would harmonize them all though it was not expressed fully in any one version. Thus the humanists stressed the continuities between historical instances, rather than the discontinuities as medieval historiography had done. Historical difference became important precisely at the moment when it became problematic. In pursuing these researches the humanists discovered the modern idea of history almost by accident; certainly it is unnecessary to attribute to conscious purpose alone what was very likely the result of a rush of cultural excitement containing many contradictions and which the participants could no more see steadily and whole than we can so perceive our own times.

Erasmus' goal was far from any sectarian ambition to support Protestants at the expense of Catholics, or to elevate the classics at the expense of Christianity; his purpose was to find the common denominator that unified them, the "invisible church" that was the ultimate authority for all sects, or, in other words, the form of the whole that alone made interpretation of particular cases possible. His writing reveals this interest in the invisible dimension and this view of physical appearances as aspects of the truth.

What Erasmus introduced was a comparative and historical method for getting from the letter to the spirit. The kind of

[40] See James McConica, *English Humanists and Reformation Politics* (Oxford: The Clarendon Press, 1965), and Gordon Zeeveld, *Foundations of Tudor Policy* (Cambridge: Harvard University Press, 1948). For discussion of the difference in "mutational energy" between Italian and Northern Renaissance painting see Erwin Panofsky, *Early Netherlandish Painting: Its Origins and Character*, 2 vols. (Cambridge, Mass.: Harvard University Press, 1964).

question the humanist asked originated in the basic premise that there exists an invisible and invariant truth which cannot be perceived in any single earthly manifestation alone but only through a comparative series of manifestations. In the Middle Ages Everyman made the same journey through sin and death to judgment; but once the differences in earthly life assumed historical importance—the differences between Zoroastrians and Cabbalists, Platonists and Aristotelians, Christians and pagans, not to mention Catholics and Protestants—questions arose as to what united them. The question, "what thing is man?" became interesting precisely because the answer was no longer self-evident, but had to be sought in a series of different instances.

This search for the hidden bond of unity extended far beyond philological research into all fields of conceptualization, and, especially in the period from the mid-1530s onward, into the field of English politics. When Henry VIII needed a theory to fit his *fait accompli*, Cromwell recruited an army of anonymous humanists who served as apologists for the king in explaining his break with Rome and produced treatises on every subject from marriage and divorce to theology and ritual. The Reformation was of course not entirely Henry's doing, and his act alone does not account for the English novel. But his act and its immediate consequences for social and political institutions, not to mention for the language of value in which those institutions were codified, owed everything to an awareness of difference and to a need for recovery.[41]

In attempting to justify the existence of two worldly religious authorities, one of Henry's foremost apologists, Thomas Starkey, looked for a higher level of generalization where differences could be reconciled. He found his text in Melancthon's Protestant revision of a Thomist law of nature, which holds that all human laws (*adiaphora*) are but approximations of God's universal law. Since this is so, arguments between human polities are absurd, because no single group has the whole truth and because together

[41] Stephen Greenblatt discusses the overt politicization of religion in the Renaissance in "Improvisation and Power," in Edward Said, ed., *Literature and Society* (New York: Columbia University Press, 1980).

they can approximate the truth better than singly. Thus cooperation and toleration are required in the search for common ground. All sects, seeing their folly in absolute claims, will then "begynne to fall into the meane, that is to say Christ's true religion."[42] This is more than a close maneuver in church politics: it reflects an ethos. Starkey's distinction between *adiaphora* and the true law is perfectly consistent with Erasmus' distinction between letter and spirit and with the realistic artists' distinction between aspect and inner form. Like the realistic artists, the humanist apologists found in difference an imperative to harmonize, to rationalize, to coordinate, and in so doing to rise to a higher level of generalization where particulars could be relegated to the status of partial aspects.

The humanists found no particular reason to emphasize dialectics in history, but Protestants subsequently did. In England the Renaissance coincided with the Reformation, and from the beginning Protestantism and humanism were paradoxical collaborators. By drawing attention away from sacraments and ceremonies toward the private soul's conversation with God, Protestantism emphasized individual conscience in ways that did not always produce reassurance. History provided some solace. In his solitary struggle the Protestant could find some comfort in the possibilities for temporal mediation that the humanist view of history offered. The sense that time could reveal the true way not only for the church but for an individual life justified the struggles of Protestant souls like those increasingly recorded in diaries and journals of the seventeenth and eighteenth centuries.[43] Time was a potential ally in unfolding the signs of salvation.

[42] Zeeveld, *Foundations*, pp. 152-53.

[43] See Ian Watt on Troeltsch, that "the really permanent attainment of individualism was due to a religious, and not a secular movement, to the Reformation and not the Renaissance" (*Rise of the Novel*, p. 74). See also John Morris, *Versions of the Self* (New York: Columbia University Press, 1966); J. Paul Hunter on the importance of Puritanism to the rise of the novel, *The Reluctant Pilgrim: Defoe's Emblematic Method and Quest for Form in Robinson Crusoe* (Baltimore: The Johns Hopkins University Press, 1966), esp. p. 94; and David Goldknopf on the importance of the Reformation in linking empiricism and science, *The Life of the Novel* (Chicago: University of Chicago Press, 1972), ch. 1, esp. pp. 9-18.

The paradoxes of Protestantism—that it was suspicious of nature and works and at the same time permissive toward reading worldly success as a sign of Grace—made the promises of history all the more appealing. The individual could find encouragement in the fact of change and special interest in fictional illustrations of successful progresses from blindness to insight. Even Moll Flanders' scandalous life can be seen to have its moral closure, its final form showing that errors are merely stages on the way to truth.

Knowledge and Power

The premises of realism are reductive in the same way as scientific laws: they reduce the welter of particulars to some abstract, categorical rule or regularity. In describing the particularizing habit of realism, Ian Watt compares readers of realistic novels with a jury in a court of law, on the grounds that in wanting to know "all the particulars" both groups take the "circumstantial view of life."[44] The problem with Watt's reading of his own analogy, which is excellent as far as it goes, is that he leaves out the law. A jury establishes all the particulars not in order to verify a circumstantial view of life but in order to make a judgment as to whether or not a law has been broken. Interest in particular details is governed by a belief that they reflect laws of human behavior accessible to everyone and universally applicable. In fact, a certain distance—or, depending on the interpretation, estrangement—from particulars is introduced into all perception by the idea that the identity of things is independent of their aspects. In a realistic painting we no longer have objects in themselves but objects as seen from a particular perspective, under certain conditions, and in particular relationships. The object-plus-subject is always represented. We cannot approach discrete objects directly; perception of them is always cluttered by the inescapable presence of the spectator. Something is forever intruding between the object and our grasp—atmosphere, point of

---

[44] See *Rise of the Novel*, p. 31.

view, distance, angle—so that our knowledge, always distanced from direct apprehension, is always mediate rather than immediate.

The realist does not imply that the object *has* no reality apart from its aspects; the squares of the parquet floor are square regardless of viewpoint, and the existence of the invariant form is what makes possible the rational perception of identity through difference in the first place. The realist says that the object can be grasped in any one instance only in aspect, and that fuller apprehension depends on the reductive comparisons made from a series of instances. What the spectator perceives, then, are not discrete objects "like" objects in experience, but a system of relationships. By showing sight rationalized in painting, or consciousness rationalized in the novel, the realistic work mimes the act of system-making. What is represented is the act of rationalization itself.

The generalizing power of this rationalization was evident to Renaissance painters and to nineteenth-century writers alike, though in different terms. Harmony, unity, centrality—values that can best be expressed when there are disparities to be harmonized—are values with moral weight for realists and humanists alike. In Renaissance painting, according to Samuel Edgerton, the central visual ray was considered "the Prince of Rays" because it was the pivot of the harmonious image and therefore the strongest and most direct; the *recta linea* or straight line was considered to be "the most Christian" and thus to have both "monumentality and moral authority." The harmony of space in realism was taken to be a testimonial to the "harmony between mathematical order and God's providence to man on earth." Like music, measurement was a divine activity because it involved the coordination of disparates.[45] Later, the language of novelists describing their own practice often reflects this interest in the projective power that arises from examining particulars. "The goal of the experimental method, in physiology and in medicine," Emile Zola wrote in his treatise defending the scientific value of realism, "is to study

[45] Edgerton, *Rediscovery*, pp. 24, 86, 164, 37-39.

phenomena in order to control them. . . . Our goal is theirs; we wish, too, to be masters of the phenomena of intellectual and personal elements in order to direct them." Whatever one's "personal sentiment," observation and experiment enable us to "control" it and to make a "conquest of the unknown."[46]

The realist consensus that makes such power available depends upon the management—one might even say the administration— of distance. One must step back from particulars in order to grasp them. In ordinary usage we say that someone is "realistic" who is able to sift relevant from irrelevant considerations and so to act in a manner appropriate to the situation.[47] While this "realism" can be seen as moral or political cynicism, a rejection of any fixed standards, in fact it implies a faith in some kind of rule according to which something can be judged irrelevant and would be so judged by anyone with the same perspective. The implication of realist technique is that proper distance will enable the subjective spectator or the subjective consciousness to see the multiple viewpoints and so to find the form of the whole in what looks from a closer vantage point like a discontinuous array of specific cases. Any move toward the margins of experience means accepting a distortion uncongenial to the realistic gambit.[48] By

[46] Zola's The Experimental Novel quoted by George Becker, ed., Documents of Modern Literary Realism (Princeton: Princeton University Press, 1963), pp. 176-95. Octavio Paz finds a control ethic characteristic of both Protestantism and capitalism, seeing both as ways of getting the future into our power (Children of the Mire: Modern Poetry from Romanticism to the Avant-garde, trans. Rachel Phillips [Cambridge, Mass.: Harvard University Press, 1974], p. 155); Paz, however, does not otherwise agree with Weber's association of Protestantism with "the irreligious movement of capitalism" (p. 117).

[47] J. P. Stern, On Realism (London and Boston: Routledge and Kegan Paul, 1973), esp. pp. 40, 139, 121. See also Ivins, Rationalization, p. 15: pictures which resemble nature, that is, which represent on the picture plane the coordinates of the world of visual perception, do so only when seen from a "definite distance."

[48] Realism is confined to "that fragile sphere we call civilized life. . . . Its terms have no meaning at the catastrophic margins of experience or in the realm of Grace, where 'the system' breaks down and 'a man's time' is no more" (Stern, Realism, p. 139). See Karl Kroeber's discussion of the contradictory directions taken by Wordsworth and Scott, Romantic Narrative Art (Madison, Wis.: University of Wisconsin Press, 1966), esp. pp. 11, 112, 181.

35

accepting the idea that the particulars of experience submit to no pressure from a formulating system, the artist moves toward that immersion in detail, that *chosisme* which Lukács laments to find in modern novels. On the other hand, by accepting the notion that a system exists that is wholly independent of particulars rather than emergent in them, the artist moves in the other direction toward an unrealistic schematism. In realism, points of view must intersect to create a uniform horizon, disagreement must be resolved so that the final picture or narrative achieves consistency in all its relationships. Realism forces its readers and viewers into a "middle distance" that makes possible the perception of a unified, single "set of meanings."[49]

These conditions of perception in post-Renaissance realism reflect a redefinition of human power to understand reality. Through systematic, abstract reductions based upon a consensus of views, realistic perception moves to higher levels of generalization. In doing this, realism suggests a new distinction between appearance and depth that removes the important meaning to a hidden place where it must be sought. Both the hidden truth and the methods for discovering it thus become abstract. If we view this development in the way St. Thomas Aquinas might have done, "we are bound to say that the European man became a thinker after he ruined himself as a knower," a "ruin" which, according to one historian, can be traced in stages "from Augustinian Platonism to the nominalistic isolation of Ockham to the despairing and desperate methodism of Descartes. For what we call the decline of medieval philosophy was really a transition from man as thinker—from man knowing the world of sensible things to man thinking abstract thoughts in separation from existence."[50] Whether we think of this change as ruin or as progress, its reality is indisputably drawn in realistic art. When an individual "never stands for itself alone but as a symbol of the system to which it

[49] See Stern, *Realism*, ch. 7, and p. 157; and George Levine's discussion of the "balance" and "tension" characteristic of the realistic method (*Realistic Imagination*, esp. p. 18).

[50] "Introduction," to *Saint Thomas Aquinas* (New York: Random House, 1948), p. xxiv.

belongs," then the goal of knowledge must be the system rather than the particulars. This does involve a fundamental estrangement between perceivers and the world of their experience. The implied spectator in realistic painting, like the implied consciousness that coordinates the temporal field in fiction, is not absorbed in the world of forms but stands outside it, as if behind a lens.

CHAPTER TWO

Perspective in Narration

My chapter title directs attention to *perspective* rather than to *point of view* in narration. For considering the narrator's function in realism the term *perspective* has the advantage over *point of view* of being free from Jamesian associations concerning individual viewpoint.[1] Point of view has come

[1] I find that others have used this term *narrative perspective*, for example Gerard Genette, *Narrative Discourse: An Essay in Method*, trans. Jane E. Lewin (Ithaca: Cornell University Press, 1980), p. 185; Jonathan Culler, *Structural Poetics: Structuralism, Linguistics, and the Study of Literature* (Ithaca: Cornell University Press, 1975), p. 7; and Robert Weiman, "Point of View in Fiction," in Gaylord Le Roy, et al., eds., *Preserve and Create: Essays in Marxist Literary Criticism* (New York: Humanities Press, 1973), p. 60. None uses it as I do here.

Beginning with James's prefaces and Percy Lubbock's *The Craft of Fiction* (Jonathan Cape, 1921; Viking Compass, 1957) and running through Wayne Booth's *The Rhetoric of Fiction* (Chicago: University of Chicago Press, 1961) to Robert Scholes and Robert Kellogg's *The Nature of Narrative* (London: Oxford University Press, 1966), "point of view" has become central to the discussion of narrative forms. Norman Friedman summarized the discussion up to 1955 in "Point of View in Fiction," *PMLA* (December 1955). See also his chapter on point of view in *Form and Meaning in Fiction* (Athens: University of Georgia Press, 1975). What James and Lubbock had in view was technique, but later critics have incorporated point of view into theoretical discussions of the genre. Scholes and Kellogg, for example, write: "The problem of point of view is narrative art's own problem. . . . In the relationships between the teller and the tale, and that other relationship between the teller and the audience, lies the essence of narrative art" (*Nature of Narrative*, p. 240). All this attention notwithstanding, point of view has not proved sufficient for defining the genres of narrative, not even for the

to be associated so closely with the subjective perception of single individuals, either characters or authors, that it will not do for my discussion of the narrator, a figure that cannot be satisfactorily explained either as a character in its own right or as a persona for the author. The following comment from Percy Lubbock represents a whole tradition in which the narrator is assumed to be an individual and, hence, to have a point of view:

> The whole intricate question of method, in the craft of fiction, I take to be governed by the question of the point of view—the question of the relation in which the narrator stands to the story. He tells it as *he* sees it, in the first place; the reader faces the story-teller and listens. . . .[2]

The difficulties of such a metaphoric formulation about the relation of reader and teller become evident immediately, because the reader is not facing anybody in particular. By avoiding the term *point of view* I avoid the assumption that the narrative consciousness I describe is an individual matter. It is precisely the narrator's function in the realistic novel to be faceless and even to be without identity in the ordinary sense of that word. The fundamental conventions of realism entail a narrative perspective without local particularity; consequently, to think of this narrator as an individual runs counter to the whole movement of realistic form. Considering perspective in narration helps to focus the

realistic novel. Franz Stanzel's discussion (*Narrative Situations in the Novel*, trans. James Pusak [Bloomington: Indiana University Press, 1971]) has the advantage of considering the whole narrative "situation" and of acknowledging fully the "one central feature of the novel—its mediacy of presentation" (p. 6); he has "Second Thoughts on Narrative Situations" in *Novel*, 11, no. 3 (Spring 1978), 247-64. See also J. Hillis Miller on the way Victorian narrators manage to stay "on both sides of the curtain at once," in "The Narrator as General Consciousness," *The Form of Victorian Fiction* (Notre Dame: University of Notre Dame Press, 1968), p. 70; also p. 82.

[2] *Craft of Fiction*, p. 251. While there may be no easy solution to the dilemma short of avoiding personal pronouns altogether, it cannot escape notice that the masculine pronoun disenfranchises half the population. Though *she* would be no better as a universal pronoun, *it* poses problems because, while allowing for the plural, collective nature of the narrative consensus, in English *it* dehumanizes the narrator altogether.

discussion of realistic fiction where I think it should be, on the comprehensive management of relationships. Chapter Three treats this question in more detail.

The Rationalization of Consciousness

What the faculty of sight is to space, the faculty of consciousness is to time. The rationalizing consensus of realism depends, in fiction, on the presence of the narrator. The realistic narrator's function, like that of the implied spectator in painting, is to homogenize the medium. Like the implied spectator, the narrator stands outside the frame of events but in the same continuum, that is to say in a time by convention coextensive with that of the represented time. In realistic painting convention suggests continuity between virtual and actual space; it seems *as if* we could walk over the threshold into that realistically rendered world. The narrative perspective maintains a similar continuity in time, and thus establishes a similar potential for agreement among multiple consciousnesses that the implied spectator establishes among multiple spatial points of view. The linear coordinates in fiction (past, present, and future) operate like the spatial coordinates in painting (front, side, and back) to homogenize the medium in which consensus becomes possible. It is the agreement, or lack of *dis*agreement, among these viewpoints that unifies the field of action and confers the illusion of perspective. The very distinction between past, present, and future is only meaningful in the first place because the periods thus distinguished are mutually informative.[3] They are the linear coordinates that make possible relative measurement in time.

The narrative perspective (or "narrator") coordinates these relative measurements into a unified, collective vision. At every moment in a past-tense narration, more than one viewpoint is represented. Every moment is grasped automatically from more

[3] See Karl Löwith's handling of this point in *Meaning in History* (Chicago: University of Chicago Press, 1949), especially his introduction and, for the specific point, p. 6.

than one viewpoint because every moment is both "present" and at the same time already past, already part of a recollection taking place some time in the future of the event. For example, in the sentence, " 'I am happy now,' she said," the present tense is embedded in the past as if in a frame, so that the present has a double, equivocal voice. It says both that she *is* happy, and also that she *was* happy (so by now she could be showing some other aspect). The momentary present is given both as emergent—in its concrete, actual appearance, in its precarious aspect; and also as contained already in a larger pattern of significance where it has become past and fixed, at least from the point of view of the implied consciousness narrating it. The present moment is transformed into a virtual present, one wearing the quotation marks that signal its transformation. It happens; it has happened. Every "present" in realism is in this way also past, so at every moment in the present story we are continuously aware of the future, which is thus implied by the very act of telling. The narrating consciousness exists in the same temporal continuum as the action but outside the arbitrary frame, in the future to which this present action will eventually (has already) led.[4] In other words, every event that is happening in realism has already taken its place in a pattern of significance, a pattern that at the same time depends upon the cumulative, serial development of those events.

Interest in the revelations of sequence, an interest that remains implicit in pictorial realism, thus finds its fullest *aesthetic* expression in the temporal medium of literature and its fullest *literary* expression in the realistic novel, where the unfolding of structure and significance receives its most thoroughgoing serial treatment. The conception of time as a common medium in which distinctions between past, present, and future are meaningful (i.e., mutually informative) is a conception predicated by realistic narrative as well as confirmed by it. The reader is led to discover the systematic rules of transformation that explain how events

---

[4] See also Leo Bersani, "Realism and the Fear of Desire," in *A Future for Astyanax: Character and Desire in Literature* (Boston and Toronto: Little, Brown and Co., 1969), p. 53: "The future of each moment is present in the account being given of it."

41

proceed from each other, rather than to focus on discrete events themselves. The past has meaning in relation to the present and this relation is reciprocal; the present can only be understood through the generalizations that emerge serially from the past. This mutual informativeness proceeds from the fact that the implied consciousness, the narrator presiding over all the fictional and temporal relationships, coordinates all moments into a single temporal series from a stance outside, in the "future" of the story.

This continuous, implicit presence of future possibility guarantees the universality, the projective extension of those basic relationships memory discerns in comparing past and present. Just as the past would have no reverberation for the present and no mystery for it if past events were discrete forms in themselves, so also the symmetries between present and past would be discrete forms, rather like the typological patterns of medieval history without the extensions to infinity implicitly granted to those relationships by the future. Futurity provides that horizon and that vanishing-point which at once mark the (arbitrary) limits of our perception and guarantee the extension beyond those limits of the order visible in the field. Futurity insures that, in a different time and place, the same familiar system will operate. Continuous with past and present, the future, like the narrator, exists beyond the arbitrarily limited horizon and it insures that, in moving toward it, we will run along the same rails that brought us from past to present. By the apparently innocent gesture of accepting the past-tense narration, then, we have accepted several rather more complex ideas: that time is a single continuum; that temporal continuities extend beyond the arbitrarily limited horizons of the text; that events point beyond themselves to a coordinating system; and that appearances are but aspects of hidden identities.

Every experience in realistic time, therefore, is mediate, because its meaning depends on the implicit presence of other states with which it must be compared to yield the abstraction we call its identity. Any given gesture only partially contains the form or regularity we take as the sign of its meaning. For example, a character like Will Ladislaw in *Middlemarch* is, in any particular instance, both identifiable and elusive. The novel presents him in various aspects, as he appears to himself, to Dorothea, to Mr.

Brooke, to Casaubon. What Ladislaw seems, furthermore, depends on what he is doing; he may be putting out a good editorial, or he may be making an ass of himself over Dorothea. Any view of him is a partial, incomplete formulation of what he really is, of the mysterious and elusive identity that the series of his actions gradually reveals more and more fully. The fact that he is always changing further refracts perception of his identity. With Ladislaw, then, as with any object or event in realistic fiction, his actual present, in which he is only very partially manifest in particular, is a very unsatisfactory thing for perception, for his "presence" lurks somewhere behind the particular speech or gesture, giving it depth and therefore meaning. Since any particular manifestation is thus equivocal, a series of them is essential in order to read the meaning of any particular, and not only one series but preferably a complex system of interlocking lives and fortunes in which the levels of generalization involve not only comparisons between different aspects of his behavior but also comparisons between his behavior and that of others.

Because this recovery of similitudes in fiction takes place temporally, the most important power in this recovery is memory. Since the meaning of any particular case cannot be read at all without comparison with other particular cases, and since the only other particular cases are past ones, the mnemonic act of recovery is crucial for perceiving the patterns in events. To recall the analogy with painting, the frontal aspect of an object in space may be called, in temporal terms, its present; its other, implied aspects are, so to speak, its past. In spatial realism the revealing series can be taken in almost simultaneously by sight; in time, the synchronizing faculty is memory. To any particular present case memory presents through its act of recall the alternate states, the comparisons, the similitudes that permit the definitive generalizations of realism. This mnemonic act of recovery in realism takes place on two levels, the primary mnemonic level of the narrator and the secondary mnemonic level of the characters.[5]

[5] All realistic novels, by virtue of this reliance on the past tense, could be considered historical novels; the fact that so many novels are literally historical novels, set back to an historical period preceding the time in which the novel first appears, is an acknowledgment of the fundamentally historical nature of this

In all realistic novels one of the chief moral problems characters face is that of making proper connections, literally by marriage, and figuratively by sustained increase of conscious grasp. The power to accomplish this often is explicitly tied to the power of memory. In Dickens, for example, the condition of life is to be surrounded by secrets, and a common motif is the search for the connections that will reveal identity. In *Our Mutual Friend* (II, xiii), John Harmon tries to get his bearings by returning to the dimly remembered place where he lost them; his effort to remember what happened is part of the larger effort to recover the continuities of his life after the blows to consciousness dealt him by circumstances. The extent of his moral problem is revealed by the faulty association he makes in this chapter between "recognition, anticipation, and failure." Part of his lesson will be that in the realistic world he inhabits recognition and anticipation, far from leading to failure, are the keys to success. In *Little Dorrit* the mysterious motto "D.N.F.," Do Not Forget, conveys a cryptic message that Mrs. Clennam misunderstands and misapplies, thereby crippling various lives, including her own. It is a motto, furthermore, that is inscribed on a watch to suggest the connection between reading moral significance and telling time.

George Eliot, also investigating the paralyzing effects of faulty memory, tends to focus more on the preemptive errors preventing characters from accumulating the experience that feeds memory and hence understanding. Characters making this mistake are apt to judge unwisely by judging prematurely, before the concording faculty of memory has had time to do its work, and then to undergo gradual disillusionment as the recalcitrant object reveals unexpected aspects. In *Middlemarch*, for example, the two major

---

fictional form, an acknowledgment that the gap between past and present in these works is essential to their generalizations. See Hans Meyerhoff for an arguable but interesting discussion of the "timelessness" of memory: "the act of recollection itself is timeless in that it seems to have no date or temporal index attached to it. It is a permanent or timeless possibility. The recollection may burst into consciousness at any time or place, which gives it the quality of being beyond time and place" (*Time in Literature* [Berkeley: University of California Press, 1955], pp. 54-55).

instances are Dorothea Brooke and Lydgate. In deciding to marry Casaubon, Dorothea makes a fatal deduction about his nature, as if his resemblance to the judicious Hooker revealed his entire identity rather than one aspect of it only. Lydgate makes the same mistake with Rosamond, who turns out to be less pliable than he had imagined on the basis of too little experience.[6] In these cases, as in the cases of suppressed or hidden facts, memory is the key to acting wisely and well.

In solving one problem of synchronization, however, the act of individual memory creates another. The reflective consciousness of any single character, that awareness structured by memory, at once unifies individual consciousness and isolates it. In spatial realism the implied multiple points of view have purely physical limitations that are relatively unproblematic because they yield their collective result simultaneously. But in temporal realism the multiple points of view are functions of memory—that is, of mental not physical position—a fact that deepens the privacy of an event and makes the homogeneity of the temporal medium dependent on the varieties of individual consciousness and therefore highly problematic for collective expression. It is the nature of consciousness, in the very act of synchronizing or "reading" experience, to build walls of difference between itself and others, so that characters in realistic novels by definition live in worlds of which others know nothing. The very force of memory that unifies the personal consciousness helps to fragment the social world and threatens the creation of that homogeneous temporal medium and of that uniform horizon requisite for the realistic effect.

Such problems on the secondary mnemonic level of the characters are solved on the primary level of the narration by the past tense. By providing a single fixed viewpoint existing always in the future of any narrated episode, the narrator unifies into a single mnemonic (i.e., past-tense) sequence the various fragments of history, each with its own point of view. This solution may

[6] Characters making this mistake are legion in realistic novels; some examples are Henry Esmond with Beatrice, Elizabeth Bennet with Darcy, David Copperfield with Dora, and Clara Middleton with Sir Willoughby Patterne.

appear to be purely formal in that it does not directly address the particular problems of social coherence raised by novels like *Vanity Fair*, *Middlemarch*, or *The Golden Bowl*. The key point here is that all episodes and viewpoints in realism perforce are coordinated into a single unified field of action by virtue of the mere fact that they exist in a single, homogeneous medium. The details of various plots in one novel tend, as by gravitational force, to reveal uniformities among themselves retrospectively.

In *Little Dorrit*, for example, the Marshalsea prison provides not only a setting for the action but also a similitude to the house where Mrs. Clennam has shut up herself and her conscience, to the psychic barricades of Miss Wade, and to the state of mind forced on so many other characters by social institutions. In *Middlemarch*, Fred Vincy's long suspense over Featherstone's will provides not only a context for the story of Fred's misplaced ambition but also one of the various forms of waiting that constitutes a similitude between his life and Dorothea's. The message in both novels is that these forms of imprisonment or these forms of waiting constitute a common property, a common basis that validates the notion of a common "human" experience. What gives these messages such force is in part the homogeneity of the medium where this activity takes place. The perceived similarities and the uniformities in human nature that they indicate will, in the future time inhabited by the narrator and the reader, provide better guidance and power of understanding for dealing with these common problems. Fragmented times become a single Time which, however provisional, persistently holds out the possibility of rationalization to the perceptive seeker of similitudes. What the past-tense narration provides is not a solution to particular problems but, more grandly and invitingly, the persistent claim that, because the medium is constant and the uniformities exist, increasingly satisfactory resolutions are possible.

The freedom initially to investigate these differences, disparities, and ambiguities comes with the confidence that these variances in individual or social expression are trivial and that an invariant, identifiable reality is present despite the refractions to which our successive angles of vision subject it. Unlike some contemporary novels and some medieval art, where change in position amounts to a change in ontological status, a dispersal of those unities of "personality" or "object" that we take for granted, change in realism offers the only way to discover identity or, in other words, that form of the whole which emerges serially from different but similar cases. Differences in realism are always concordable, never irreducible; they invite us to reach for the inner dimension where differences are reconciled. The multiplex realistic sequence discovers different aspects of what, nevertheless and by means of this very process, can be identified as the "same" object and the "same" world. The centrifugal forces of multiplicity, variety, disparity, ambiguity always exist in tension with centripetal forces of the centering, rationalizing, synchronizing motive. Concordable differences always exist to be overcome.

The relation between narrator and character, or in other words the relation between the primary mnemonic level and the secondary, demonstrates in one way the peculiar equipoise in realism between the forces of unity and the forces of dispersal. This tension between aspect and recovery has many varieties and manifold possibilities for complexity—a richness of formal convention that I can only suggest here and that subsequent chapters can only begin to develop. The mediate perception (always a provisional generalization) that gives depth to an individual character can also, in a wider and more comprehensive series than a strictly personal one, give depth to a whole field of social activity in which the balance between form and dispersal involves events not only of personal but also of interpersonal history.

The premises of realism thus foster a language of mediation that maintains tension between inside and outside, between surface and depth, between public and private. What is shareable (public) is the common denominator, the form of a whole series of aspects collected and reduced; what is not shareable (private) are the secondary aspects, the appearances incidental to the form of the whole. The realities of depth, perceivable only through the mediations of consciousness, exist in constant tension with the secondary characteristics, the *adiaphora* of experience unsorted.

47

This tension between aspect and depth gives realistic form its characteristic resistance to closure. The identifying form in realism is a function of a series, something that is inherent in it but not available except through a consensus. In Cassirer's terms, the real object is not the individual forms of sensuous experience but "the various species of dependency that can subsist between forms" (see above, Chapter One, note 33). Recent discussions that emphasize the semiosis of experience or the dialogism in novels tend to slight this crucial dependency. In realism closure is always provisional but always available. At the level of character and event every limited system is relativized, opened to dialogue with others, but at the same time the past-tense narrator focuses attention on the species of dependency between them and not on the individual forms or systems themselves. Realism does not produce either a system with final closure or a system with complete open-endedness; the balancing between the two is itself a form, and a powerful assertion of mutual relevance that potentially extends to infinity and ends only arbitrarily.[7]

[7] Marshall Brown, seeing realism as "an underlying type of semiosis," emphasizes the dialectical nature of these intersections ("The Logic of Realism: A Hegelian Approach," *PMLA*, 96, no. 2 [March 1981], 233). Walter Reed also discusses the "semiosis of experience" (*An Exemplary History of the Novel* [Chicago: University of Chicago Press, pp. 263-70]), although he suggests, together with Michael Holquist, that the "realism of the novel" lies in the encounter between literary and nonliterary codes in an "open-ended series of realisms" ("Six Theses on the Novel—and Some Metaphors," *New Literary History*, 11, no. 3 (Spring 1980), 413-24. Peter Garrett makes his way "between the monological rock and the deconstructive whirlpool" by emphasizing "dialogical" form—something, however, that seems to suggest a degree of autonomy in narrative voices uncongenial to realistic consensus (*Victorian Multiplot Novel* [New Haven: Yale University Press, 1980], esp. p. 13). David Miller recognizes the tension between form and dispersal, although his tension between openness and closure works better for Jane Austen than for George Eliot because closure becomes the symptom of definition (*Narrative and Its Discontents* [Princeton: Princeton University Press, 1981]). In treating the tension in realism between desire and limitation, George Levine's *The Realistic Imagination* (Chicago: University of Chicago Press, 1981) does much fuller justice to the dependency between form and sequence by accommodating the historical qualities of realism and by stressing the importance of balance between individual and collective consciousness (esp. pp. 12, 18). Robert Caserio stresses the connection between sequence and value in his discussion of *Plot, Story, and the Novel* (Princeton: Princeton University Press, 1979).

The language of "inside" and "outside" especially has vertiginous possibilities of paradox. What is characteristic of an individual, i.e., the depth dimension of Will Ladislaw that remains constant through a series of partial glimpses, can also be, in wider social terms, what is least characteristic of a social group, what is most marginal, or idiosyncratic, or discardable among the manifestations of a society. The inner depths that are the stable form of Ladislaw's personality can also be the arena of possibility, the private reserve from which we derive the stable, verifiable, public forms. The tradition that defines history in terms of public event and public personality is, nevertheless, a tradition that draws upon a reserve of privacy, a reserve which, at the more restricted level of individual character, in turn depends for definition upon a distinction between manifestation and deep structure.[8] "The idea of inwardness," as Stephen Toulmin suggests, "is almost as perplexing a notion for us nowadays as the idea of time was for St. Augustine."[9] Despite perplexities, however, the important constant in realistic fiction at all levels is maintaining a tension between the centripetal and the centrifugal impulses: between a potential for mobility and the form of mobility contained; between the arena of freedom or even dispersal on the one hand, and, on the other, the arena of stable, verifiable meanings. What is crucial in this language of inside and outside, of surface and depth, is the need for *both* terms of the opposition to any fully realistic conception. Whatever the individual or social transaction, realism always presents *both* the series of possible, partial meanings, *and* the form of the whole that remains implicit in them, nowhere appearing free of particular instances but consistently giving depth to them all.

The fact that reality is mediate accounts for the centrality of

[8] Leo Braudy discusses the distinction between public and private as a developing norm in eighteenth-century historiography in *Narrative Form in History and Fiction* (Princeton: Princeton University Press, 1970), esp. pp. 11, 34.

[9] "The Inwardness of Mental Life," *Critical Inquiry* (Autumn 1979), p. 3. So important is this distinction between hidden and revealed response that, as Dorrit Cohn shows, it is maintained in fiction even in silent, inner thought-processes. See *Transparent Minds: Narrative Modes for Presenting Consciousness in Fiction* (Princeton: Princeton University Press, 1978), p. 59ff., on Amy Dorrit's monologue.

institutions in realistic fiction. A realist fiction, in the words of Raymond Williams, creates and judges "a whole way of life in terms of the qualities of persons. The balance involved in this achievement is perhaps the most important thing about it."[10] Society is not background in any trivial sense, essential to the understanding of individuals and particulars; in fact, individuals and particulars are also, as Smollett suggests in the preface to *Ferdinand, Count Fathom*, merely ways of specifying the system. The genial consensus of realistic narration takes place in a middle distance, where both the concrete particulars and the coordinating patterns can appear, where the difference between the two can be maintained in all its importance. "The realist must somehow bridge the gulf between the exceptional-unique in its chimerical isolation, and the common-respectable."[11] When a balance between private and public life cannot be conceived, realism tends to tip either into lyrical fantasy or into tidy telic motion. Institutions that have lives of their own, as they often do in Dickens, destroy the creative tension among individuals that sustains institutions in the first place. On the other hand, individual characters who overshadow a narration, as they sometimes do in Henry James, also can tip the balance away from consensus.

The more complex and paradoxical the array of individuals, plots, and particulars, the more thoroughgoing the final perception of order and depth will seem. The loose bagginess of realistic novels reflects not some disagreeable authorial limitation but rather the author's close adherence to the logic of realism that insists on the serial expression of truth. The subjection of characters to various kinds of journeys, the proliferation of episodes and of sequences in realistic novels, are devices managed with the reader's developing depth-perception in mind. The more the char-

[10] Raymond Williams, "Realism and the Contemporary Novel," in *The Long Revolution* (New York: Columbia University Press; London: Chatto and Windus, 1961), p. 278.

[11] J. P. Stern, *On Realism* (London and Boston: Routledge and Kegan Paul, 1973), pp. 139, 103. The collective truth avoids extremes of radical alienation ("domination of unaccommodated self") and of naturalism ("domination of milieu").

50

acters see of the world, the more we see of the characters and, consequently, the better able we are to identify in the variety those deep consistencies both within individuals and between them that temporal continuities gradually reveal. The realistic novelist actually seeks to emphasize and even to exaggerate differences, ironies, paradoxes, since without these painful gaps and troublesome disparities there would be no need for the embracing abstraction. If there were a true congruence between characters and their possibilities—between Jane Eyre and her true marriage, for example—then there would be no need for bridges. If, on the other hand, the gap between characters and their images of fulfillment proved absolute and irreducible, there would be no basis for those continuities between things that hold out the hope of comparative discoveries. Because differences are always concordable in realism, the doubleness of character and ambiguity of events consistently hold out the promise of recovery and fruitful resolution.

The power of the past-tense convention can be appreciated if we imagine a novel written wholly in the present tense—for example, a novel by Robbe-Grillet. The use of the present tense in *Jealousy* sets the controlling viewpoint in motion; there is no stable narrator standing safely outside the frame and implying the possibility of connections without ever having to draw any in particular. The present tense brackets out the future and the past, in other words it brackets out the linear coordinates that make possible relative measurements in a stable world, and the continuous present thus destroys the continuity of time and democratizes all moments and all viewpoints. Any emergent patterns dissolve, any comparisons have uncertain foundation. These effects are possible because there is no common denominator in time for making reductive comparisons. Details stand for themselves alone, unavailable to the reclamation that the realistic consensus implicitly encourages. The loss of the past tense means the loss of the future and, therefore, the loss of that continuity of time in which causal sequences can unfold their meanings.

These meanings depend upon the realistic narrator's presence but in a strictly formal sense, in the way that the rationalization

51

of sight in painting depends upon the implied spectator. In its construction of a consistent and uniform world out of the material of consciousness, the realistic narration coordinates into one single mnemonic sequence the various points of view that are themselves coordinated mnemonic sequences. What most distinguishes realistic from other kinds of narration is the fact that the narrative perspective is, by virtue of this mnemonic act, a consensus. The realistic narrative maintains the unity of the temporal field not in spite of multiple viewpoints but as a consequence of them. In contrast to the heroic visions of Piers Plowman or of Dante or of the poet in *Paradise Lost*, the coordinating consciousness in realism is not visionary; it consistently remembers. It is not an heroic act of anticipation but an heroic act of recall, one that the characters would do well to emulate, could they but see the model. Even where no pattern may be evident, in the most immediate moments of experience, the presiding consciousness posits, by its doubling act of memory, the possibility of hidden meaning, of emergent pattern. Not absorbed in the particular world of events, the narrator, like the implied spectator, stands outside it, as if behind a lens: a witness whose indistinct faceless presence maintains the consensus that supports the realistic world. The sheer fact of this consensus is far more powerful a generalization than any ornamental remarks the narrator might make along the way. The powers of the convention can scarcely be overstated, especially when we still take them so much for granted.

The presiding consciousness, by virtue of its position in the future of the story being recalled, functions effectively to keep the realistic system open to infinity. The basic mnemonic structure that relates past and present does so solely because the discontinuities between them invite us to search for their meaning in some interior dimension, some level of generalization beyond particulars. The whole scheme depends upon the perpetuation of the gap between Is and Seems, the preservation of the mystery which, ostensibly, the narrative exists to unfold. The known past and known present are limited, determinate, and therefore they yield only partial meanings. The hope of closure that makes the whole mnemonic enterprise of consciousness worthwhile is contained in the existence of future possibility. That possibility must therefore be kept open. Since permanent closure would end the enterprise, closure must always be provisional, always a matter of horizon. The unfulfilled promise of closure must remain unfulfilled.[12] Paradoxically, the future both maintains the hope of closure for the time-bound consciousness and at the same time it insures that the irresolution of the pattern will be maintained so that the universality of the system, its projective extension to infinity, will be maintained.

Since futurity is a fiction essential to the realistic convention, any solution that is permanent kills the system. When we finally believe that everyone has an Electra complex or an Oedipus complex, we will have revealed the interior heart of things and dispersed the very mystery that led us to pursue our discoveries and hypotheses in the first place. Walter Benjamin describes what becomes of history that has no future, taking his cue from Klee's painting, *Angelus Novus*. Klee's angel stands with its back to the future and its face to the past.

> Where we perceive a chain of events, he sees one single catastrophe which keeps piling wreckage upon wreckage and hurls it in front of his feet. The angel would like to stay, awaken the dead, and make whole what has been smashed. But a storm is blowing from Paradise; it has got caught in his wings with such violence that the angel can no longer close them. This storm irresistibly propels him into the future to which his back is turned, while the pile of debris before him grows skyward. This storm is what we call progress.[13]

---

[12] J. Hillis Miller comments that characters in novels, while they have different experiences, nevertheless share the "temporality of the present" with its connectedness to a past and its "reaching toward a future" (*Form of Victorian Fiction*, p. 15). For a related point see Robbe-Grillet's discussion of tragedy in *Essays for a New Novel*, trans. Richard Howard (New York: Grove Press, 1965).

[13] "Theses on the Philosophy of History: IX," in *Illuminations*, trans. Harry Zohn, intro. Hannah Arendt (New York: Schocken Books, 1969), pp. 259-60. For discussion of this problem of presence and absence see Paul de Man, "The Rhetoric of Temporality," in Charles Singleton, ed., *Interpretation: Theory and Practice* (Baltimore: The Johns Hopkins University Press, 1969), pp. 173-209;

What Klee's "new" angel views is a universe of discontinuities that results from the loss of the future. The realistic novelist, by contrast, manages to keep the dead awake and to maintain the unity of the temporal system by keeping our minds steadily on the future, while memory works its shuttle between present and past.

The triumph of time in Victorian realism is a collective achievement that is the most important fictional event. It is a triumph of collective awareness, a matter not so much of public conscience as of public consciousness. The past-tense narration stimulates the imagination toward reconciling past and present for the sake of projection into the future, a process that establishes the existence of a single, collective perception. This event, this collection by the narrator of all voices, is not just ancillary to fictional events; it is the chief event, the one toward which, at least for readers, the writer's whole creation moves. The community of understanding may exist primarily outside the text, as it does for example in *Bleak House*, or the community may be dramatized in the text in various ways, such as through addresses to readers, the narrator's personal voice, or scenes of communal observation or judgment punctuating events. But, despite all differences in expression, the basic activity of the past-tense narrator is the same: a confirmation of collective experience, literally a recollection of all points of view and of all private times under the aegis of a single point of view and in a common time.

The objectivity of the picture resulting from such a linear narrative thus depends on a collection of voices for which the narrator acts as a kind of administrator, coordinating the novel's various moments into a single sequence that confirms the mutual relevance of one moment for another. The consensus not only establishes an agreement of meanings; it literally establishes the continuity of time. This continuity in time, common sense might object, is what makes collective agreements possible. What I'm urging is that the reverse is true: that collective agreement makes historical continuity possible.

and Frederick Bogel's excellent "Structure and Substantiality in Later Eighteenth-Century Literature," in *Studies in Burke and His Time*, vol. 15 (1973-74).

The Ethic of Mobility

Realistic fiction gives still more symphonic treatment than painting to the motion implied by realistic conventions, with their multiple viewpoints, measured distances, and suggested infinity. Realistic fiction thus confirms what might be called an ethic of mobility. This phrase is suggested by Leo Bersani's description of the "ethic of stillness" behind *Mansfield Park*, a novel that presents a social universe inimical to the values of realism. In a hierarchical social order that depends upon maintaining position, Fanny Price is the moral center, and the Crawfords, who like role-playing and mobility, are "ontological floaters." "What dooms the Crawfords morally is the ease with which they move around among various, even contradictory sorts of behavior."[14] Viewed in terms of the realistic ethic of mobility, however, the Crawfords seem the reassuring characters, and the reader who accepts this ethic would find their contradictoriness "realistic" and the novel's refusal to identify the reconciling unity in their personalities "unrealistic."

The ethic of mobility works against the establishment of hierarchical social patterns, especially those of the family which, as *Mansfield Park* makes so apparent, is the microcosm of social hierarchy. The ordering patterns in a hierarchical universe compartmentalize the world of experience and work against the temporal continuities that tend to unify it. In the realistic universe people have to recognize that their identity depends upon themselves and their actions, rather than on family, class, or some such "mark" of identity that has nothing to do with their wills or self-consciousness. Many, perhaps most, of the main figures in realistic novels are orphans: Jane Eyre, Lucy Snowe, Becky Sharp, Henry Esmond, Esther Summerson, Pip, and nearly all of George Eliot's main characters. Characters who do have family ties are usually expected to rise above them, as with George Eliot's Catherine Arrowpoint, whose position and inheritance are af-

---

[14] Bersani, "Fear of Desire," *Astyanax*, pp. 75-76. For a discussion of mobility in relation to stasis see Edward Said, *Beginnings: Intention and Method* (New York: Basic Books, 1975), pp. 94-97.

flictions to her. The natural family often is a center of stillness and a source of paralysis for its offspring: the Sedleys and Osbornes in *Vanity Fair*, the Vincys in *Middlemarch*, the Meagles in *Little Dorrit*. Adam Bede's parents, like so many in Dickens, require parenting. Even successful families like the Garths in *Middlemarch* or the Poysers in *Adam Bede* have something of the rural idyll about them, and their harmony is both limited in range and terribly vulnerable to the forces of growth and change that surround and sometimes destroy them.

Because change is so important in the realistic ethic of emergence, the imagery of failure in realistic novels often has to do with stasis and discontinuity. Dickens's Krook, a rag-and-bone-shop collector, is a moribund, dried-up, decaying wreck. The great Merdle, although his collection of wealth makes him arbiter of society, is nevertheless, as his name indicates, nothing but a collection of effluvia: a fact that he finally recognizes when he decides to take his own alleged life. In George Eliot's works there is Casaubon, who lingers in labyrinths of his own devising, there is Grandcourt, who is described as reptilian, white, dead, still, and there are her hoarders, Featherstone and Silas Marner, who have the same hollow power and the same lifelessness as Merdle. The failures of these characters can be measured not only in moral terms but in ontological terms as well. In seceding from the world of relationship and change they have withdrawn from all possibility, including the most fundamental self-realization. Trying to profit from the ethic of growth by capitalizing on their detachment, they eventually die.

Great expectations about resolution may not be fulfilled in particular cases, but even the gaps unbridged, the marriages not made, function as comments on the need for bridges and marriages. The striking thing about the realistic premise of depth is its power of recovery.[15] Incomplete realization of meaning or even outright failure may merely suggest the limits of the horizon in which the search for rewards was conceived, and not impropriety in the search itself. In *Little Dorrit*, for example, the various

[15] This is Robbe-Grillet's phrase for the tendency of all "habitual" humanism.

parallels of plot, scene, and image conspire to suggest that deeper continuities unify the world of experience despite the failures of individuals. Even though William Dorrit dies without ever recognizing Amy's true worth—or for that matter true worth of any kind—still this failure of realization does not disturb the deeper patterns of relationship that connect into a "commanding structure of significance"[16] not only these two characters but also everyone in this populous novel—a structure of connection that is reinforced by the commanding metaphor of the book, the prison, which echoes in every corner of the world and confirms in its negative way the ethic of mobility. Particular connections may fail, but the effort to make them does not go unrewarded.

By successfully coordinating apparently disparate elements, the realistic novelist asserts the existence of a common ordering system; apparently unrelated particulars sooner or later reveal a connectedness, a pattern. Whether it be of a collective life, as in *The Old Curiosity Shop*, of a single life, as in *Henry Esmond*, or of part of a collective life, as in *Adam Bede*, finally differences are resolved, patterns become clear, ignorance is punished or educated. Whether the characters see the emergent pattern or not varies from novel to novel; at the end of his life Henry Esmond sees for the most part what the reader sees; Mr. Dorrit on the other hand does not. But sooner or later, for somebody and from some perspective the series reveals a form, and this revelation of order is the closest we get to closure in realistic fiction. However the shared system may be "distorted by vice, by social circumstance, or by ignorance and weakness," the system proves in the end that it "carries meaning and moulds experience itself."[17]

Because of this power of recovery, the most various and disparate field can be organized, rationalized by experience in time. Similitude can be found in the most dissimilar figures. To recall the analogy with geometry for a moment, we remember that even

[16] Bersani, "Fear of Desire," *Astyanax*, p. 53. "The realistic novelist can wander, linger and digress as much as he likes; he will absorb any material—as the Balzacian digression supremely illustrates—into a commanding structure of significance."

[17] Ioan Williams, *The Realist Novel in England* (Pittsburgh: University of Pittsburgh Press, 1975), p. 155.

the differences between a triangle, a cone, a circle, and a line can be mediated by opening levels of generalization where these different forms can be seen to flow into one another: a cone has the properties of the triangle and of the circle, the arc of the largest circle is a straight line, and so on. In a similar way realism expresses this reassuring power of recovery, one which Robbe-Grillet claims is characteristic of all humanism. The tendency "to recover *everything*, including whatever attempts to trace its limits, even to impugn it as a whole," is "one of the surest resources of its functioning."[18] We must be convinced of the multiplicity, the resistance to resolution, in order for the final form to surprise and please us and not seem merely conventional, but the particulars exist for the sake of that hidden order they however reluctantly reveal. Given enough time, enough distance, any anomaly (so the premise goes) has its proper place in the final system. The more an event or a personality—some gratuitous crime or cruelty—threatens one's faith in the hidden order, the more triumphant will be the rationalization that finally draws the disparate elements together in a unity. The mastermind controlling this unity is the consciousness, which, the past tense implies, presides over the temporal continuities and enforces consent. The powers and limits of that presence are the subject of the next chapter.

A novel that achieves a final consistency of horizon where a final form of the whole emerges from similitudes is not necessarily a good novel—it is merely a realistic one. Artists can choose to distort or to abandon realistic consistencies for purposes of their own, and in so doing to produce not bad works but only unrealistic or partially realistic ones. Several Renaissance painters who understood quite well Alberti's system for achieving a single vanishing-point nevertheless chose to paint pictures where this uniformity was wrenched somewhat, perhaps producing several vanishing-points in close proximity to each other for the sake of a

---

[18] *Essays for a New Novel*, p. 51.

particular effect.[19] The same suspension of realistic continuities can be found in fiction.

In *Clarissa*, for example, Richardson presents us with a series of single viewpoints that, however consistent in themselves, are increasingly difficult to place in terms of a common location or common sequence, not to mention common values. When the novel begins, a certain temporal and spatial coherence is produced by the fact that we see most of the world through Clarissa's eyes, and at the end Belford's primacy as teller has the same unifying effect. But in the middle, as the action reaches its tragic peak, the sequence of letters garbles the sequence of events so that it becomes difficult to establish a sense of sequence or causality except by heavy reliance on the date beginning each entry. These threats to temporal continuity present problems of judgment that are acute and sustained, most of all during the prolonged crisis. The only loose, slack moments in the novel occur between letters, so that the spaces that in a past-tense narrative would permit some continuity are turned into abysses. The action takes place mainly in a foreground, and the perspective and relationships that would provide a sense of background are increasingly disrupted. We must endure the power of Richardson's slow revelation, adjusting our judgment of the characters as we walk around them again and again, our hopes perpetually roused and dashed. If one judges the characters wrongly, as some eighteenth-century readers misjudged Lovelace (to Richardson's horror), one cannot understand the action at all. These problems in judgment are no accident, and Richardson poses them for us partly because he suspends the continuities by which we ordinarily measure and judge. The emergent pattern is threatened and not recovered, as it would be in realism, on the same plane and in the same world. The consistency that a unified horizon entails is not necessarily

[19] See, for example, Samuel Edgerton's account of Pisanello in *The Renaissance Rediscovery of Linear Perspective* (New York: Basic Books, Inc., 1975), pp. 52-53. See also Jonathan Goldberg's discussion of the way early perspective painters avoided "illusionist" results, "Quattrocento Dematerialization: Some Paradoxes in a Conceptual Art," *The Journal of Aesthetics and Art Criticism*, 35, no. 2 (Winter 1976), 153-68.

a value held by every artist, and even those who use realistic techniques may modify them for a purpose.

While Richardson modifies realist conventions more than Dickens does, and Dickens more than George Eliot, all three deal with time and consciousness in ways that show their similarities markedly by contrast with nonrealistic narratives like *Pilgrim's Progress* and *Paradise Lost*. These latter two are especially instructive examples because their authors were practically contemporary with Defoe and shared a spirit of dissent. But both Bunyan's fictional narrative and Milton's epic take an apocalyptic view of time that influences their views of individual action and social discourse and consequently their formal conventions.

Pilgrim's Progress turns gospel into a universal story, but it is not history. There are none of the interesting differences between individuals or events that create the resistance and atmosphere of realism. The conception of Christian's identity is generic. Qualities like obstinacy, pliability, worldliness, or hope exist not as aspects of an internalized individual identity but as externalized personifications. The plot, too, is typological, moving from one "place" or *topos* to another in a rhetorical rather than an historical sequence. These "places"—Vanity, Despair, Destruction, Despond—like the personified qualities constitute an environment through which the pilgrim progresses. His medium is far from neutral and homogeneous time and space; it is the qualitatively differentiated environment of a moral universe. The qualities are not in the pilgrim, he is in them—a complete reversal of realist convention.

In Bunyan's text point of view is either right or wrong and thus not congenial to consensus. The true voice is God's and it comes to Christian through scripture (which Bunyan allows him to quote frequently) interpolating its familiar texts into his own. The Word is what counts. Knowledge is *a priori*, not experimental; reference is vertical, not horizontal. It takes time to make mistakes—to digress—but not to discover truth. In this profoundly antisocial and antihistorical vision, all men are pilgrims, working out their private salvation, and that is the most interesting thing about them. Christian has a negative relation to his environment on the whole, and to his fellows. He pities Ignorance, and avoids him; together with Hopeful he even sharpens his piety at Ignorance's expense. Foolish Ignorance, meanwhile, voices the values associated with realism. He trusts the human heart and thereby reveals his depravity. The mind and heart are good only if they agree with the (essentially negative) "judgment which the Word giveth of both."

The past-tense narrator has a precarious hold in this text where prophetic utterance holds the central place. The overwhelming effect is one of temporal discontinuity and absolute separation between right and wrong. Where differences of aspect are not interesting, no collaboration is possible. The stable, past-tense narrator—a figure here derived from medieval dream allegories—is minimally present, a fascinating trace of the presence that becomes so important in subsequent realistic fiction. Although *Pilgrim's Progress* can be seen as an archetype for plots in later more realistic novels like *Robinson Crusoe* and *Tom Jones*, it belongs to a visionary tradition with roots in medieval conventions, and its premises are essentially uncongenial to the empirical spirit of realism.

Even though it is a poetic narrative, *Paradise Lost* develops realistic conventions more fully than *Pilgrim's Progress*, and some of Milton's central values appear to encroach on the preserve of realism. He emphasizes the inward heart and mind, going beyond Bunyan's ideal of emptiness and receptivity; his characters are more individualized than Bunyan's figures; and perspective is an important tool in the poem. The strange power of *Paradise Lost* owes something to its partially realistic treatment of supernatural events. But Milton deliberately evokes the values of realism in order to contain them. History is an arena of confusion and not, as in realism, an orderly linear sequence with forms recoverable by memory. It is visionary, not recollective history, informed by typological not chronological motifs. Only Satan appears to believe primarily in projects and in temporal opportunity, and his example hardly recommends his faith. His debates are rigged, his consensus a fraud, and his projects doomed. His mind is not sustained by holy power, so he needs troops. The poet, on the other hand, who invokes the Holy Spirit, has little need of a human resource like consensus and little need of history to support and illumine his mind. Louis Martz's image of the poem, a dark circle with a bright center, aptly suggests the way in which time and space are curved in *Paradise Lost*, warped by holy power into a universe that is finite and closed.

The poem is composed of one story that is delivered by means of stories within stories—both in the similes and in the whole pattern of narration. The narrative is told by various voices—the poet, Adam, God, Christ, and angels singly (Uriel, Raphael, Michael) and in chorus. The story is the same story, that of the Fall and Redemption, repeated over and over again in everything from the falling Icarus to the rising mists. It is a story that is always present.

The mobile narrative perspective involves precipitous shifts in position (that in Book One, for example, from the prologue to the floor of hell) and abrupt changes of focus from large to small (the fallen angels, introduced as giants, become insects). The whole poem produces the effect of simultaneity by shifting backwards and forwards in time, confirming the final apocalyptic view of historical sequence. The central vision of creation, framed by two versions of hell and chaos, is a flashback that acts as a parable or warning for Adam and Eve and serves the visionary and prophetic movement of the poet's song. Even the language, with its inflected rhythms, suspends the ordinary sentence sequence and unifies the impression by paratactic means. These discontinuities in the medium distort the patterns and rhythms of ordinary perception and force readers to attend to the system as a whole and to the simple elegance of its architecture.

In aid of this vision memory has a function quite different from its recollective function in realism. Memory here is a faculty of praise and is linked with the creating word, the "powerful Word/ And Spirit coming to create new Worlds" (VII, 208). Memory for Adam and Eve is the key to success or failure. Adam promises never to "forget to love/ Our maker" (V, 550), and Raphael warns him, "Remember, and fear to transgress" (VII, 912). After they fall the poet insists "For still they knew, and ought to have still remember'd/ The high Injunction" (X, 12). They fall because they forget, as Satan is always trying to do. The unfallen angels show how memory is properly used as an instrument of creation. They praise Christ in chorus: "never shall my Harp thy praise/ Forget, nor from thy Father's praise disjoin" (III, 414); Uriel tells the story of creation to Satan disguised as a cherub: "For wonderful indeed are all his works,/ Pleasant to know, and worthiest to be all/ Had in remembrance always with delight" (III, 695-705). These mnemonic choruses are scarcely distinguishable from action, and this is because retelling the story has an active and creative consequence. "Whatever was created, needs/ To be sustain'd and fed" (V, 414), and the divine word raises and supports creation not only once but repeatedly. The angels, shuttling back and forth across creation, act as a kind of cosmic memory that feeds and maintains the universe, everywhere adjusting its harmony. "Cherubic songs by night from neighboring Hills/ Aerial Music send" (V, 447) to Adam and Eve in paradise, before their world falls to ruins in the last four books.

In Milton's epic, concord depends on differences that are absolute. The meaningful relationship is vertical, not horizontal, a reflex between God and his creation. Any change of position in this vertical axis has absolute consequences. We may change our nature for the worse, like Satan and his victims, or "by steps we may ascend to God" (V, 512). "Ascending and descending" on the golden stair, the bright figures of creation reenact the Word, God's "trace" in the fallen world. The mobility and freedom of the narrative perspective is possible because the cosmos is eternally stable. The historical past is the result of sin, and so history is a disorder expressive of human solitariness and need for redemption. In realism, by contrast, order depends on memory of the past, something that cannot be stable without the collaboration of others.

Realistic novelists exploit for various ends the tensions between difference and concord, between the centrifugal forces that fragment and multiply experience and the centripetal ones that unify and reduce it. But whether the conclusions are pessimistic or optimistic, the very terms in which realist writers conceive the world posit a faith that the sequence of appearances contains a hidden order and that knowledge of it increases control. Unlike the classical hero, whose fate is determined and who can only strive for the fullest momentary expression of his physical power, the character in realistic fiction faces an open horizon and has a hand in destiny. Such a character can, by moving around, by remembering well and by careful projecting, create powerful reserves of knowledge with which to guide crucial choices. Heroic characters have only to be fully manifest; realistic characters, like the world they inhabit, have depths that can never be expressed fully in one heroic action nor ever fully understood except as an abstraction of consciousness. This power of understanding, this capacity for mediate knowledge, belongs mainly to the narrator in realistic novels. Viewpoint in fiction is not (despite the spatial metaphor) a matter of space and sight, it is a matter of time and consciousness; the rationalization of consciousness in realistic novels, comparable to the rationalization of sight in painting, depends upon the heroic recollection of an invisible and dematerialized narrator.

CHAPTER THREE

The Narrator as Nobody

T he genial consensus of realistic narration implies a unity in human experience which assures us that we all inhabit the same world and that the same meanings are available to everyone. Disagreement is only an accident of position. However refracted it may be by point of view and by circumstance, the uniformity at the base of human experience and the solidarity of human nature receive confirmation from realistic conventions. All individual views derive from the same world and so, with enough good faith, enough effort, enough time, problems *can* be solved, tragedies *can* be averted, failures in communication *can* be overcome. The death of Jo in *Bleak House* and a myriad of other less dramatic defeats need not have happened if enough people had shared enough information and if enough buried secrets had come to light. At the level of consciousness we can transcend the accidents of physical limitation. However, this saving awareness takes on an impersonal cast precisely because it exists independently of particulars. The conventions of realism confirm both the collective nature of human consciousness and also its abstraction from particulars, qualities that confer on the consciousness thus conceived both its characteristic power and its chief disability.

The narrator is "nobody" in two ways already suggested by my discussion of narrative perspective: it is not individual, and it is not corporeal. First, the narrator is a collective result, a specifier

65

of consensus, and as such it is really not intelligible as an individual. Second, since the general consensus thus specified exists only through a dissociation, at a distance from the concrete, the narrator-specifier is also not intelligible as a corporeal existence.

The collective nature of consciousness is implied by the fundamental premises of realism. If one believes—and it is the business of realistic convention to make us believe—that an invariant, objective world exists, then consciousness is always *potentially* the same, interchangeable among individuals, because it is consciousness of the same thing. All consciousness derives from the same world and so, if total consciousness were possible, it would be the same for everyone. This implication of invariant nature is an implication that also follows from the realist view of time. Since time is inseparable from consciousness in realistic fiction, and since time is a continuous medium, again it follows that consciousness is *potentially* one single continuum. Neither time nor consciousness has material existence or simple location; the narrator, who most closely approximates pure consciousness, has no material existence either. As Dowden said of the "second self" that narrates George Eliot's fiction, it is, unlike its author (or even any of the characters), a being "unencumbered by flesh and blood and daily living."[1] Existence somewhere between particulars, mediate existence, the existence of consciousness and time, is a de-individualizing, unlocated thing, an abstraction that exists in order to break down the discontinuities that limitations introduce into experience, to bridge the manifest gaps in material existence. As the coordinating viewpoint, the narrator, or that collection I have been calling narrative perspective, realizes most fully this potential for collective and even continuous consciousness. It exists apart from, between, particulars; it is everywhere

---

[1] The "chief centre of interest for the imagination" in George Eliot's works, Dowden writes, "is that 'second self' who writes her books, and lives and speaks through them. Such a second self of an author is perhaps more substantial than any mere human personality encumbered with the accidents of flesh and blood and daily living. . . . It is more than an individual. . . ." (*Contemporary Review*, 1872). Cited in Gordon S. Haight, ed., *A Century of George Eliot Criticism* (Boston: Houghton Mifflin, 1965), p. 64.

and nowhere, brooding over the realistic work like an energy source, available to the characters who manage to tap it.

The individuality of the narrator, then, like the individuality of the implied spectator in painting, is not an issue in realism. Each is a collective result, a presence without location, density, or concrete particularity. Though its influence is everywhere felt, essential to the formulation of the whole realistic work, this perspective depends upon a consensus among multiple viewpoints—which is to say that it represents not an individual consciousness but a collective consciousness. Its power of generalization belongs to any witness, to any implied spectator or reflexive consciousness at a certain distance. Such power is not a special privilege of the narrator but merely the condition of consciousness generally—which is, by definition, to be distanced or estranged from particulars. The narrator thus represents at least a partial response to an urgent question in realistic fiction, the question as to what extent and in what terms collective experience is possible. It is both a moral and aesthetic problem, and one that is traceable to humanist values. "The primary assumption of all attempts to understand the men of the past," says Herbert Butterfield, "must be the belief that we can in some degree enter into minds that are unlike our own. If this belief were unfounded it would seem that men must be forever locked away from one another, and all generations must be regarded as a world and a law unto themselves."[2] Like the historian, the past-tense narrator recognizes the possibility of overlap between minds, and even embodies it. Realistic novels demonstrate the power of narrative consciousness to occupy one mind after another; and in so doing, they confirm the potential continuity of consciousness between minds and even implicitly extend that continuity beyond the arbitrary limits of the text to include the reader. The narrator transgresses the boundaries of individuality not only between persons but also between persons and texts.

I will return to this capacity to see from all viewpoints, but

[2] Herbert Butterfield, *The Whig Interpretation of History* (London: G. Bell and Sons, Ltd., 1963), p. 9. The historian's "chief function is to act in this way as the mediator between other generations and our own" (p. 10).

first, in order to clarify how the narrator transgresses by being both inside and outside the text, I want to invoke a pictorial analogue that has received some attention, Velasquez' *Las Meninas*. Behind the foreground figures (the child, her servants, and the painter at an easel) a mirror hangs on the wall. The reflection in that mirror is a crux of discussion. Given the laws of perspective observed in the painting, that mirror should reflect the artist, Velasquez; that is the standing-point of the implied spectator, i.e., the standing-point from which the uniform horizon is specified. This position, what John Searle calls "point A," belongs to the implied spectator, whose viewpoint coordinates the scene into a uniform horizon. But instead of the artist we find that position ("point A") occupied by two figures, King Philip and his wife; the artist himself appears in the picture, standing at his easel and looking out, along with the other foreground figures, at point A and at us. "The heart of the paradox presented by the Meninas is in that mirror. The mirror shows us point A but it shows it occupied by impossible tenants." The artist, in short, is not in his proper place; he is outside and inside his picture at once. "So that in the *Meninas* the 'I' of the 'I see' is not that of the painter but of the royal couple. Point A is after all not a natural point in the world. . . . A is in an important sense the subject matter of the picture."[3] "Point A" in fiction is occupied by the narrator and, to the extent that it can be considered a character, the narrator does what Velasquez' artist does: enters the picture and returns the gaze in an overt acknowledgment of the mutual responsibility in constructing a world.

"Point A," we should notice, also potentially includes any implied spectator, and not just the original one of the implied artist. The king and queen stand in for all these implied presences (the artist and all other spectators), while the implied artist, perhaps to escape the disembodiment of existence at Point A, takes up residence in his picture. In any case the "I" of the implied spectator becomes dissociated from the particular artist and be-

[3] John Searle, "*Las Meninas* and the Paradoxes of Pictorial Representation," *Critical Inquiry*, 6, no. 3 (Spring 1980), 486-87.

comes a general "I," for which Velasquez has found not one but two representatives: and two whose representative power as king and queen far exceeds that of any discrete individual. The very discreteness is called into question by the artist even though he affects to seek refuge in particularity by getting into his own painting. "The function of that reflection," writes Foucault, "is to draw into the interior of the picture what is intimately foreign to it: the gaze which has organized it."[4] Velasquez thus at the same time subscribes to the conventions of realism and calls attention to them. The organizing gaze doubles itself—a multiplication that could extend to infinity—and in doing so calls attention to the fact that the convention is sustained by agreement.

This continuity between organizing and figural apprehension characterizes realistic narrators as well. Describing this continuity in James, Percy Lubbock says:

> Nobody notices, but in fact there are now two brains behind that eye; and one of them is the author's, who adopts and shares the position of his creature, and at the same time supplements his wit . . . bringing another mind to bear upon the scene. It is an easy and natural *extension of the personage's power* of observation.[5] (Italics mine.)

[4] Michel Foucault, *The Order of Things: An Archaeology of the Human Sciences* (*Les Mots et Les Choses*) (New York: Random House, Vintage, 1973), pp. 15-16. There are various ways of conceptualizing the reconciling third term. Searle's "Point A" is one; Rene Girard (*Deceit, Desire and the Novel* [Baltimore: The Johns Hopkins University Press, 1966]) and Alistair Duckworth (*The Improvement of the Estate* [Baltimore: The Johns Hopkins University Press, 1971]) speak of "triangulation" as a phenomenon of narrative; and Propp's "donor" function is similar (see Fredric Jameson's discussion in *The Prison-House of Language* [Princeton: Princeton University Press, 1972], pp. 67-68): the folk tale depends for interest not on the *what* but the *how*—and behind every how is a *who*. This "donor" is "the element which explains the change described in the story." Another formulation of this mediating function is Freud's superego (see Leo Bersani, "The Subject of Power," *Diacritics* [September 1977], esp. p. 16, and Martin Price, "The Other Self," in Maynard Mack and Ian Gregor, eds., *Imagined Worlds*, [London: Methuen; New York: Barnes and Noble, 1968] p. 283).

[5] Percy Lubbock, *The Craft of Fiction* (New York: Viking, 1957), p. 258.

The collection of perspectives extends the power of any individual perspective and the possibility of modulation between minds that constitutes one unique pleasure of reading realistic fiction. Whether the narrator is Jane Austen's in *Emma*, or George Eliot's in *Daniel Deronda*, or Meredith's or Dickens's or many others', the reader's interest focuses again and again on the modulations from one mind to another: from character to character, from narrator to character, from reader to narrator. Following the connections between minds, however inexplicit those continuities may be, permits the reader to rise above individual limitation and particular constraint. Although critical discussion has until recently attended mainly to one or another discrete position of narrator and character, the reader's interest remains on the potential for connection between them, the manner in which such connection can develop, and the extensions of power thus confirmed.

The narrator, considered as a collective and not individual matter, has no particular "privilege," except insofar as consciousness itself is always privileged by being dissociated from particulars and superior to them. Its privilege is arbitrary and changeable. The collective nature of consciousness in realistic narration thus causes to evaporate one of the major critical problems with the so-called omniscient narrator, namely, its capacity to see from an "impossible number of viewpoints."[6] This power has seemed unrealistic because it appears to violate the relativism implicit in realism by transcending the ordinary limitations of individual viewpoint—limitations that are the chief condition and problem for the characters. Where characters struggle unsuccessfully with the powerful isolation of consciousness and where taking another's viewpoint requires a nearly impossible subjective leap, the narrator seems to move around with annoying ease. "Poor Lydgate! Poor Rosamond! Each lived in a world of which the other knew nothing." This famous phrase in *Middlemarch* is a model of the narrator's mediating behavior, bridging gaps that the characters are unable to cross. In the same way Thackeray's narrator in *Vanity Fair* bridges the gap between Amelia, dreaming of her

[6] Morroe Berger, *Real and Imagined Worlds: The Novel and Social Science* (Cambridge, Mass.: Harvard University Press, 1977), p. 181.

immortal hero-husband, and the real George, who lies on the field at Waterloo with a bullet in his heart. In both cases the narrator provides a unifying bridge of ironic paradox where the regret for unachieved unity, reunion, mutuality is a form of insistence on its possibility. In the very act of commenting on the disparity between viewpoints, Thackeray's puppeteer and George Eliot's wise voice seem to force intersections between them and so to bend the probabilities of the fictional world where such mutuality, such meetings, seem manifestly impossible.

But considered as a collective presence, the narrator's awareness is merely a potentiality of consciousness as derived from the various individual viewpoints that constitute it, including those of the characters; it is implicitly the future extension of the characters' own powers of insight and projection. The narrator's privilege is thus an extension of ordinary consciousness, one theoretically available to anyone able to go the distance. While this insight follows from the premises of realistic narration, it is an insight confirmed by ordinary experience as well. The activity of knowing other minds and of projecting results is not so unfamiliar or extraordinary an activity as it might at first seem. In fact, the narrator's activity is in some ways an accurate representation of familiar habits. Imagining the motives of others, carrying on mental conversations with them, anticipating their actions, and generally scripting events are activities with which even the most self-disciplined individuals may have some experience. Such self-confirming mental scenarios and interpretations, sometimes verbalized in the form of gossip, represent a kind of activity essential to knowledge in an equivocal universe, and they are part of what we ordinarily mean by consciousness. The silent conversation scholars have with the books and articles written by others is only one of the silent conversations of everyday, conversations that presuppose a vast, invisible arena of common endeavor.[7] "The *audition* of another voice in another head" is not only, as

[7] Such arenas, for example, as intertextuality and intersubjectivity. Homer Brown likens this communal nature of narrative to the "anonymity of gossip. . . . It is precisely this parentless drift, this unresolvable ambiguity that the novel has 'inherited' from gossip" ("The Errant Letter and the Whispering Gallery," *Genre*, 10, no. 4 (Winter 1977), 578-79.

71

Dorrit Cohn says, part of "the convention of the transparency of fictional minds"; it is a convention of common life as well.[8]

Stephen Toulmin argues, in fact, that "in real life, reading the minds of others often proves to be easy enough while knowing our own minds may well be much harder; so whatever may be the prime obstacle to mental lucidity and psychic candor, it can scarcely be the opacity of flesh and blood!" He cites Unamuno's remark that "to think is to talk with oneself, and each of us talks to himself because we have had to talk with one another. . . . Thought is interior language, and interior language originates in outward language. So that reason being linked to thought and so to inner speech is properly both social and communal."[9] Setting aside the special question of relations between written and spoken language, this description fits realistic premises closely. The analogy with painting is illuminating once again. Potentially sight is infinite. We could see everything—if we were not too old, too lazy, too busy—simply by moving around infinitely in space; sight is infinitely expandable. But given human limitation, we rely on the sight of others—their pictures, their reports, their microscopes—to supplement the seeing we do ourselves. The same is true of consciousness, which is to time as sight is to space: we could become conscious of everything—if we were not too old or too lazy or too busy—simply by expanding our awareness and, perhaps, without ever leaving our armchair.

Most treatments of realistic narrative that consider the narrator individualize it, and the results have been very unsatisfactory, often devolving into classification and taxonomy rather than into terms that accommodate the powerful continuities of realistic narration. This state of affairs in criticism is instructive and worth

[8] Cohn argues for the "realism of interior, subauditory monologue and for the sense when we are reading 'fiction' that we are mind-reading" (*Transparent Minds* [Princeton: Princeton University Press, 1978], pp. 60-61, 78, 87). Such mind-reading is not inconsistent with empirical epistemology, though it may be inconsistent with an Einsteinian universe, in which case the unanswerable objection to such powers of consciousness would be an objection not to the phenomenon itself but to empirical epistemology.

[9] Toulmin, "The Inwardness of Mental Life," *Critical Inquiry* (Autumn 1979), pp. 3, 7.

some attention here. Over and over again in even the best crit-icism spatial metaphors lurk in discussions of viewpoint, inter-fering even with efforts to discuss narrative continuities. A case in point is Geoffrey Tillotson's discussion of "the author" in a passage from Kingsley. His point is that narrative sequence moves subtly from detachment into and out of the mind of a character. "The author . . . is felt to be near" but has "not yet intruded as it were physically"; a later passage begins "deep in the mind of a personage" then moves to an "ambiguous" position and then one that is "the author decisively."[10] What Tillotson points to here is crucially important—the shifts in consciousness sometimes in mid-sentence from one to another temporary location—and his plea for more attention to this feature is eloquently put; but his vocabulary works against the insight. Dorrit Cohn's *Transparent Minds*, an especially valuable book for its fine delineations of the modulating narrative consciousness, also demonstrates how thoroughly spatial metaphors (quite different from my explicit spatial analogies) have permeated our discussion of narrative per-spective and how much these metaphors enforce arbitrary divi-sions upon what is actually a process and a continuity.[11]

These spatial metaphors, submerged in the critical language about point of view, arise from several sources. One is the der-ivation of critical vocabulary from other genres or from limited examples of fiction. Much critical language for describing nar-

[10] Geoffrey Tillotson, "Authorial Presence: Some Observations," in Maynard Mack and Ian Gregor, eds., *Imagined Worlds*, pp. 221-31.

[11] Cohn's threefold order for describing third-person narration often seems to be established as a basis for exceptions, so that, having established three different positions of the narrator relative to character, she draws our attention to the "overlap" between one and another, or the "insensible shading" or even "radical fusion" of narrating and figural voices. Her study shows conclusively how the narrator provides continuities unavailable to epistolary fiction and how past-tense telling makes available an astonishing range of spoken and unspoken language, verbal thought, and other mental states. She even returns several times to the indefiniteness of the gap between teller and told. But all of this notwithstanding the vocabulary of discrete spatial position often works at odds with the intended points and occupies the reader with distinctions whose arbitrariness is not ac-counted for. (*Transparent Minds*, esp. pp. 26, 75, 107, 126, 134, 137.)

73

rative ("scene," "dialogue," "monologue," "gesture," "action," "character") has been imported from discussion of drama, without allowance for the fact that a narrative is something more than a supine play. Another source of obstructive vocabulary is the practice of Henry James and his own critical use of pictorial, sculptural, and architectural metaphors. Percy Lubbock's work and others' have codified the practice of James and at the same time borrowed his metaphors.[12] Despite the symbiosis of space and time in fiction it is important to remember that even the structural principles of a novel must be discovered sequentially, and, even where two actions take place simultaneously in the story, they still must be discovered sequentially in the discourse. Linear, serial narration necessarily turns spatial gaps into temporal ones, transforming even a spatial absence into a past, just as it always transforms every present into a virtual present.

One final and important reason for the individualizing of narrators, however, has less to do with spatial analogues than with exigencies of criticism. "Identifying narrators," as Jonathan Culler has explained, "is one of the primary ways of naturalizing fiction." Naturalization restores literature "to a communicative function," gives it "a place in the world" as defined by a culture, situates it by reducing its strangeness. "The difference which seemed the source of value becomes a distance to be bridged by the activity of reading and interpretation. The strange, the formal, the fictional, must be recuperated or naturalized, brought within our ken, if we do not want to remain gaping before monumental inscriptions." The identification of narrators, which involves individualizing them, is a way of contraverting realistic convention

---

[12] Wayne Booth, for example, juggles degrees of distance with some skill to accommodate the fact that the novel dramatizes a continuity of different stages of consciousness. Distance "may be moral . . . physical or temporal" (*The Rhetoric of Fiction* [Chicago: University of Chicago Press, 1961], p. 156). See also Joseph Kestner, *The Spatiality of the Novel* (Detroit: Wayne State University Press, 1978): "In the spatial arts, time constitutes the *secondary* illusion; in the temporal arts, space is the secondary aesthetic illusion" (p. 19; also p. 28). And see W.J.T. Mitchell, "Spatial Form in Literature," *Critical Inquiry*, 6, no. 3 (Spring 1980), esp. 552; and, in the same issue, Robert Morgan's "Musical Time/ Musical Space," 527-58.

for the sake of another. "This convention may be seen as a last-ditch strategy for humanizing writing and making personality the focal point of the text."[13]

Attempts to find terms adequate to the intersubjective nature of narrative consciousness can be found in some recent interpretations of narration (although they do not distinguish consistently between realistic and other kinds). Erich Kahler traces *The Inward Turn of Narrative* from the eighteenth century, and acknowledges the unspecific, impersonalized, and intersubjective nature of this new narrative consciousness. "The later modern narrator is an impersonally objectified artistic consciousness caught up in the labor of expression, addressing itself to a no longer specific, an imaginary recipient. This imaginary recipient is included within the work of narration; he is immanent in the narrative and the narrator."[14] This recognition of mediation between narrator and reader or implied narrator and implied reader evokes reader-oriented critics like Wolfgang Iser and Stanley Fish, who attend to the text as a transaction that confirms the continuities between what is "inside" the text and those extensions of the consciousness (otherwise known as readers) implied "outside" of it.[15]

---

[13] *Structural Poetics* (Ithaca, N.Y.: Cornell University Press, 1975), pp. 200-201, 134-39. Culler cites Julia Kristeva on a parallel phenomenon in criticism of *intertextualité* or the relation of texts to other texts: " 'Every text takes shape as a mosaic of citations' " and thus validates the existence of "intersubjectivity" (p. 139).

[14] Erich Kahler, *The Inward Turn of Narrative*, trans. Richard and Clara Winston (Princeton: Princeton University Press, 1973), pp. 47, 178.

[15] For discussions of this implied reader see the following: Kestner on the "virtual reader" in *Spatiality of the Novel*, p. 177; J. Paul Hunter on the communal imperatives of the novel in "The Loneliness of the Long-Distance Reader," *Genre*, 10, no. 4 (Winter 1977), 455-84; Seymour Chatman on reader-drawn inferences ("reading out") as an element of story, in *Story and Discourse* (Ithaca, N.Y.: Cornell University Press, 1978), pp. 41-42; Douglas Hewitt to the effect that "realistic novels do not affect us as being like life; they are like the experience of being told about life by someone whom we trust," in *The Approach to Fiction* (Totowa, N.J.: Rowan and Littlefield, 1972), p. 55; and Tzvetan Todorov, "The Categories of Literary Narrative," trans. Joseph Kestner, *Papers on Language and Literature*, 16, no. 1 (Winter 1980), 31: "The image of the narrator is not a solitary image but is from the first page accompanied by 'the image of the reader.'

This intersubjectivity is not, as J. Hillis Miller pointed out some time ago, "omniscience." The "general consciousness" of the narrator he links to a collective mind that "has been brought into existence by the living together of a group rather than imposed from the outside by divine Providence"; it is a "sovereign inwardness" belonging to "the collective awareness of the community." This means, among other things, that consciousness is by definition impossible in solitude because it is a "consciousness of consciousness of others" in time.[16] What saves the narrator from the limitation of viewpoint is not omniscience, personalized as the author or as a surrogate "god," but the extension to infinity provided by inclusive consensus. The continuities between minds have a modal quality of the kind especially obvious in Proust, who intentionally blurs the boundaries between character, narrator, and author. In Proust, according to Gerard Genette, we have the "focalization" of narrative perspective by one or another character rather than a more discrete series of shifts between one mind and another.[17]

. . . These two images are proper to every work of 'fiction' confirming the general semiologic law that sender and receiver, I and You 'always appear together.' " For discussion of narrators as mediators between author and text see Wladimir Krysinski, "The Narrator as Sayer of the Author," *Strumenti Critici*, 11 (1977), 45, and Franz Stanzel, *Narrative Situations*, trans. James Pusak (Bloomington: University of Indiana Press, 1971), and "Second Thoughts on Narrative Situations," *Novel*, 11, no. 3 (Spring 1978), 247-64.

[16] *The Form of Victorian Fiction* (Notre Dame: University of Notre Dame Press, 1968), pp. 67-68, 23. Auerbach also recognizes that the "multipersonal representation of consciousness . . . has to do with the treatment of time" and that "depths of consciousness" have to do with "depth of time," and he places the shift to this kind of narrative around 1800; but because of his intention to include all the great works of Western literature into one continuous tradition Auerbach does not allow for distinctions between realism and other kinds of telling (see *Mimesis*, trans. Willard Trask [Princeton: Princeton University Press, 1953], pp. 474, 477).

[17] Gerard Genette, *Narrative Discourse: An Essay in Method*, trans. Jane E. Lewin (Ithaca: Cornell University Press, 1980). See also Timothy Reiss's interesting discussion of the mediating function in language and its power for maintaining public discourse ("Discursive Criticism and Epistemology," in Mario Valdés and Owen Miller, eds., *Interpretation of Narrative* [Toronto: University of Toronto Press, 1978], esp. pp. 39-40, 46).

In stressing the continuities between the minds in realistic narration and in conceiving the narrator as a collective rather than an individual consciousness, I want to avoid any suggestion that my subject is some preverbal "stream" of consciousness.. The term "stream of consciousness," as Robert Humphrey and Dorrit Cohn have argued persuasively, refers to the whole of mental operations, including preverbal awareness. Collective consciousness of the kind I am describing does not linger in the psychic depths revealed to Freud, Jung, Bergson, and others. The consciousness available to consensus in realism always depends upon distance and memory and thus upon the conscious formulation that these imply.[18]

In its treatment of perception the realistic convention of consensus entails a certain circularity (some may prefer *reflexiveness*), a circularity that may reflect only the self-confirming nature of systems in general but nevertheless one that the convention somewhat masks. The circularity I mean concerns the relations between consciousness and the objective world. Subject and object are born together in Western culture, and this is nowhere so evident as in realism. On the one hand the realistic consensus produces and supports the existence of an objective world; consensus literally "objectifies" the world. The narrative discovers different aspects of what, *by means of this very process*, can be identified as an autonomous reality. What is so, *is* so, because many different viewpoints *agree* that it is so. A stable, invariant world is there (at least to human perception)—solid, as in itself it really is—*because* everybody agrees that it is so. On the other hand, the objective world produces consensus. All consciousness

---

[18] Humphrey distinguishes stream-of-consciousness fiction by subject matter, not technique: specifically the prespeech levels of awareness favored by new subjects like "Gestalt psychology, psychoanalytical psychology, Bergsonian ideas of *durée* and the *élan vital*, religious mysticism, much symbolic logic, Christian existentialism, etc." (*Stream of Consciousness in the Modern Novel* [Berkeley: University of California Press, 1954], esp. pp. 3-5, 8). See Cohn's related discussion of the difference between the inner speech of adults, evolved from "the vocal egocentric speech of children," and their public speech. Inner speech is not "speech minus sound," but an "entirely separate speech function" (*Transparent Minds*, pp. 87, 95-96).

is epiphenomenal: a reflex from, a response to an objective, invariant world that remains the same regardless of spectator mobility. The narrator is, in W. Blok's words, "a function of his own narrative. He is summoned by it."[19] The same is true for all minds in the narrative; all are summoned in this way by the objects that they mutually perceive. We are dealing, therefore, with a reversible premise. Since the objective world of realistic narration is a collective result of consciousness, one to which the narrator also contributes, the narrator's consciousness is to some degree consciousness of itself. The realistic convention does not force these circularities on us, but we should be aware of them when considering the function of the narrator in the realistic convention, because this epistemological state of affairs suggests, among other things, the precariousness of the realistic consensus.

The insubstantiality of the narrator is a prerequisite condition for the narrator's power. The values of realism—consensus, continuity, mobility, distance, infinity—are relatively careless of the concrete. Particulars remain mere concretia until, combined with other cases of a similar kind, they yield their abstraction; concretes are appreciated not in themselves but as tools and as keys that unlock hidden secrets. Particulars have value only quantitatively, multiplied until they permit consensus to form or measurement of distance and relationship to take place. The insubstantiality of the narrator, then, comes as no surprise. But as Panofsky cautions, "modern perspective . . . is a two-edged sword." It can make both solids and voids equally real. "Perspective permits the artist to clarify the shape and relative location of corporeal things but also to shift the interest to phenomena contingent upon the presence of an extracorporeal medium."[20] The

[19] "Ergocentric Analysis of the Novel and the History of Literature," *Dutch Studies* (1977), p. 80.

[20] Erwin Panofsky, *Early Netherlandish Painting*, 2 vols. (Cambridge, Mass.: Harvard University Press, 1964), p. 6. See also Alan Kennedy, *Meaning and Signs in Fiction* (New York: St. Martin's Press, 1979), p. 129: "It is erroneous to suggest that in its history the novel shows any tendency to forsake the mysterious unseen for the world of the observable."

extracorporeal medium of light or of consciousness can even become an object of focus itself, supplanting more corporeal things. Foucault, for example, calls attention to the profound dematerialization implied in painting by the continuities of sight: "the profound invisibility of what one sees is inseparable from the invisibility of the person seeing."[21] As with the "point A" of a realistic painting, so with the realistic narrator: the occupant of that position implies dematerialized, nondiscrete, even indiscreet powers of mind and eye, powers that support and sustain realistic representation. The narrator presiding over a literary consensus "offers the reader nothing but a collection of positions which it presents in a variety of relationships, without ever formulating the focal point at which they converge. For this point lies in the reader's imagination, and in fact can only be created by his reading."[22]

This estrangement from the concrete is what gives consciousness its power in realistic conventions, a power that constantly overwhelms the nice distinctions among narrator, reader, and author, among narrator, character, and fictional structure. One place where the peculiarity of this narrative consciousness appears most clearly is the relation between the narrator and the formal elements of the novel: those patterns of imagery, parallel episodes, paired characters, or any of the rhythmic, repetitive features whose function is to confirm the orderliness of human experience. In *Our Mutual Friend*, for example, the allusive dust image, the

---

[21] Foucault, *Order of Things*, pp. 15-16.

[22] Wolfgang Iser, "Indeterminacy and Reader Response," in J. Hillis Miller, ed., *Aspects of Narrative* (New York: Columbia University Press, 1971), p. 24. Iser finds this "indeterminacy" to have been on "continual increase" since the eighteenth century (p. 23). See also Douglas Hewitt's useful chapter on "The Conventions of Realism: The Shared World," in his *Approach to Fiction*, pp. 45-66.

For discussions of the ontological insecurity associated with this kind of narrative see Edward Said, *Beginnings* (New York: Basic Books, 1975), esp. pp. 85-93; for discussion of anxieties over the insubstantiality of the self see Patricia Spacks's *Imagining a Self* (Cambridge, Mass.: Harvard University Press, 1976), and Hans Meyerhoff's *Time in Literature* (Berkeley: University of California Press, 1955).

parallels between marriages, between deaths, between forms of diving, all belong to a "single spectrum of scenes and sentences and meanings"[23] that seems to exist beyond the narrator's consciousness and to reveal the regularities of human nature to the watchful reader without particular aid from the narrator. Form thus generalizes the strings of private moments in which individual characters are isolated in their own consciousnesses. Whereas the narrator coordinates a temporal sequence in much the same way as any individual consciousness would, the narrative structure coordinates present and present, past and past, so that the various points of view all belong to a single temporal continuity that approaches clock time. This time is a continuous temporal medium distinct from the narrator's remembered sequence; it remains invariant despite the formulations of any point of view. Although shared moments and true meetings of mind are rarities in realistic novels, the possibility of such mutuality is perpetually held out by the synchronizations of time that these submerged metaphors produce.[24]

[23] J. P. Stern, *On Realism* (London and Boston: Routledge and Kegan Paul, 1973), pp. 82-83.

[24] A word is in order here about Bakhtin's important study of *The Dialogic Imagination*, translated by Michael Holquist and Caryl Emerson (Austin: University of Texas Press, 1981), which appeared after my book was completed. Although our terms agree in various ways, we do disagree on some important points concerning the narrator and concerning time. In seeking a field theory for "the novel," he takes on a subject too large to allow for the kind of discriminations I am making about two kinds of narrative time and about the collective nature of consciousness in realism; in discrediting "monologism"—something partly intelligible in terms of his particular audience—he blurs what I take to be important distinctions. Thus, for example, he personalizes the narrative voice so much that he leaves undeveloped openings that lead to the connection between language and consciousness. He does touch on problems of "consciousness" and "intention" of the sort I deal with here, but does not pursue them (see pp. 292, 295, 303). In treating different forms of time he assumes methodologically a single kind of time as a common denominator; so he speaks of "the past," "the present," or "memory" as if they had the same status universally, where I argue that even these values change with the currency. Different kinds of time as evident in plots for him still exist "in history." These habits of thinking about narrator and about time permit him to stress differences between voices, an important discrimination but one that I argue has a different value when one assumes a common temporal denominator than when one does not.

One of the most important of these synchronizing devices is the "meanwhile" clause, which brings the action in one plot into synchrony with the action in another. While Hetty Sorrel is flirting with Arthur Donnithorne, Adam Bede is entertaining hopes of her; while Amelia Sedley is dreaming of George, George's father is ordering him to marry someone else; while the Stranger is searching London for Little Nell's grandfather, the old man is journeying farther and farther away. Each particular episode is narrated in isolation, as the characters experience it, but the narrative shifts call attention to the fact that these episodes belong to the "same" time and hence to a unified field of relationships that cannot be perceived by any individual consciousness. The narrative order thus reassures the reader of the possibility, essential to realism, that the gaps between one point of view and another can be mediated and therefore that the problems of discontinuity that the characters face are solvable.

The paradoxical side of these connections is one of the chief sources of interest in realistic novels. While the possibility of mutual experience is held out by the novel's formal conventions, the characters more often than not fail to bridge the gaps that separate them. Dickens makes heavy use of the "meanwhile" device to show connection between characters who, although they are mutually invisible to each other, are mutually present in a temporal sense. For example, one action in *The Old Curiosity Shop* concerns the efforts by the Stranger to find Nell's grandfather who, it turns out, is his brother. The more he searches, however, the wider the gap between them becomes and, when he finally catches up with Nell and her grandfather at the farthest reach of their journey, the reconciliation proves impossible. The Stranger begs his dying brother to remember him, that is, to recall and recover their kinship, their shared life. Given the importance in Dickens of such recognitions of common nature, in this case literal brotherhood, it is a terrible moment when Nell's grandfather responds not to his brother but to his own obsession. Such moments of union or reunion do occur in some novels, but they are rare. In *Middlemarch*, for example, Dorothea's meeting with Rosamond at first fails but then succeeds, and the two women

81

momentarily achieve a mutual understanding that asserts the possibility of such meetings across immense psychological distances. But bridging such gaps, as Gwendolen Harleth finds, requires "mountainous travel," and few are equipped for the expedition. That the gaps are bridgeable is shown less by successful examples than by the existence in the temporal field of similitudes that signify regularity, order, intelligibility in the world of common experience.

Repeated images like those of prisons, webs, rivers, mirrors quietly insist on the similitudes between apparently disparate things. Without calling attention to themselves, they invite the reader to levels of generalization about patterns of experience that are higher than any reached explicitly by either the narrator or the characters. These synchronizations, while they have metaphorical value of enormous power, have their most important effect on the reader's sense of time. They suggest the connections between one character's present and another's, one person's experience and another's, and in so doing these synchronizations reinforce the implication that all the human activity in the scene takes place in the "same" time and the "same" world, and is part of the "same" human nature. The mutual informativeness of events could, by dint of this increasing power of generalization, extend to infinity and, because this is so, it exceeds the particular vision of the narrator.

These formal patterns can get ambiguously intertwined with the narrator's consciousness, because such repetitive patterns resemble the doubling action of memory as it perpetually shuttles between past and present, collecting the similar instances separated by time. In *Little Dorrit*, the reader can ask, *is* society really a prison or is that just the way Somebody sees it? In *Villette*, *is* society a carnival or is that only Lucy Snowe's view? In *Great Expectations* do Magwitch and Orlick really have some deep kinship with Pip, or is that merely the nervous impression of Pip's sensibility? If the reader supposes that form is meaning because it implies a meaner, then the reader will search for the final, conclusive point of view and the search will extend in easy (and increasingly less satisfactory) stages from the narrator to the author, from the author to social conditions, and so will go the unsuccessful search for closure, or, to use Culler's term, for ways to naturalize the narrator.

These compositional elements cannot be naturalized satisfactorily either to the narrator or to the author. The important thing about them is the ambiguity they introduce into the relationship between author and narrator. Where the ambiguity is not preserved—as when either a character or an implied author explicitly takes possession of them—the realistic effect is disturbed. In *Middlemarch* or *The Old Curiosity Shop* the narrative structure signifies the regularities in the world that are independent of viewpoint and the narrator merely presents that order as it is perceived by a single mind; but in *The Ambassadors* the perceived structures are the only structures. James's scrupulous adherence to a single viewpoint produces a powerful coherence, but it distinctly sacrifices both the social interest and the objectivity of realism. James's novels are almost like a realistic painting with only one visual cone, that is, without the intersecting viewpoint that generalizes the scene viewed. In fact, it is precisely at those moments of intersection, like the moment when Strether finally sees events through Mme de Vionnet's eyes, that Henry James drops his inquiry—respectful, perhaps, of the tremendous difficulty and power, even the violence, implicit in the leap from one subjective view to another. It is as if James believed with difficulty in the possibility of a shared, common set of meanings derived from a common order that could validate and reinforce the private ones, and had confidence only in leaps from one subjective set to another in an exhausting (albeit exhilarating) series of encounters. In any case, his novels show how a narrative, to the extent that it associates all structure with a single mind, departs from the premises of realism and their requirement of having both an independent, invariant order and a subject to view it.

The pressure of realistic conventions, however, works against any efforts to personalize the controlling consciousness. The entire effect of verisimilitude depends upon the collectivization of perception: in the case of painting, the collectivization of sight,

83

in the case of fiction, the collectivization of consciousness.[25] Narrative perspective consists both of narrator and of structure, and the two are both separable and yet not wholly distinct precisely because they are epiphenomena of the same world. The repetitive patterns, the insistent similitudes, the relative measurements of the realistic fiction belong not to a single consciousness but to a kind of consciousness that is not significantly an individual matter. At one extreme, the narrator may be very like the characters: possessed like Thackeray's or Conrad's narrators of a particular voice and particular opinions. At the other extreme the narrator's consciousness can be wholly generalized: a vessel of accumulated awareness like Austen's or James's that breaks the bonds of any personal experience.

Insofar as the signs of form in a novel are not traceable to a single consciousness, they present an orderly world that is independent of any center of self[26] and cannot be got outside of or distanced because it extends beyond the limited horizon and is the same for all times and places. To the extent that the narrator takes personal possession of these forms, as Thackeray's narrator does for a moment at the end of *Vanity Fair*, their realism is compromised, they are unrealized because their projective extension, their futurity, is compromised. This rarely happens, however. Even in first-person narratives like *Great Expectations* and *Henry Esmond*, the universality of the generalizations in those novels is saved by the persistent doubt about how much the narrators, Pip and Esmond, see of the full significance that the reader sees in their histories. Even though the first person narration forces the reader to remain always in the company of the central character, the reader can easily see more than the char-

[25] See Ivins's discussion of this rationalization in painting, *On the Rationalization of Sight* (Papers, no. 8 [New York: Metropolitan Museum of Art, 1938]; repub. Da Capo, New York, 1973).

[26] See Leo Bersani on how "the networks of metaphorical correspondences" in Proust are "psychologically disintegrating in the sense that they make it impossible for us to locate any fixed center of the self from which all its images might proceed." ("Realism and the Fear of Desire," *A Future for Astyanax* [Boston and Toronto: Little, Brown & Co., 1969], p. 85.)

acter at every point because significance in a realistic world depends on emergent forms and these are never evident in a single physical arrangement or episode. While the single point of view, then, is essential to the rationalization both of sight and of consciousness, still both the spectator and the narrator look upon a world they have not made. Its regularities can be seen only from a single perspective, but they do not depend for their existence on that perspective. The controlling point of view is the most powerful, since the viewer and reader alike are forced by the realistic artist to see from that fixed vantage point, but the order thus perceived extends beyond the horizon to infinity; it exceeds the coordinating vision and implicitly reveals its partiality.

The perspective administered by the realistic narrator reflects most fully the potential of consciousness for continuous extension of power, but this potential is realized only at a price, the price of estrangement from the particulars of experience and from the actual present—the price, in a word, of disembodiment. Questions about the identity or location of the past-tense narrator cannot be answered, because the narrator literally is nobody. Like Odysseus in the cave of Polyphemus, the narrator is a survivor stripped of all the distinguishing marks of human identity except a voice: in Odysseus' case an almost pure human heroism stripped of family, kingdom, retinue, name; in the narrator's case, almost pure consciousness, stripped of physical embodiment, gesture, concreteness. To revise Descartes' dictum, substituting "consciousness" for "time," we might say that "consciousness, without things, is nothing else but a mere ideal possibility."[27]

Standing forever in a continuous actual present that has no concreteness or measurable change and consists only of remembering, the narrator has no perceptible identity. Since identity in realism is a residue of motion, a residue of change, the changeless narrator who stands fixed in a continuous actual present has no identity. In the material and intelligible universe of realistic

[27] Descartes quoted by Kestner, *Spatiality of the Novel*, p. 15. George Eliot's Lydgate reflects in similar terms on how imagination creates its "ideally illuminated space" (*Middlemarch*, ch. 16).

85

fiction the narrator is, in Leo Bersani's phrase, "the one psychologically empty or at least incomplete presence in the novel," the one being unavailable to discourse.[28] Like time and consciousness, the narrator is everywhere and nowhere, suspended from participation in actions and choices by the very reflective consciousness that presumably makes reasoned choice and action possible. The inescapable condition of consciousness in realistic fiction is perpetual distance from the actual present—a distance that is also estrangement. The actual present, the moment of possibility, is always virtual, always distanced, always mediate for consciousness. The actual present, if it can be said to exist at all, is the most difficult reality to know because to know anything means to be outside it.[29] In any consistent past-tense narration the teller is forever after the fact, existing in a present that is perpetually displaced by the past that is being told. The past acts like a trap in which the narrating consciousness is caught and held, and so prevented from assuming its actual present. The narrator has the kind of abstracted and helpless lucidity that succeeds experience; but without local habitation that narrator has no arena in which to exert this mastery.

The purification of narrative consciousness, the development of language unaccompanied by other performance, is a kind of existence increasingly reflected in English fiction of the eighteenth and nineteenth centuries. Kahler treats the inward turn of narrative as a progressive "alienation," a progressive "displace-

---

[28] Bersani characterizes the realistic universe as one of "compulsive intelligibility" ("The Subject of Power," *Diacritics* [September 1977], pp. 16-17). See Julio Cortázar's treatment of the ontological dangers for those fixed behind a lens. In *Blow-up* it is the photographer, Michel, who is "dead," fixed by the lens, while the world (both the one in his photograph and the one outside his window) continues to move.

[29] Gertrude Stein's own prose captures something of this difficulty in her comment on the problem of prose since its "separation" from poetry in the eighteenth century. The problem lies with thinking about how you know anything. "And then slowly they came to know what they knew might mean something different from what they had known it was when they knew simply knew what it was" (*Narration: Four Lectures* [Chicago: University of Chicago Press, 1935], pp. 27-28).

ment of outer space by what Rilke has called inner space, a stretching of consciousness."[30] In James the narrator is "no longer a figure that leans and looks out of a window, scanning a stretch of memory." In *The Ambassadors*, for example, the prevailing view "is given as nobody's view—not his [Strether's] own, as it would be if he told the story himself, and not the author's as it would be if Henry James told the story. . . . The novelist passes on towards drama, gets behind the narrator, and represents the mind of the narrator as in itself a kind of action." Despite the fact that consensus in James is hard won and precarious, this description captures the essential development toward consciousness as the subject of fiction that still retains the consensus of realism. "The story passes in an invisible world, the events take place in the man's mind," which is "a mind grown visible."[31] This is an advanced stage in the development from man as knower to man as thinker. This fact about realistic narration, still implicit in the novels of the eighteenth and mid-nineteenth centuries, has become explicit by the time of Proust, who shows in *Remembrance of Things Past* how it is that the only true life is literature. Proust, in Dorrit Cohn's words, defines "the narrative process as the retrospective cognition of an inner life that cannot know itself at the instant of experience. It is therefore essentially a method for rendering past consciousness that Proust has in mind in the frequently cited sentences: 'True life, life at last discovered and illuminated, the only life therefore really lived, that life is

---

[30] Kahler, *Inward Turn of Narrative*, p. 5. See also Leo Braudy's interesting discussion of the growth of mind in eighteenth-century historical writing, from the serene detachment of Hume to the mental portrait of Gibbon. Historiography develops from the separate treatment of mind and fact to their treatment as part of one conception. "The final impression of the *Decline and Fall* is of the mind that created it" (*Narrative Form in History and Fiction* [Princeton: Princeton University Press, 1970], p. 268). Lewis Beck gives a condensed account of how, in philosophy between Newton and Kant, time gradually replaces eternity as a philosophical problem, and thus introduces consciousness as a problem for philosophy ("World Enough, and Time," in Paula Backscheider, ed., *Probability, Time, and Space in Eighteenth-Century Literature* [New York: AMS Press, 1979], esp. pp. 116-17, 122, 125).

[31] Lubbock, *Craft*, pp. 146-48, 156, 162.

87

literature.' "[32] By the late nineteenth century the disembodiment of intellect receives some negative treatment. A well-known example is Conrad's Kurtz, who has become "just a voice": a disembodied intellect, a legend mainly on paper (as literature), deranged by its own abstraction and turned destructive.[33]

Differences between first- and third-person tellers do not appreciably alter the effect of disembodiment. This is not to say that there are no interesting differences between first- and third-person narrations. For one thing, the narrator who stands both inside and outside the fictional world, i.e., is both actor and teller, tends to confirm more conclusively that continuity between virtual and actual time upon which fictional realism rests. But the difference between first and third person is not definitive in realism.[34] A realistic novel may be written in either third or first person, but it can *only* be written in the past tense. Autobiographical narrators like Pip in *Great Expectations* or like Henry Esmond appear as characters during the course of the story and as such they submit to the encumbrances of circumstance; but the full consciousness they assume as tellers tends to dissolve their corporeality and to make them, as tellers, weightless and disembodied like third-person tellers. They share the ontological uncertainty of the tellers of *Middlemarch* or *Our Mutual Friend*. Who and where is the narrator of *Middlemarch*? The question cannot be answered. As tellers, Pip and Esmond are in the same disembodied condition. Who and where is Pip at the time of the telling? There is scarcely a clue. Even in *Henry Esmond* the few clues

---

[32] Cohn, *Transparent Minds*, p. 146.

[33] Frederick Bogel claims that a faith in a "paradoxical nexus at the heart of things," faith in a "central reconciling substance," is lost in the eighteenth century and along with it confidence in "our capacity for substantive experience" ("Structure and Substantiality in Later Eighteenth-Century Literature," *Studies in Burke and His Time*, 15 [1973-74], 146-47).

[34] Cohn notes the ease with which first-person narration can be transformed into third (*Transparent Minds*, pp. 100-101). The very ease of this transformation, it seems to me, hints at the primary importance of continuity between minds and at the secondary importance of distinctions between third and first person, certainly secondary to the distinction between present and past tense in import for narrative.

scarcely matter. First-person tellers keep referring to an "I" that has no present state except in the act of telling; they too are only lenses for seeing the past states of their existence which cumulatively fill out the identity of the "I" who tells and who, nevertheless, remains beyond particularization. Autobiographical narrations that actually continue into the narrator's present moment of telling (like *Moll Flanders* or *Jane Eyre*) are rare, and they have an unsettling effect because the control provided by a distanced consciousness is threatened.

So dematerializing is the position of controlling consciousness in James that, as Lubbock points out, it presents a danger to any character that becomes for long the "vessel of sensation." Such a center of consciousness—like Strether or Isabel—is in danger of becoming a transparency, in danger of seeming light, weightless, by comparison to other characters with more "objective" images, i.e., physical outline and presence. So the one who "ought to bulk in the story more massively than any one, tends to remain the least recognizable of the company, and even to dissolve in a kind of impalpable blur. By his [James's] method . . . the author is of course forbidden to look this central figure in the face, to describe and discuss him; the light cannot be turned on him immediately."[35] Even in Richardson's epistolary fiction, and for all the immediacy of his writing "to the moment," we know little about Pamela at the actual moment she writes her letters. However close in time that writing may be to the actual event, it can never overtake it and remain realistic. Fielding's joke at Richardson's expense (*Shamela*) was based on the reduction to ab-

---

[35] Lubbock, *Craft*, p. 259. Gerard Genette makes this point in his discussion of Proust in *Narrative Discourse*: "One of the fictions of literary narrating—perhaps the most powerful one, because it passes unnoticed, so to speak—is that the narrating involves an instantaneous action, without a temporal dimension" (p. 222). "We know more or less where Proust wrote the *Recherche du temps perdu*, but we are ignorant of where Marcel is considered to have produced the narrative of his life, and we scarcely think of worrying about it" (p. 216). For discussions of similar questions see Robert Weimann, "Point of View in Fiction," in Gaylord Le Roy et al., eds., *Preserve and Create* (New York: Humanities Press, 1973), esp. pp. 56-57, and Norman Friedman on "Point of View" in *Form and Meaning* (Athens: University of Georgia Press, 1975), esp. pp. 142, 153.

surdity of this gap between teller and event. ("Odsbobs! I hear him just coming in at the Door. You see I write in the present Tense, as Parson *Williams* says. Well, he is in Bed between us. . . .") Whether it is *Robinson Crusoe* or *Emma*, the gap between teller and tale remains indistinct, and it does so because that gap is essential both to the power of generalization inherent in the realistic convention and to the power of consciousness generally.

The situation of the narrator thus reveals with special force the ontological tensions entailed by realistic premises. There is in the realistic fiction always a gap between consciousness and event, even for characters directly engaged in the action. Estranged by its privilege, consciousness thus defined necessarily moves from the changeable to the changeless, from *adiaphora* to the "true church," as Erasmus would put it. Since in a given moment *adiaphora* is all that ever appears, the main arena of knowledge is in the abstractions of consciousness that are the residue of many *adiaphora* experienced in time. The invitation to ever-closer approximation of truth spurs the consciousness to accumulate the experience that will ultimately enable knowledge to accelerate the pace of life for the sake of this experience, perhaps even to stretch the limits of endurance in order finally to grasp the formal abstraction that will give meaning to experience thereafter. This is the happy state at which Newman and Mill arrive in their autobiographies where, they tell us, revelation is complete and they have "no more history to tell."[36] The narrators of realistic fiction, who inhabit an open-ended time, are less comfortably circumstanced. Their consciousness is an epiphenomenon of the regularities presented by the world to perception in time; it is bound to that world and to the consensus

[36] Newman writes, "From the time that I became a Catholic, of course I have no further history of my religious opinions to narrate. In saying this, I do not mean to say that my mind has been idle, or that I have given up thinking on theological subjects; but that I have had no variations to record. . . ." (*Apologia Pro Vita Sua* [Boston: Houghton Mifflin, 1956], p. 227). After describing his conversion Mill writes: "I have no further mental changes to tell of, but only, as I hope, a continued mental progress; which does not admit of a consecutive history" (*Autobiography* [New York: Columbia University Press, 1924], p. 155).

90

that marks its stability. The narrator's privilege is but an accidental result of an arbitrarily chosen position; its disembodied
consciousness is only a sustained example of the condition of
consciousness generally, which is to be perpetually estranged by
its own abstractions from any particular scene.

So long as we accept the narrator's transparency, the regularities we perceive through the lens are not compromised by the
tension between teller and tale—the tension of that indefinite
gap between consciousness and particulars—any more than the
order perceived in a Vermeer is compromised by the primary visual
angle. The governing point of view merely specifies the set of
relationships, those generalizations of realism that project beyond
the arbitrarily limited horizon to all times and places. The realistic
world is consistent only so long as we accept the narrator as a
specification of general agreement, a medium for seeing that coordinates the temporal field and registers the world's variety in a
manner common to all consciousness.

As soon as we start asking after Marlow's mother, his motives
for curiosity, or inquire of George Eliot's narrator why we are
being told all this, we have shifted the focus from the field to
the viewer, we have assumed an opacity in the narrative consciousness that requires us to put *it* in perspective, to see it from
the outside. This refocusing translates the objective field that the
narrator describes into a subjective vision that requires further
distance to be objectified, a distance unavailable in the realistic
work. We have prepared ourselves for Humbert Humbert, not
the teller of *Middlemarch*, and we have made it impossible to get
more than fleeting glimpses in the novel of an invariant, objective
world.

When we lose the faith (and perhaps the operative word is
faith) that these regularities exist, then at the same time we lose
the possibility of that distance from which we could view them.
When we cannot maintain distance, because it yields nothing or
because the world does not require it, then the peril and possibility
of the present are both enormously enhanced. A story that does
not permit the generalizations to form actually prevents the consciousness from remaining disembodied, and the reader becomes

the accomplice of the story, an unwitting participant, a victim like the hapless reader in Cortázar's story, "Continuity of Parks": "he" settles back into his green velvet armchair to read a novel, and gradually detaches himself like a good realistic reader from his particular cares in order to get involved in the story of two lovers whose final meeting results in their agreement that the woman's lover should venture out of the woods, into the great house, up the stairway, down the hall to the library, into the library with knife poised, and up behind the man sitting in a green velvet armchair reading a novel. The virtual present, in which the realistic reader enjoys his detachment, becomes an actual present, in which the reader cannot maintain distance from the story. The potential violence of this transition under-scores the difference in premises between the kind of narrative that does not contain the present in a controlled pattern of sig-nificance and the realistic narrative that does.

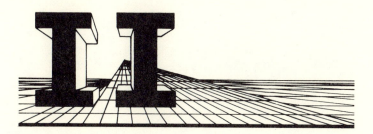

PROBLEMATICS
OF AGREEMENT

CHAPTER FOUR

Time and Eternity:
The Cases of *Robinson Crusoe* and *Pamela*

The rationalization of consciousness, together with the idea of identity based upon it, remains problematic in Defoe and Richardson. Each demonstrates in his first novel the way in which realistic conventions can be used to limit such realistic values as consensus, mobility, depth, and recollection. Despite the presence of plot, character, and detail, despite sensational action, elaborate records of consciousness, the realistic conventions in *Robinson Crusoe* and *Pamela* are attenuated. This does not mean that these are limp or inconsiderable novels, but rather that they qualify realistic techniques and premises in illuminating ways. Both novels are kinds of past-tense narration, but in neither does the author exploit the full power of that convention. In *Pamela* we stay continuously in the heroine's mind, and yet the epistolary style breaks up the continuities of time and space even more than it does in *Clarissa*, where multiple narrators at least attempt (though finally they fail) to focus on the same events. In *Robinson Crusoe* we have a past-tense narrator reflecting from some distance on past experience, but it is a narrator that scarcely capitalizes on its power. When the recollective powers of memory are so attenuated, neither the single consciousness nor the sequential narration is sufficient to produce verisimilitude.

Despite their differences as protagonists, Crusoe and Pamela share similar concerns and gestures: the anxiety about psychic preservation in the face of unstable, even wildly fluctuating, experience; the recourse to enclosure and barricade; the recourse to writing and to other symbols in the effort to maintain the mind; the depreciation of memory's power; and the obsession with decoding worldly signs in order to maintain alignment with the eternal Truth. To assess their positions they resort not to forms of mobility but to fortification. They create sacred spaces, places discontinuous with their context that differ from it qualitatively and must be maintained against its encroachment. Crusoe's private space may be small and Pamela's smaller; but since their private territories differ *qualitatively* from their neighborhoods, mere quantitative measures have little importance. When the point of reference is another world, relationships in this world have mutual relevance only by having a common point of reference outside it. In the eye of God, human timekeeping is a paltry measure—a necessary one, perhaps, but one with a defensive and mainly negative value. When the vanishing-point of time lies outside the temporal world, time does not extend to infinity on a human horizon; it is stopped in God.

In such a context the continuities and provisional resolutions of realism have little meaning. Robinson Crusoe says as much in his poem on "Eternity":

What we have been, and what we are,
The present and the Time that's past
We can resolve into nothing here,
But what we are to be in thee, at last.

From the sequel to *Robinson Crusoe (Serious Reflections During the Life and Strange Adventures of Robinson Crusoe with His Vision of the Angelic World)*, this poem directs attention to the margins of experience and depreciates the value of historical relations which, it says, come to "nothing." The here-and-now makes sense not relative to a there-and-then but to a world outside time and experience, the "angelic world" where all linear developments become stopped, permanently synchronized and perfectly fixed. "Eternity," Crusoe says elsewhere in the same poem, is a "mighty

Circle."[1] This important conventional image for time appears in *Pamela* as well. Like Crusoe she is confined to nearly total solitude during the first half of her story; like Crusoe she then moves back during the second half into society and the problems of worldly life. When she does this, however, she takes up residence in a state of blessedness; the refractory episodes disappear, and she passes every period in "the same agreeable manner. And thus, in a rapturous circle, the time moves on."[2] The cycles of Pamela's life may be smaller than Crusoe's and more closely synchronized with daily domestic routine, but the difference in scale should not obscure the affinities between her "blest" existence and Crusoe's, when he is capable of perceiving it.

These novels share with the traditions of spiritual autobiography this anxious concern for relations between temporal and eternal existence. Spiritual autobiographies, as G. A. Starr suggests, depreciate temporal sequence. "Between two successive episodes, in other words, a direct, causal connection may be altogether lacking; nevertheless they will be significantly related by virtue of having a common point of reference."[3] When the

---

[1] Quoted in Paul Alkon, *Defoe and Fictional Time* (Athens: University of Georgia Press, 1979), p. 92. Alkon quotes the 1903 edition of the sequel (Boston: Dana Estes & Co., pp. 187-90). For an argument that Defoe's main concern was the conflict between this world and the next and that his main object was to make readers experience this conflict through ethical crises, see Anthony James, *Daniel Defoe's Many Voices: A Rhetorical Study of Prose Style and Literary Method* (Amsterdam: Rodopi, NV, 1972). "Such ethical crises are not only central to Defoe's fiction, but are also stylistically and dramatically highlighted by the author" (p. 157, n.22).

[2] Samuel Richardson, *Pamela, Or, Virtue Rewarded* (New York: W. W. Norton & Co., Inc.), p. 387. All references will be to this edition and will be included parenthetically in the text. Calling attention to the religious conventions in Pamela's forty days "in the wilderness," Mark Kinkead-Weekes remarks that "accounts of the novel which recognize the central concern with faith are remarkable by their absence" (*Samuel Richardson, Dramatic Novelist* [Ithaca: Cornell University Press, 1973], pp. 35, 57). Alkon points to similar patterns in Crusoe, noting that "Crusoe's life is perceived as a movement away from historical time toward the encounter with private and sacred time on his island, followed by a return to participation in the era which he left" (*Fictional Time*, p. 64).

[3] G. A. Starr, *Defoe and Spiritual Autobiography* (Princeton: Princeton University Press, 1965), p. 43.

97

crucial change of condition occurs, it can be, like Crusoe's conversion or Mr. B's, "somewhat abrupt" or even "instantaneous," partly because no special value accrues to temporal continuity, while considerable value accrues to breaks with or escapes from worldly contexts. The invisible world at every step transcends the visible, and emblematic stories express the relation between the two better than continuous histories.[4] Inconsistencies between past and present can be tolerated easily because they are insignificant to the real unity, which is God's. Chronological time offers merely a "mechanical sequence of second causes" whose ultimate source is outside time.[5]

The conception of time as a fluctuating sea, a conception uncongenial to the linear time of realism, appears compatible both with the spiritual autobiography and with the two novels considered here. To a spiritual pilgrim time is a necessary evil; like the sea, it is a destructive element to which one must not submit. Robinson Crusoe lives at the mercy of the sea currents, emblems of the tides of his "folly" and of the shifting nature of human circumstances generally. The seamen are, he says, "the least of all mankind given to fore-thought"; "how strange a chequer-work of providence is the life of man! and by what secret differing springs are the affections hurry'd about as differing circumstances present! To day we love what to morrow we hate; to day we seek what to morrow we shun; to day we desire what to morrow we fear, nay, even tremble at the apprehensions of. . . ."[6] Both Pamela and Mr. B conceive their experience in similar terms. After an outing with Mr. B, Pamela writes to her parents begging them not to cease their prayers for her,

> for, perhaps, this new condition may be subject to still worse hazards than those I have escaped; as would be the case, were

[4] J. Paul Hunter makes this point in *The Reluctant Pilgrim: Defoe's Emblematic Method and Quest for Form in Robinson Crusoe* (Baltimore: The Johns Hopkins Press, 1966), esp. p. 102.

[5] Starr, *Spiritual Autobiography*, p. 64.

[6] Daniel Defoe, *The Life and Adventures of Robinson Crusoe*, ed., Angus Ross (New York: Penguin Books, 1965), pp. 251, 164. All references will be to this edition and will be included parenthetically in the text.

conceitedness, vanity, and pride, to take hold of my frail heart;
and if I was, for my sins, to be left to my own conduct, a frail
bark in a tempestuous ocean, without ballast, or other pilot
than my own inconsiderate will.   (Pp. 349-50.)

Her master confesses in the same language his past unworthiness:

For let me tell my sweet girl, that, after having been long
tossed by the boisterous winds of a more culpable passion, I
have now conquered it. . . .

and, having found "so stable a foundation" for his affection, may
"promise" for himself more boldly (p. 360). The spirit of these
passages, as of the central metaphors in *Robinson Crusoe*, resembles spiritual autobiography in its conception of temporal experience as a kind of chaos, unredeemable by unaided human will.[7]

For both Defoe and Richardson, temporal continuity has secondary importance at best. Although they do invoke realistic
conventions, part of the power in these works derives from the
ease with which they qualify those conventions. Both novels, for
example, assume continuities (what Crusoe calls the "converse
of spirits") between temporal and atemporal states of being that
we tend to consider discontinuous. At the same time they neglect
continuities between temporal states where we assume them, thus
giving an appearance of inconsistency, especially in character,
that we find at once charming and troublesome. *Robinson Crusoe*
is an especially interesting case because it is written in the past
tense and yet makes little use of its available powers. The insights
of the moment are often permanently at odds with the stable
hindsight that cuts across the record of experience with its warn-
ings and exhortations. Both novels focus intensely on the present
moment and court none of the slackened attention common in

[7] The purpose of Oliver Heywood's autobiography is "to inferre a good caution
from the by-past for the remaining part of my life, that where I have seen danger
of a shipwreck I may observe such rocks, and quicksands, and charge mine owne
hart with more jelousy and watchfulness, and make a covenant with my sense,
members, facultys, and know satans devices, and where my strength and weaknes
lyes: o what a helpful improuement may former experience proue to future close-
walking." Quoted in Starr, *Spiritual Autobiography*, p. 29.

the recollected temporal sequences of realism. Patterns do not develop; they are either perceived or not perceived, and they are elemental, even heroic, in outline. The pattern of alternating attack and resistance in *Pamela*, the pattern of alternating lucidity and forgetfulness in *Robinson Crusoe* repeat themselves over and over again with the increasing intensity of accumulated threat until the breaking-point. The important action takes place on the margins of experience, in extremity, in the moments when spiritual life can be won or lost.

Discontinuous Time and Rhetorical Sequence

By attending to other matters than development, Defoe and Richardson produce first novels full of temporal disjunctiveness. Before turning to the kinds of rhetorical sequences that mainly concern them, I want to consider their treatment of time, beginning with *Pamela*. By using the epistolary style, Richardson makes temporal disjunctiveness a condition of his form, so that the reader experiences a temporal instability similar to that which constantly plagues Pamela. Repeatedly she is "forced to break off" (pp. 7, 41). Her fear of time becomes almost formulaic. "I begin to wish I had ventured everything and gone off, when I might. O when will this state of doubt and uneasiness end!" (p. 161); "What will be the end of all this?" she asks, on the eve of her long-awaited departure for home (p. 254); "O this frightful tomorrow; how I dread it!" (p. 27); even marriage (as it is for Moll Flanders) is a leap in the dark the significance of which is wrapped in "the dark bosom of futurity, and only to be proved by the event" (p. 359). The writing of letters and the keeping of her journal permit Pamela to take some distance from her experience, but the distance is minute—only what is consistent with the need to write down an experience. Writing "to the moment" permits a margin of temporal distance from experience, but one that is always precarious, always threatened. The gaps between letters and between journal entries are the blanks that represent her periods of immersion in experience, and their blankness constantly suggests the presence of threats to the stable consciousness Pamela maintains with the help of her writing. After an early encounter with Mr. B she goes away blushing "to the ears; for, though there was no harm in what he said, yet I did not know how to take it" (p. 12). At every point in *Pamela* events have yet to reach their conclusion. There is no continuous hindsight to permit the discovery of overarching patterns, and there seems in the novel no felt need to recover time in this way. One event supplants another; each moment is absolute.

The epistolary form thus confines the reader's consciousness to a discontinuous medium that jeopardizes it at every step. Every moment is a potential cliffhanger, even in the second half when immediate threats are withdrawn. Since Pamela's strategy for survival depends on keeping track of herself in writing, the gaps between letters threaten the central enterprise. Any interruption can mean unexpected change. When Pamela is "forced to break off hastily," the break portends some event that may threaten more than just the continuity of the report. When psychic survival depends upon maintaining a militant watchfulness, and when such watchfulness depends upon maintaining the record, then the gaps between letters are gaps in time that amount, for the reader, to gaps in consciousness. It is a breathtaking fact about epistolary fiction that the reader loses power in these moments. The experience of reading *Pamela* or *Clarissa*, as compared with the continuous past-tense narrations of the nineteenth century, closely resembles the heroines' own struggles to maintain consciousness and memory against overwhelming odds. When events press too closely on Pamela, she actually does lose consciousness momentarily, and one moment lost, as she is so well aware (and as *Clarissa* unfortunately learns), may mean permanent loss of that "mind" which she so scrupulously maintains through verbal exercise. Unlike Tom Jones, who can rely on the narrator to maintain some continuity, Pamela can never go off duty without threatening continuity altogether. Richardson exploits these gaps and silences to even greater effect in *Clarissa*, but the effect is present in *Pamela*, where in our more distant readerly way we experience her "pit-a-pat" of the heart at the

101

brush with unformed, unregulated events: undigested potential that lurks in the interstices of consciousness. In the epistolary style, hindsight has only the slenderest hold. It is discontinuous, interrupted, qualified at every step, and keeps even the most wary reader, like Pamela, in a prolonged "state of doubt and uneasiness."

When Pamela looks backward, it is only over the shortest periods of time. We get nothing at all of the married woman, looking back on her courtship and marriage; even after the marriage, when the record is less breathless and less pressured by threats of interruption or alteration, the story is still told to the moment.[8] Even when she has opportunities to recollect an experience from a greater distance, she does not take advantage of it. When she finds her manuscripts missing, for example, or when she prepares to deliver them up to Mr. B, she summarizes their contents exactly, repeating in miniature her previous accounts without attempting to add or to interpret the data.[9] The scene with Lady Davers is reported twice in the same journal entry, written presumably after she had faced Lady Davers, fled to the neighbors, and told them about it. She describes the scene to her parents (pp. 403-21), and then immediately reports to them the detailed report of the same scene she gave at the Darnfords' (pp. 430-36), a second account that, though it is interrupted and abridged, contains verbatim transcripts of the first report (for example the episode where Pamela refuses Lady Davers' orders to pour her wine, pp. 410 and 434). This iteration and reiteration has a flattening rather than a deepening effect; the differences in time and place have no effect on the account, thus depreciating the importance of differences between times and places. Time has passed, circumstances have changed, but that fact yields noth-

[8] Kinkead-Weekes observes that "Pamela's journal doesn't break Richardson's form, since the experience of living from moment to moment, day by day, is more important than the letter convention" (*Samuel Richardson*, p. 397).

[9] Pamela's report of her escape (pp. 177-90) is repeated on p. 247 and p. 251; her account of Mr. B's proposals and her response (pp. 197-202) is repeated on p. 247 and p. 262; all events "to Wednesday the 27th day of my distress" are repeated on pp. 236-37.

ing. The continuous flow of time is constantly impeded: by the double columns in the report of Mr. B's offer, that make the reader stop and consider which way to read and that force simultaneous consideration of their opposition; or by the repetition with misreading, as when Lady Davers misinterprets at length Mr. B's letter to Pamela; or by the miniatures of events which, interposed into the narrative, have a microcosmic relation to the whole rather than any significance in sequential arrangement.

Events in *Pamela* are consigned to temporal order mainly through language, and there is no attempt in the narrative itself to keep track of relative time. Sequence is unimportant to the project of the novel. It is a shock to discover, if one makes the effort required to do so, how little time has passed altogether in *Pamela*: only thirteen weeks, but thirteen that seem like an eternity. There is no slack, no sense of relative measure, no sorting of significant from insignificant details. The sequence of events is more like an accumulation than a development, a sequence in which Pamela is engaged in the same activity first and last. "I find I am watched and suspected still very close; and I wish I was with you; but that must not be, it seems, this fortnight. I don't like this fortnight; and it will be a tedious and a dangerous one for me, I doubt" (pp. 217-18). This passage, written just before she leaves Lincolnshire near the end of her captivity, could well have appeared at the beginning when she was making the waistcoat back in Bedfordshire. Every moment presents the same challenge to Pamela; nothing develops. The only history where development takes place gradually and depends on marking comparisons over time— the history of Mr. B's change of heart—is almost totally suppressed in the novel. In Pamela's story every moment is The Moment, and nothing is insignificant, except perhaps temporal continuity.[10] Every moment is a pivot, a potential turning-point for which

[10] Consciousness of chronological sequence is, according to Kinkead-Weekes, "indefinite" at first and last, and is most acute during the most trying time. In *Clarissa* the "interplay of 'personal' time and clock time . . . is clearly a major factor in the book's verisimilitude" (*Samuel Richardson*, pp. 414-15). Elasticity in time can be consistent with realism if it is measured against a regular chronology; but in *Pamela*, as I am arguing, it is not.

103

Pamela must be ready with her whole mind. The patterns that do develop—the pattern of attack and resistance relieved intermittently by uncertain pauses—have the iterative or even rhythmic quality of a heartbeat or pulse that marks time without changing.

Even though *Robinson Crusoe* is putatively a past-tense narration, it is one that demonstrates the degree to which the past tense can be used against itself. Defoe uses the mnemonic power to insist on the *disjunctiveness* between past and present, not on the continuity—a fact that helps to account for the irresoluteness of the time scale in this novel. The convention that the novel is mainly Crusoe's journal keeps the writing close to the moment, just as Pamela's journal does, and permits a degree of inconsistency to exist between event and hindsight that prevents temporal continuities (as well as the consistent consciousness that might be based on them) from forming. Like *Moll Flanders*, this novel raises questions about the force of memory and of moral awareness in the face of the intrigue of the moment. Crusoe's providential reading of his experience coexists uneasily with the descriptions of the castaway craftsman making boards and bread. There is an instability in the narrative perspective that confirms the instability of human will and the tenuousness of the best-laid plans. Crusoe reads his own experience in two ways alternately: as prophetic allegory and as a series of survival problems. The two are laminated together rather than reconciled, a fact that is proof of the fragility of consciousness in time. The narrative of his "folly," in which we take such interest, is interpreted by Crusoe himself as a loop in mythic time: not as an open-ended sequence but as a series of discrete episodes whose meaning derives from a source independent of history.

The unstable narrative viewpoint gives the reader an experience similar to that of a viewer watching movies made with a hand-held camera (for example the description of seeing remains of the cannibal feasts for the first time, p. 172). Navigation, a metaphor for consciousness in the novel, suggests very well the mobility of the narrative viewpoint. Every point in the description is potentially a turning-point, a pivot, just as it is in *Pamela*, because the sense of relative position in time and space is so tenuous. We squirm with Crusoe every step of the way;[11] and part of our difficulty stems from the elasticity of the time scale, which focuses at length on a detail of carpentry and then passes several months in a paragraph. We are forever adjusting to a new vantage point, a process resembling Crusoe's continuous efforts to maintain psychic equilibrium in the face of threats.[12] In such a world Crusoe wisely relies on Providence as the only source of stability.

The description of Crusoe's life on the island as it proceeds from the first pages to the middle of the book first distorts the normal, customary time scale and finally obliterates it altogether, except for references to daily cycles. Crusoe comments himself, at first, on how much time the simplest matters take. "For example, I was two and forty days making me a board for a long shelf." He describes this procedure in detail from the felling of the tree to the thickness of the board: "I only observe this in particular, to show the reason why so much of my time went away with so little work, viz. that what might be a little to be done with the help of tools, was a vast labour, and required a prodigious time to do alone and by hand" (p. 127). The cumulative effect of such descriptions is to replace chronological sequence with sequences of activities and concerns. Initially Crusoe marks time in annual periods, so that we learn when each of seven years has passed; but gradually, as if the focus on small tasks has superseded the regular but arbitrary sequence of years, the scale is distorted so that we begin to be surprised by how much time has passed.[13]

[11] Benjamin Boyce says of the reader of *Roxanna*: "He squirms with Roxanna every step of the way." ("The Question of Emotion in Defoe," in *Daniel Defoe: A Collection of Critical Essays*, ed., Max Byrd [Englewood Cliffs, N.J.: Prentice Hall, 1976], p. 1).

[12] "Crusoe fortifies to restore his psychic equilibrium; whenever he has brought his defenses to seeming perfection he is again disturbed" (Everett Zimmerman, *Defoe and the Novel* [Berkeley: University of California Press, 1975], p. 26). On Crusoe's anxiety about psychic survival see Homer Brown's splendid article, "The Displaced Self in the Novels of Daniel Defoe," *ELH*, 38, no. 4 (December 1971), 562-90.

[13] See Paul Alkon's discussion of variants in "the ratio of event to narration"

The significant markers of sequence in fact soon cease to be chronological at all; sequences begin to be marked according to tasks completed or even according to fluctuations in Crusoe's state of mind. The first year ("three hundred and sixty-five days") is accounted for in some detail (pp. 65-117), and so is the second (pp. 117-26). But the third and fourth pass together (pp. 126-39), and measurement by task begins to take over. "In the middle of this work, I finished my fourth year," he says (p. 139), as if the significant marker is temporal; but soon he is saying things like "In this government of my temper I remained near a year" (p. 153) and notifying us immediately afterwards that five years have passed.[14] This disengagement from chronological sequence proceeds in proportion to his adjustment to a timeless, repetitive life whose only important cycles are daily. When he sees the footprint, for example, the relative temporal position is "noon." At the end of the novel his reengagement in chronological sequence proceeds in proportion to his forced reentry into the society of man.

In getting his true bearings, then, Crusoe shifts out of time into a providential universe where ordinary measures, especially temporal ones, are meaningless. Crusoe's fortifications are defenses against an external threat that never materializes. Experience will always surprise him with five canoes full of cannibals (instead of one). "The number of them broke all my measures" (p. 204). So although, as he says, "I took all the measures humane prudence

---

and his general discussion of tempo in Defoe's novels, in *Fictional Time*, esp. pp. 17-18, 179, 214.

[14] Eight pages account for years five and six (pp. 139-47); the next seven pages take the account to year eleven (p. 154). During the account of his twelfth to fifteenth years Crusoe remarks that he is prepared to feed himself for as long as it is necessary, "if it were to be forty years," thereby invoking conventional time and measuring his prospects by it (p. 161). After that an unmarked length of time passes before he again marks the anniversary at fifteen years. Since this period follows his discovery of the footprint and yet brings no further contact with any human beings, this account doubles the surprising impression of how much time has passed. Gradually toward the end of the book more space is devoted to less time, the longest section (forty-three pages) being given to his last year on the island (pp. 230-74).

could suggest for my own preservation" (p. 169), ultimately it is Providence and not his own measures that preserves him. The great moments in Crusoe's island life—his conversion and the arrival of Friday—are heralded not by historical probability but by dreams.

This depreciation of temporal continuity means that Defoe, like Richardson, is a master of incident because he conceives of temporal experience (unaided by Providence) as being in itself discontinuous. Life is radically unstable and fluctuating, full of discrete, disconnected incident and inconsistent motive. What redeems it is not recollection in tranquillity but ever active, ever vigilant contact with Providence and obedience to its dictates. Crusoe is most explicit about the spiritual continuum that breaks the boundaries of temporal existence and connects heaven and earth.

> Men should not slight the secret intimations of providence, let them come from what invisible intelligence they will, that I shall not discuss, and perhaps cannot account for; but certainly they are a proof of the converse of spirits, and the secret communication between those embody'd and those unembody'd. . . . (P. 182.)

With such "converse" between embodied and unembodied spirits available, it is no wonder that Crusoe and Pamela should slight social exchange.[15] They are living on the edge of time, where typological patterns of forty days or forty years are the most valid kind of measurement. Crusoe's first shot on the island—"I believe it was the first gun that had been fired there since the creation of the world" (p. 72)—takes place in a solitude never before broken and in a context that stretches back to the creation of

---

[15] Arthur Secord has noticed that Defoe is a "master of incident" and that this enables him to imitate the "shapelessness" of life; but it does not follow that Defoe is "deficient in the construction of plot," if by that Secord means to suggest that Defoe would have constructed plots if he had known how. Such "construction" of time would be inimical to Defoe's purpose. See *Studies in the Narrative Method of Defoe* (Urbana: University of Illinois Press, 1924), p. 1.

the world. In such circumstances there is something almost comical about Crusoe's obsessive timekeeping.[16]

Relative location in time and space, then, means little in both these novels; by comparison the soul's disposition toward extraworldly reality means everything. "Where are you? Where have you been? . . . How come you here?" a voice startles Robinson Crusoe in his slumber (*Crusoe*, p. 152). The indeterminate source of these questions and their ambiguous reference give them, momentarily, a kind of absolute validity and universal reference. Their very indeterminacy suggests the unimportance of time and place; they are questions for all times and places—always present, always urgent—and temporal answers to such questions can only be reductive. On this point Defoe has a joke at Crusoe's expense by putting these important questions in the mouth of a parrot. Crusoe accepts the most immediate explanation; it is left for the reader to reflect that the parrot's questions are a version of Crusoe's own voice, a projection of his deep uncertainty about psychic survival; that the questions cannot be answered meaningfully in temporal terms; and that Crusoe's productions—his pots, enclosures, records, and talking parrot—all have limited value as self-confirming artifacts. Crusoe's ontological insecurity is such that he looks for ways to assuage it; but by discovering that the voice is "only" his bird he seems to settle for a natural explanation that is no explanation at all and merely postpones the question about whose voice it really is and what the answers to those important questions really are.

The only meaningful temporal markers in *Robinson Crusoe* are those that mark cycles rather than progress. September 30 is an anniversary: the "same" day Crusoe begins both his "wicked life"

---

[16] The comedy is especially evident in Crusoe's straight-faced anxiety about one lost day in his record of twenty-five years. The comedy lies partly in his confessed attempt to close the very gap that made possible his passage to the other side of time. Of this transition, Paul Alkon says the following; "In the midst of awakening to God, who dwells in eternity, Crusoe is wrenched outside time in the only way possible apart from death, which his sleep simulates. . . . Defoe makes Crusoe's lost day as well as his calendar emblematic of relationships between ordinary time and sacred time" (*Fictional Time*, p. 61).

at sea and his "solitary life" on the island; on the "same day of the year" he escapes from the Yarmouth wreck and, one year later, from his captors at Sallee; on the "same day of the year" that he ran away from home he also is taken a slave in Sallee (p. 144). If this is a journey, it is a ritually repetitive one. Even Crusoe's efforts to maintain his physical existence and a record of himself have a kind of circularity most evident in the episode with the parrot. He teaches his bird to talk, and the bird then parrots back to him only what he has taught it. He scans the horizon with his perspective glass to no avail, because his location and horizon in themselves provide no clue to the real coordinates of his life. Even the past-tense recollections, interspersed in his journal account, yield no sequential patterns because the coordinates of his life have little to do with the temporal and spatial world. The clues are in his Bible and his dreams, not on his horizon.

In *Pamela* temporal and spatial coordinates are equally irrelevant to the heroine's real state. Pamela seems to know from the start what the reader learns with difficulty, that such questions about spiritual location have an urgency that no temporal or spatial answers can satisfy. Where she is in space or time matters little in comparison with the condition of her "mind," which is to say, her soul and honor. Unlike Crusoe, however, Pamela is never caught slumbering. Her suspicion of all temporal solutions, her degree of self-doubt, her awareness that keeping track of herself is at best a means to prevent backsliding and in no way self-creation, her reference at every point to the will of Providence, her perpetual sense of her danger—all make her a model that would dazzle the soul of an inconsistent, backsliding Robinson Crusoe. Her situation in space and time is not irrelevant to her spiritual well-being—though in her retreat from vile encroachments she never meets the ultimate test as Clarissa does— but she always knows how misleading temporal solutions can be and how much she has to fear from temporal success.

In both *Robinson Crusoe* and *Pamela*, then, the relation of the soul to the fluctuations of temporal experience occupies both authors intensely, but time is periodic not continuous. To the

109

extent that patterns and meanings emerge from events and are not arbitrarily enforced on them, the novels are realistic; to the extent—and I think on balance it is a greater extent—that the governing patterns are conventional and mythic, the more arbitrary is the relation between sequence and meaning and the more limited the effect of realism. In these two novels temporal disjunctiveness is primary.[17]

Sequence of course remains important, but sequence that is mainly rhetorical, not historical. The habit of treating events as examples and considering sequences rhetorical transforms history, as Paul Alkon rightly observes, "into a species of deliberative rhetoric, a species of persuasion most concerned with the future."[18] When time is not a continuum, events are merely discrete occasions that yield their meanings typologically, not chronologically. Exempla are not parts of a process. Their meanings are not arrived at over time, through the sorting of relevant from irrelevant aspects. Exempla have a more arbitrary relation to general meaning; meaning does not emerge from them so much as it dictates them. "What a force example is" exclaims Pamela of her husband (p. 399) in terms that might as well apply to her for she is an example to her sex—a cautionary one for some, an inspiration for others; Mrs. Jervis is an example of a good servant, Mrs. Jewkes of a bad.

It is not only characters but whole sequences that are exemplary in *Pamela*. The scene where Mr. B devises a moral speech about

---

[17] Paul Alkon makes the important observation "that the very fact of time-consciousness may be as important as the direction it takes in prompting a writer to experiment with various temporal structures" (*Fictional Time*, p. 82). But discussions of time often assume that "time" has a simple referent, implying all our assumptions about temporal continuity where they may not be applicable. According to G. A. Starr, what distinguishes the autobiographer from the diarist is "having to cope with the phenomenon of time"; and yet time can have "an element of pattern or direction by means of which it resolves parcels of time into discrete periods of unfolding stages" without necessarily having the continuities of time that make possible realistic effects (*Spiritual Autobiography*, p. 36). To say *Robinson Crusoe* or *Pamela* have discrete periods, even unfolding stages, is not to say that such time is continuous, or more than conventional and disjunctive.

[18] Alkon, *Fictional Time*, pp. 37, 39.

110

politics on the occasion of a whist game is one instance that typifies the whole narrative strategy. The classic instance is the description of seating arrangements at dinner.

> When supper was brought in, Lady Darnford took me by the hand, and said to my master, Sir, by your leave; and would have placed me at the upper end of the table. Pray, pray, madam, said I, excuse me; I cannot do it, indeed I cannot. Pamela, said my master, to the great delight of my good father, as I could see by his looks, oblige Lady Darnford, since she desires it. It is but a little before your time, you know.

The action at hand here seems too trivial to bear the vocabulary, with its mingled suggestions of lovemaking and childbirth. The great delicacy of the matter becomes more enhanced when neither Lady Darnford nor Pamela nor Sir Simon can figure out how to manage the proper disposition of persons at table. It is a disposition in the full, rhetorical sense of *dispositio*. Mr. B finally accommodates the differences by arranging them in a manner significantly different from customary usage and yet inoffensive because of the invocation of special categories and circumstances:

> Dear, good sir, said I, pray don't command it! Let me sit by my father, pray! Why, said Sir Simon, here's ado indeed! Sit down at the upper end, as you should do; and your father shall sit by you, there. This put my dear father upon difficulties. And my master said, Come, I'll place you all: and so put Lady Darnford at the upper end, Lady Jones at her right hand, and Mrs. Peters on the other; and he placed me between the two young ladies; but very genteelly put Miss Darnford below her younger sister; saying, Come, miss, I put you here, because you shall hedge in this little cuckow; for I take notice, with pleasure, of your goodness to her; and, besides, all you very young ladies should sit together. This seemed to please both sisters; for had the youngest miss been put there, it might have piqued her, as matters have been formerly, to be placed below me; whereas Miss Darnford giving place to her youngest sister, made it less odd she should to me; especially with that hand-

some turn of the dear man, as if I was a cuckow to be hedged in.

This nice arranging confirms more than mere finicky sensibility. It confirms the rhetorical value of all personal and social gesture.

The delicacy of the seating, its almost ontological significance, Pamela's assumption of the head—spoken of as "her time," as if she were about to deliver something other than another exemplary performance—all this strains the sense of probability concerning what is due at dinner. But probability is not a concern for the author or the characters here, and this is no mere dinner. The fact is that in rhetorical terms the hints of lovemaking and child-birth are no accident. Pamela will soon deliver up that heir about which so much fuss will be made and for the sake of whom her marriage was so difficult in the first place. The heir is the clincher, and the very thing that stands between servants and upward mobility. Such an episode would be easy to mock or to read ironically in context of continuous historical time and realistic depth; but in context of the rapturous circle of time and rhetorical altitude we can see here lessons in form and assertions of signif-icance that vastly exceed the moment, and for which the moment is only an occasion.

The ability to recognize the occasional value of all moments, in fact, is one of Pamela's major feats. A sequence is really a series of examples of lessons, a fact that becomes most evident in *Pamela* when Mr. B forgoes his refractory behavior and co-operates in giving lessons: lessons in distributing money (p. 374), lessons in proper dress (p. 388), lessons on the values of all the "good old family rules" (p. 389) that receive ritual confirmation in the second half of the work. Recognizing the rhetorical and ahistorical value of sequences helps to make sense of passages that seem clumsy or obscure when read according to the historical lights of realism.

As with *Pamela*, so with *Robinson Crusoe*: the rhetorical inter-pretation of sequences can be keys to revelation. The importance of casuistry to Defoe's novels has been demonstrated by G. A. Starr, who claims that "casuistry appears to be one of the factors

responsible for their disjointedness" and for the fact that chronological connections have no causal connection.[19] It is worth
looking closely at a passage for confirmation, since the extent of
the rhetorical disposition of events in *Crusoe* is still insufficiently
accepted. The description of Crusoe's first landing is a case in
point. Describing how Crusoe is washed ashore, Defoe offers a
little vignette of life in time. At the beginning of this passage
Crusoe seems to have reached shore—the waves leave him "upon
the land almost dry, but half-dead"—but then "another wave
. . . as high as a great hill" swamps him and he is again swimming
"towards shore," which now seems a distance away. And as his
description proceeds we begin more and more to lose bearings in
space. One minute he is "upon the land" and "about dry," the
next he is "buried" twenty or thirty feet under water. How close
could he be to the shore? Without certain contact either to the
bottom or to the shore, he can only fight for the surface every
time he is buried again. Finally, he says, "I strook forward against
the return of the waves, and felt ground again with my feet."
Then he takes to his heels and runs toward shore, but is not
delivered; "twice more I was lifted up by the waves and carried
forward as before, the shore being very flat," and again he struggles
for breath and takes blows. Finally he "resolves to hold fast by a
piece of the rock" until the waves abate; he "then fetched another
run, which brought me so near the shore that . . . the next run
I took, I got to the main land" and "clambered up the clifts . . .
quite out of reach of the water." Only now, paragraphs after he
first put his feet down on land, can he safely say "I was now
landed and safe on shore" (pp. 64-65).

This passage teems with allegories: about the momentary and
precarious nature of deliverance; about the need to hold fast to
a rock; about the incommensurability of human powers to deal
with waves of influence beyond its measure; about the danger of
depths. The experience is emblematic of Crusoe's spiritual life,
in which he recognizes and then forgets the importance of Prov-

[19] G. A. Starr, *Defoe and Casuistry* (Princeton: Princeton University Press,
1971), p. x.

113

idence in his affairs. This passage recapitulates in miniature his life's repetitiveness, especially the alternating reliance on and despair of his own powers to shape his destiny. It is an experience that cannot be adequately measured or controlled except by escape from the medium (the sea of time) altogether and by holding fast to some rock.[20] Crusoe's fluctuation between fear and religious hope, a constant theme after his conversion, results from the discovery of some new circumstance that breaks his measures and reminds him of his weakness. His response after he sees the footprint is an example.

> Thus my fear banished all my religious hope; all that former confidence in God, which was founded upon such wonderful experience as I had had of His goodness, now vanished. . . .
>
> How strange a chequer work of providence is the life of man! and by what secret differing springs are the affections hurry'd about as differing circumstances present! (P. 164.)

The sequence in which he is washed ashore has most meaning in rhetorical not historical terms.

Because of the essential discontinuity of temporal experience in *Robinson Crusoe* and in *Pamela*, meaning does not develop so much as it proliferates. Few speeches and gestures are univocal, a fact that accounts for much of their charm. Their multivocality cannot be explained in terms of recoverable ambiguity or irony. The multiple voices of a speech or gesture do not harmonize, they splinter, proliferating their meanings in ways that depreciate the value of time and defy recovery. For example, Pamela complains early in the novel that Mr. B's remorse vanishes as soon

[20] In this analysis I agree with John Richetti, who finds in this passage a competition between "unruly and therefore fascinating forces" and the patterning response ("occasional analytic details which establish human understanding of the relation between surf and shore"). *Defoe's Narratives: Situations and Structures* (Oxford: The Clarendon Press, 1975), pp. 37-38. What this passage and the novel as a whole do, I think, is to weaken our sense of the firmness of human understanding and control. The fact that, as Richetti says, "position is always relative" in the novel (p. 24) still leaves open the question: relative to what? Defoe portrays a restlessness that can only be quieted outside itself and outside the world's resources altogether.

as he finds her alone. She is making here a statement about a mythic struggle, of which the local one is merely an example—in particular, a statement about the embattled soul's solitude. Her complaint, made in the first few pages, could be made anytime and, if not of Mr. B, then of others (Lady Davers for instance). It is always appropriate. The plot merely tries to find out how many ways it can be tested, but there is no development because interest focuses on the multivocality of the single *sentence* or paradigm, represented by the master and maid—a paradigm as old as the 137th Psalm and as new as its revision by an eighteenth-century waiting-girl (pp. 334-39). This mythic element in *Pamela*, which has not gone unnoticed,[21] is perhaps more evident in the second half, but it is present from the beginning. The repeated encounters with Mr. B or his agents, the symbolism of barricades, the efforts at communication baffled by walls and limited to key-holes, the lengthy extractions of meaning from a card game or a seating arrangement—all have the ritual repetitiveness of myth.

The same multivocal proliferation of mythic meaning appears in *Robinson Crusoe*, and perhaps even more obviously. Crusoe's fraternity with Milton's Adam and Bunyan's Christian is, as Tillyard remarks, the kind of identification that tells us to "expect some kind of multiple meaning" at every point. "As soon as we assert (or admit) that Crusoe is something more than the chief figure in a lively narrative, being the type both of the merchant adventurer of his own day and of mankind itself in certain difficulties, we have to decide whether to push such multiple significances farther."[22] Such multiplication of meanings resists resolution; the multiple voices are not intended to harmonize. Counterpoint is intentional. Unable to make either allegory or realism out of this narrative, the reader "must," as Tillyard puts

[21] See, for example, Margaret Doody, "*Pamela* is an extended fable with human characters . . . closely related to fairy tale, folk-tale, and ballad" (*A Natural Passion: A Study of the Novels of Samuel Richardson* [Oxford: The Clarendon Press, 1974], p. 34).

[22] E.M.W. Tillyard, "Defoe," in *Twentieth-Century Interpretations of Robinson Crusoe*, ed. Frank Ellis (Englewood Cliffs, N.J.: Prenctice Hall, 1969), pp. 74-75.

it, "be ready for the unusual and the richly significant." This proliferation of meanings is an advantage of narrative which depends on mythic outline instead of historical development. Crusoe's parrot sounding the unanswerable question, "Where are you? how come you here?"; Pamela's seams that "grow large" with papers: these are exempla that have value completely apart from the continuities of realistic narration and realistic context and viewpoint. This is a spiritualizing of particulars like those of early autobiographers. "Here indeed was occasion for 'mighty wit' of the sort ascribed to John Machim: occasion, that is, for *discordia concors*, the discovery of occult resemblances in things apparently unlike."[23] Unlike the concordable differences about which realistic narrators are so serious, the occult resemblances have interest, have wit, because in any temporal terms they are not alike at all. These concordances cut across common sense, invading continuities, lacing them with fissures and interstices through which another world can be glimpsed that contradicts or even reverses the appearances of this one.

The depreciation of sequence means that in these two novels, despite their attention to particulars, details lack the density of those embedded in historical sequences and containing secret meanings. In spiritual autobiography, Starr says, fact serves "purely as ground for reflection," and "little stress" is laid "on the actual recording of experience." Behind the details of spiritual histories is a "belief in the essential uniformity and sameness of Christian experience,"[24] not a conviction that invites interest in relative measurements. Consequently, details can be chosen from the field of experience with a certain arbitrariness to convey perennial truths. In *Pamela*, for example, the descriptions of her bundles of clothes, or her fishing in the pond, or her hiding letters under the sunflower, or even her ability to cut up a turkey "in a trice," all yield up their abstractions easily, without reference to a series of cases which would give them dimension and depth. The danger

[23] Starr, *Spiritual Autobiography*, p. 26.
[24] Ibid., pp. 27, 14.

116

of the carp, as Pamela reminds us, is equivalent to her own in life; the symbolic value of clothes is stressed repeatedly; the sunflower specifies humility.

Details have the same yielding quality in *Robinson Crusoe*. Crusoe's failure to float the boat he has laboriously constructed too far from the water proves "the folly of beginning a work before we count the cost, and before we judge rightly of our own strength to go through with it" (p. 139). Overproduction of food brings a moral about covetousness (p. 140). The sailing mishap that nearly carries him away from his island proves that things can always get worse and that "we never see the true state of our condition till it is illustrated to us by its contraries" (p. 149). His "constant apprehensions" about cannibals prove that the expectation of evil is worse than the evil expected (p. 189). The peace of mind that comes with ignoring danger proves that what we don't know doesn't hurt us (p. 200). All such details have rhetorical value. "Once spiritualized," Starr observes, "all objects and activities" are commensurable.[25] Such a scheme equalizes biblical precedent with historical precedent. There is no temporal resistance to perceiving their meaning, no historical drag from reliance on a series of cases.[26]

Defoe especially has been praised for verisimilitude in his use of detail,[27] although some attention has been given to the way

[25] Ibid., p. 26.

[26] "Defoe shared with the majority of his readers the typological habit of mind involved not only in the assumption that Old Testament events prefigure those of the New Testament but, more generally, that the past offers archetypes of the present and future." Crusoe is a "powerful myth" because of Defoe's "avoidance of chronological placing," since "myths depend on some detachment from ordinary chronology" (Alkon, *Fictional Time*, pp. 40-41). For further discussions of the place in literary tradition of this treatment of time see Alkon, *Fictional Time*, p. 256; and Tillyard, "Defoe," in *Twentieth-Century Interpretations*, ed. Ellis, p. 75.

[27] Arthur Secord (*Narrative Method*, p. 11), E. Anthony James (*Defoe's Many Voices*, pp. 125-56), and de Quincey (quoted in Norton edition of *Robinson Crusoe*, pp. 292-93) all regard judicious selection of detail as the key to Defoe's verisimilitude.

117

his treatment of "things" places emphasis *not* "on their sensuous fullness but on their moral function."[28] Crusoe's description of his tent and the fence before it is an example:

> Before I set up my tent, I drew a half circle before the hollow place which took in about ten yards in its semi-diameter from the rock, and twenty yards in its diameter from its beginning and ending.
>
> In this half circle I pitched two rows of strong stakes, driving them into the ground till they stood very firm like piles, the biggest end being out of the ground about five foot and a half, and sharpened on the top. The two rows did not stand above six inches from one another. (P. 77.)

The passage continues to defy visualization. Even with diagrams, these details do not yield scenes with primarily dramatic value, because the space in which they occur is not conceived as a unified and homogeneous medium any more than is the temporal succession in which they occur. Given the lack of consistent relationships in space or time, "one may well conclude" (as Leo Damrosch says of Defoe's story on "The Apparition of Mrs. Veal") "that the many fine strokes of verisimilitude are essentially decorative."[29]

There is a pristine quality, an atmosphereless simplicity, in *Pamela* and *Robinson Crusoe* that owes something to this freedom from the constraints of temporal and spatial continuities and from the relative measurements necessary for experience in such media. When all the restless activity is done, the stories are beautifully simple in outline, mythic, unencumbered by the qualifying weight of relative measurement and detail. Defoe's books have been

[28] Martin Price, *To the Palace of Wisdom: Studies in Order and Energy from Dryden to Blake* (New York: Doubleday, 1964), p. 268. See also Dorothy van Ghent, "On *Moll Flanders*," *The English Novel: Form and Function* (New York: Harper and Row, 1961), to the effect that objects are "entirely desensualized, inaccessible to sense, abstract" (p. 36).

[29] "Defoe as Ambiguous Impersonator," *Modern Philology* (November 1973), 155. Damrosch says this of "The Apparition of Mrs. Veal," but it applies as well to *Robinson Crusoe*.

discussed as experiments with "the atmosphere of anxiety" which "interest us by their evocation of some sort of fear."[30] Pamela's prolonged state of doubt and uneasiness depends on the same emotion. "Did I not do well now to come back?—O could I get rid of my fears of this sham marriage (for all this is not yet inconsistent with that frightful scheme)" (p. 273). In the atmosphere of anxiety and without the reassurance of connectedness in space and time, these fictional worlds take on a porousness, a transparency, which accounts both for their charm and also for the incompleteness of their verisimilitude.

The temporal continuities of realistic narration provide one means of giving meaning to particulars, but a means inconsistent with the intentions of Defoe and Richardson. Both *Robinson Crusoe* and *Pamela* lack the narrative language that, as Homer Brown describes it, removes the contingency and absurdity of the "lived moment by abstracting that moment from the field of open possibility and directing it toward a certain outcome which will define it and give it significance." This description fits realistic narratives better than it fits either *Robinson Crusoe* or *Pamela*. It is because "the point of view of narrative is precisely a providence"[31] that neither Crusoe nor Pamela can rely upon it. To their religious apprehension no power but Providence can be trusted, not even their own powers of recollection. However well Crusoe understands his debt to Providence, he forgets; however unyielding Richardson's "precise, perverse, unseasonable Pamela" remains (p. 253), her strength is insufficient to win of its own accord— something her brush with suicide confirms. Though her resolve does not fluctuate like Crusoe's, even Pamela grows weary of her

[30] Boyce, "The Question of Emotion," pp. 47, 50, 41. Boyce cites the whole tradition springing from Leslie Stephen's view that there is "no sense of sin" and no passional element in Defoe. James Sutherland mentions the "isolation and unexpectedness" of the footprint in *Robinson Crusoe* and the purse in the *Journal of The Plague Year*, which is described lying in the middle of a yard, "cleverly framed by empty space" (*Defoe*, Writers and Their Work Series, no. 51 [London: Longmans Green & Co., 1965], pp. 16-17). The isolation of such details from continuous relationships with the surrounding environment corroborated the more important isolation of the psyche, in Crusoe the psyche of the hero.

[31] Brown, "Displaced Self," p. 587.

life. Power comes from the Almighty alone, and the human agent can best focus on the moment's choice by recalling the Bible, not experience. Thought is full of mediations, but life is full of choices. The disengagement implied by recourse to thought is not an option for Crusoe or Pamela; they must remain situated in the midst of their affairs, always engaged, always on guard, but never "at ease."[32] The stable, detached hindsight of the nineteenth-century narrators, even (as *Robinson Crusoe* shows) where it is available, yields comparatively little.

The Dangers of Mediation

The temporal discontinuity in *Robinson Crusoe* and *Pamela* actually prevents space and time from becoming rationalized: prevents, in short, the firm establishment of verisimilitude. The rationalization of space or time in realism depends on the mutual relationships between collaborating viewpoints. That second, harmonizing viewpoint—the past moment in time or the side view in Albertian spatial perspective—makes relative measurement possible and homogenizes the medium of perception. Without that agreement there can be no consensus, and therefore no way of estimating relative value. The mediating viewpoint that corrects and supplements the controlling one performs essential acts of mediation in realism; and in *Robinson Crusoe* and *Pamela* these mediations are mainly absent.

One key symptom of Defoe and Richardson's skepticism about the possibility of such mediation lies in their depreciation of memory. "It is the function of narrative, with its double perspective, to remember," says Homer O. Brown.[33] But in *Robinson Crusoe* and *Pamela* memory has little value in moral life; where passing time yields nothing but the same old history of error and confusion, memory holds few powers. The written record can

[32] In the preface to *Clarissa*, Richardson disclaims any interest in the detached narrator "perfectly at ease." Paul Alkon astutely observes, such "perfect ease can only be expected in Eternity" (*Fictional Time*, p. 183).

[33] Brown, "Displaced Self," p. 587.

serve as a mnemonic device, but neither Crusoe nor Pamela uses writing that way (although Pamela's friends do). To Pamela writing is a present exercise with present value, which helps her to "sink the impression" of her lessons "still deeper" and to make available an unchanging account to which she can turn "as often as I shall mistrust my memory" (p. 475). For Pamela's memory is at best a holding action, at worst misleading: "You say, said I, that he was sorry for his *first* offer in the summer-house. Well, and how long did his sorrow last?—Only till he found me by myself; and then he was worse than before: and so became sorry *again*. . . . How then, Mrs. Jervis, said I, can I *ask* or *wish* to stay?" (p. 37). This is an early version of doubts Pamela sustains clear up until marriage. Had she profited by experience, seen the pattern developing in events, she might have mistaken the true situation utterly, rejected Mr. B, and lost her golden opportunity. Reliance on temporal experience and her own powers of inference could have produced a dismal result indeed.

This passage is especially interesting because it shows Pamela struggling with a problem familiar in realistic fiction: the double consciousness entailed by awareness of the past. Like other instances, this affinity with realism invites us to suppose the novel to be a full-fledged version of realistic narration, but what Pamela finally does with this passage explicitly reverses the values of realism. Since her knowledge does not come from experience, she does well to listen to her own experience with only half an ear.

> Smartly said! says he: Where a d——l gottest thou, at these years, all this knowledge? And then thou has a memory, as I see by your papers, that nothing escapes. Alas! sir, said I, what poor abilities I have, serve only to make me more miserable!— I have no pleasure in my memory, which impresses things upon me, that I could be glad never *were*, or everlastingly to *forget*.
> (P. 241.)

Pamela bears out this latter sentiment, one that is blasphemy in a realistic canon. Repentance and forgiveness erase the past. Though her child holds some promise of continuity, Sally Godfrey repents sincerely and thereby makes an absolute "break with the past."[34] Mr. B repents, and in the second half there is little or no residue of his former near-pathological suspicions. Pamela's need for her excellent memory lessens with her need to suspect depth in Mr. B. What's past is past, and from their marriage onward Pamela and Mr. B's whole purpose in life seems to be in taking time by the forelock and subduing it to exemplary value.

Richardson uses realistic technique to criticize realistic values, a most interesting case being his use of point of view. "Richardson is the pioneer of 'point of view' in fiction," according to Mark Kinkead-Weekes; he "formally banishes himself" and by a "process of dramatic projection" sees and speaks through characters who cannot be identified with the author.[35] Certainly there are instances that not only support this claim but even do so in terms consistent with the definition of realism offered here: in terms of temporal continuity and of vantage-point in time. Pamela frequently refers Mr. B to his past behavior in order to explain her present behavior or motivation:

> When I recollect upon your former proposal to me in relation
> to a certain person, not one word of which is now mentioned;
> and upon my being in that strange manner run away with, and
> still kept here a miserable prisoner; do you think, sir . . . that
> your general assurances of honour to me, can have the effect
> upon me, that, were it not for these things, all your words
> ought to have. (P. 143.)

She says of Mrs. Jewkes: "I should have thought her virtuous, and even pious, had I never know her in another light" (p. 399). But in these instances the different viewpoints of past and present are mutually exclusive; there is no possibility of harmonizing them, because they do not belong to the "same" worlds. Of the two views of Mrs. Jewkes, one is right and the other wrong, just as Mr. B's letter has a wrong reading (Lady Davers') and a right (Pamela's). The struggle between Pamela's honor and Mr. B's is

---

[34] Kinkead-Weekes, *Samuel Richardson*, p. 69.
[35] Ibid., p. 397.

a mortal struggle that is resolved only by a ritual transformation of the terms. This involves some important redefinitions. Pamela's proper place is not a servant's, so both Mr. B's honor and hers can be accommodated by raising Pamela to the higher place where she really belongs and not, as in realism, by rising to a higher level of generalization.

In *Robinson Crusoe* it is even clearer than in *Pamela* that action is forgetting; but here, too, memory is an unreliable instrument of repair. The hero struggles from beginning to end with lapses of memory. Crusoe gets comfortably involved in some position, only to forget where he is and how he came there. After about two weeks on the island, he resorts to written records in order to preserve his memory from lapses (p. 81), suggesting that the longest Crusoe can remember clearly is about a fortnight. Soon after his first seafaring disaster "remembrance . . . wore off" (p. 38), and this pattern continues. Unaided experience seems to be an inadequate teacher; its lessons wear off after short periods and leave no residue. The intermittence of memory corresponds to the intermittence of human resolve generally; this is something that does not change for Crusoe, who continues after his conversion to have difficulties and backslidings. These journal-novels offer no model for the kind of distance available to the narrators of nineteenth-century novels.[36]

Both Defoe and Richardson chose the same metaphor for life unmediated by time and consciousness: the metaphor of enclosure. Compared with the metaphors of a river or a web that Dickens and George Eliot use to support their ideas of continuity and connectedness, the enclosure or barricaded space denies the possibility of continuity and creates problems of access. Crusoe builds fortifications within fortifications; Pamela locks up her letters and Mr. B locks up Pamela. This metaphor, central in each novel, suggests in spatial terms the presence of differences inaccessible to mediation.

In using this metaphor of enclosure, Richardson nearly reverses

[36] Such detachment is difficult to conceive in a providential universe because, as Starr says, even "god is never a mere spectator"; individuals can hardly exercise a privilege unavailable to the Almighty.

the procedures of realism. Instead of temporalizing spatial relationships, *Pamela* spatializes temporal ones in a way that aggressively neutralizes sequence. "What is remarkable in this book," Robert Folkenflick says, "is the extraordinary number of spatial locutions, one after the other, with few other 'realistic' or descriptive details. The emphasis is on the movement from one room to the next—the flights, pursuits, withdrawals and entrances take place in a maze of passages, halls, alcoves, bedrooms, dressing rooms, summer-houses and closets." He sees this ordering of space as a "bourgeois analogue of the mythic ordering of the cosmos in Shakespeare and his contemporaries."[37] Even older traditions lie behind the imagery of the walled garden, which echoes distantly the Christian iconography of the Virgin. The separate space Pamela reserves to herself, however small, differs *qualitatively* from its surroundings. It is a space she reserves for her immortal soul and one she defends more successfully than Clarissa. Her maidenhead is her final barricade against being ravished—in Crusoe's terms being swallowed up or cannibalized; next to that are her papers, sewed into the seams of her clothing. To have one is almost to have the others, or so Mr. B seems to think in his attempts to "get at" Pamela (p. 237). The final barrier, as well as the intermediate ones that reinforce it, has the greatest ontological importance.[38]

Crusoe's survival strategies depend even more fully upon enclosure. He builds his first fortification to surround his first shelter, his cave; after the cave has fallen in and been refortified, he periodically takes measures to improve his wall, including building another wall to enclose the first. At his "country seat" he makes enclosures for himself and for his animals; he reinforces his en-

[37] Robert Folkenflick, "A Room of Pamela's Own," *ELH* 39, no. 4 (December 1972), 586-87, 593, 595.

[38] Kinkead-Weekes, discussing the dramatic value of epistolary style, speaks of Richardson's pattern "of enclosure within each point of view, and of dramatic exploration towards a more inclusive vision" (*Samuel Richardson*, p. 461). The connection thus implied between enclosure and point of view is suggestive, so long as the two are not conflated. Enclosure, rather than representing point of view, is an alternative to it: a way of shoring up against moral chaos and imperfection.

closures with a fence that actually begins to grow, making it even more invulnerable to invasion—a sign of the cooperation of nature in his strategies for natural survival. The whole system on the island—one that as Homer Brown shows can be read as a projection of himself—is a vast and increasingly complex system of enclosures. Like Pamela at the table, Crusoe is comfortably "hedged in" by a support system that is regarded both as a confirmation and an extension of his power. Crusoe fortifies, and when more materials wash ashore, refortifies, so that the activity of fortification becomes a sign to himself of his continuance, like his other productions and records, a sign of his power to maintain himself against any external threat. No one can "get at" Crusoe where he can keep them out. Like Pamela's, his circumstances unexpectedly trap him and, like Pamela, he attempts to improve not his mobility but his security in one place. His mobility is a symptom only of his folly.

Although Pamela and Crusoe both feel intensely the need for mediation in their experience, neither accepts (or is offered) the terms whereby realism makes mediation possible. Neither trusts or should trust time. By acknowledging a need to stabilize experience in writing, they consign their consciousnesses to the linear powers of language, but they do not really put much trust in the power of consciousness to sustain itself without constant reference to its records. Their narratives do represent a kind of retreat from threatening immediacy, from the different forms of engulfment they both fear.[39] But, rather than retreat to some distance, they make a more desperate flight into a separate space or territory that differs qualitatively from what surrounds it.

It is the absence of the continuities sustained in more realistic novels, or at least the fragility of those continuities, that makes reading *Robinson Crusoe* or *Pamela* at once delightful and difficult. Confined to the moment, readers must experience a series of events without the benefits of continuity. The mediating power

[39] For a discussion of Crusoe's fears of being swallowed up, see Homer Brown's essay "The Displaced Self." See also Zimmerman, *Defoe*, p. 32: "The ubiquitous references to being devoured point to a generalized fear: of being dematerialized—the reversal of the desire to accumulate."

of the narrator is missing because it is irrelevant to the relation between consciousness and Providence. In *Pamela* the corrective point of view, Mr. B's, is almost totally suppressed,[40] so that the reader and Pamela alike have no earthly assistance in judging events: "For, to be sure, the world, the *wise* world, that never is wrong itself, judges always by events. . . . But how would my censurers act in my case before the event justifies or condemns the action is the question?" (p. 265). In *Robinson Crusoe*, the past-tense narrator does not take advantage of his distance to show readers how to reach the same conclusions he reaches about the providential pattern in his life. The distance either is insufficient to permit the telling patterns to form or (in the case of the repeated yielding to "folly") does not give us sufficient evidence to regard it as a pattern. Consequently the reader's sympathy can belong (without seeing the folly of it) to the castaway craftsman making himself a world and not to the Christian autobiographer.

In sum, both Crusoe and Pamela reinforce their immortal souls by standing still. For both the central motive is to control access to their vital center. To do so they exert all their force and attention to establish a territory that they associate, quite rightly, with their continued existence, and that differs qualitatively from the territory outside it. Their confinements are really blessings in disguise. The ebb and flow of worldly possibilities may lap at the edges of Crusoe's consciousness but, like the island, his converted mind is stable in spite of time and circumstance. He considers his island life "my reign, or my captivity, which you please"

---

[40] "The greatest of all the formal flaws in *Pamela*," according to Kinkead-Weekes, "is the failure to give access to the hero's mind." This alleged failure "is the result of the single focus" that "causes fissures in all sorts of directions" (*Samuel Richardson*, p. 96). Kinkead-Weekes is quite right, I think, to suggest that the central way of misreading the novel is "to adopt Pamela's view of her master," but, as I have tried to show, there are many good reasons to suppose that this is precisely the "mistake" the novel invites us to make. Negative judgment of the effect depends on an assumption, tenuous in my opinion, that Richardson's goal was full dramatic representation. Zimmerman makes similar points about Defoe in a generally useful discussion of disjunctive narrative perspective (*Defoe and the Novel*, esp. pp. 75, 80, 106).

126

(p. 147). Pamela, too, has nowhere to go and no pressing urge to go there. When she finally does unlock the garden gate, she faces a world of highwaymen and general danger, almost sub-human forces of which the frightful bull (in this case a literal one) is emblematic: threats from which she recoils, as Crusoe recoils from the cannibals, and retreats to the protection of her prison. Eventually her prison becomes a palace. Once she and Crusoe recognize that spiritual danger is the same everywhere—in Hull as in Brazil, within the walls at Lincolnshire as well as without—they accept staying put. Physical mobility is merely distracting and, like the sea, is associated with changeability and threat. Although neither one chooses solitary confinement, each finds that being trapped helps direct the prisoner's mind in a vertical direction toward Providence and not urgently toward the horizon. Scanning the horizon gives Crusoe a better view of precisely nothing. Mr. B directs Pamela's attention upward, not backward, "recounting the uncommon gradations by which we have ascended to the summit of that felicity, which I hope we shall shortly arrive at" (p. 280). The goal is not common ground but a high, more secure, place in an increasingly refined and differentiated hierarchy of social and spiritual values. The progress stops at the summit, and there is no infinity beyond the horizon to tempt their human powers, or to make the activity of mediation between instances a meaningful activity.

Accommodating Difference

Discontinuous territory and discontinuous time create signifi-cant problems of consistency in *Robinson Crusoe* and *Pamela*. Inconsistencies in society at large can be made intelligible even to modern readers with hierarchical metaphors; personal incon-sistencies are more troublesome. Modern readers of these two novels have had recourse to irony as an interpretive key to such problems of inconsistency. Irony thus rescues Defoe and Rich-ardson from inconsistency by providing a higher level of gener-alization to reconcile apparent contradiction. From his other writ-

127

ing it is clear that Defoe was thoroughly conscious of irony as a technique; and Richardson, even in *Pamela*, demonstrates the capacity for irony that was later so obvious in *Clarissa*. Unfortunately for modern rescuers, neither Defoe nor Richardson shares our norms for behavior. Their norms of veracity are not those of verisimilitude; the norms of narrative consistency we enforce by resorting to irony are not Defoe's or Richardson's norms, and so in enforcing them we only run against the current of their novels or, what is worse, attribute to accident or ineptitude effects that are quite consistently striking. In fact, the inconsistencies we solve with "irony" may be the very problems each novel consistently strives to create.[41]

An important consequence of the disjunctive time schemes in these novels is that they do not require modern conceptions of "self" and of "society" as discrete, substantial, internally unified entities. Such conceptions depend upon consistencies that Defoe and Richardson do not sustain. In *Robinson Crusoe* and in *Pamela* the apparent inconsistencies of character are not mistakes and, what is more unsettling, they are not accessible to mediation in the terms familiar from realism. When Lady Davers changes her mind about Pamela, the difference between her past and her present view is explained by recourse to magic. "I was bewitched!" says she (p. 459). Her inconsistency cannot be reconciled with the idea of "self" as a unified product of experience. Whatever self-definitions are possible are conceived in terms of territory, in terms of external constraint not internal coherence. Hierarchy is a means for accommodating such inconsistencies in society, but in terms of personality that is harder, and our authors give us little help with the dilemma.

The characters' view of clothes is a case in point. Pamela seems to revere her apparel in an unseemly way, until we reflect that a

---

[41] It is most important to recognize the extent to which both Defoe and Richardson have "a very unmodern notion of veracity." Leo Damrosch thus characterizes Defoe, and I think the characterization applies as well to *Pamela* ("Defoe as Ambiguous Impersonator," p. 154). See also Frederick Bogel, "Structure and Substantiality in Later Eighteenth-Century Literature," *Studies in Burke and His Time*, vol. 15 (1973-74), 143-54.

set of clothes literally means a different ontological condition. Changing from her plain cloth to her finery is a means of moving from one state of being to another, so dependent is the personal life upon its place. The same spirit is evident in Crusoe's attitude toward Friday's nakedness. Nakedness, appropriate in a savage, is inappropriate in the civilized (converted) man; clothes are a sign of self-consciousness about sin.[42] Without a sense of contradiction the self changes suddenly from one ontological condition to another. This disjunctiveness in personality has proved especially troublesome to modern readers.

Character treatment in *Pamela*, for example, can raise some of the following questions. What are we to make of Mr. B, when in the midst of a shameless persecution of Pamela before the servants he responds to her pleading thus: "My master himself, hardened wretch as he was, seemed a little moved, and took his handkerchief out of his pocket, and walked to the window: What sort of day is it? said he" (p. 72). Are these tears as affected as they seem? Or is Richardson merely mixing in an exemplum too baldly for our taste? Surely his intent here is not comic, nor is it comic when Pamela leaves the room "holding by the wainscot all the way with both my hands" (p. 73), as if to give an authentic performance of terror. What is the intent when Mr. Williams prefers to walk home rather than ride, so as to reflect on Mr. B's goodness: "If you will go, Mr. Williams, said he, shall my chariot carry you home? No sir, answered he, I thank you. My time will be so well employed all the way, in thinking of your favors, that I choose to meditate upon them, as I walk home" (p. 329). Accustomed to novelists who use conversation and gesture to reveal character, we might find Mr. Williams merely sappy, whereas Richardson may wish us to take a point more like the one verbalized by Pamela: "O! What a godlike power is that of doing good!" What we might read as a bit of preposterous characterization may be fully intended as a device for teaching truth by example and quite regardless of context.

[42] Maximillian Novak comments, "to be ashamed of nakedness is a sign of reason" (*Defoe and the Nature of Man* [London: Oxford University Press, 1963], p. 47).

129

Finally, we are likely to regard Pamela's virtue with some suspicion as a disingenuous bid for fortune. She seems overly rigorous at some times, and strangely slack at others. "I have been *vilely tricked*, and, instead of being driven by Robin to my dear father's, *I am* carried off, to where, I have no liberty to tell" (p. 97). Is Pamela merely a subtle casuist here? If she thinks she has been vilely tricked and really wants to go home, why does she not reveal her whereabouts? If Pamela must be consistent, she cannot have it both ways. Her treatment of clothes and money seems likewise inconsistent with her unworldliness. She characterizes her new clothes as "too fine" in the same breath as she gives a detailed account of them; she confirms her pledges of kindness to the servants by giving them "five guineas a-piece" and a "God bless you every one!" (p. 495). These are instances of a general blend of cash and piety that may be too much for the modern reader to take straight, so long as we assume that cash and piety have some necessary relationship one way or another, either close or distant. But if Richardson assumes no such necessary relationship, then the demand for consistency is inappropriate, something that may account for "the more than two centuries of debate about exactly how artful and how conscious Pamela is in the process of getting what she wants."[43]

Problems of irony in Defoe are a special case. The difficulties of locating "Defoe's perspective" in his various novels and tracts is notorious, and extends to the general context of Defoe's life. Defoe himself "played contradictory roles with remarkable vigor"[44]—

[43] Patricia Spacks, *Imagining a Self: Autobiography and the Novel in Eighteenth-Century England* (Cambridge, Mass.: Harvard University Press, 1976), p. 310.

[44] Richetti, *Defoe's Narratives*, p. 6; Zimmerman, *Defoe and the Novel*, p. 14. Ian Watt summarizes the debate about irony in *Moll Flanders* in "Recent Critical Fortunes of *Moll Flanders*," *Eighteenth-Century Studies*, 1, no. 11 (September 1967), 109-26. In his first chapter, Richetti summarizes critical difficulties in finding ways in which Defoe can be "rescued from inconsistency" ("Defoe and the Problem of the Novel"). Others have addressed the problem of confusion in point of view. In his discussion of Defoe's essays, Leo Damrosch finds that a common result of his method, in narrative and essay alike, "is that Defoe has left us in confusion. It is easy enough to propose possible readings for each passage; the trouble is that so many of them are possible. None of these works is presented as fiction, and

a fact that is often explained by the need to survive amidst turbulent political change; but this interpretation rescues Defoe from the charge of inconsistency only to level at him a charge of hypocrisy. Especially important for someone of nonconforming background like Defoe was the claim of unity against uniformity: national unity, requiring religious tolerance, against the uniformity of the universal Catholic church. Uniformity, according to Defoe in *The True Born Englishman*, belongs only to the kingdom of the devil: "no Nonconforming sects disturb his reign."[45] Defoe "always claimed to be 'a constant follower of moderate principles, a vigorous opposer of hot measures of all parties.' "[46] In its suggestion that Defoe resisted taking any human solution as final, this comment aligns him with the Henrician apologists who regarded all worldly solutions as *adiaphora* or partial hints of truth. If all parties have partial truth and no party has the whole truth, then the ability to enter into a variety of different points of view with partial but not complete commitment becomes an important moral activity. Defoe's education at Charles Morton's dissenting school included practice with "the assumption of authorial masks," a practice which, Anthony James suggests, may be a clue to Defoe's political and literary behavior.[47] Masks are discardable, they are ways of getting a narrative viewpoint without necessarily getting a stable distance: something which the tradition of dramatic monologue developed more fully in modern literature, up to and including Humbert Humbert. In his ironic impersonations Defoe causes interpretive problems by his refusal to provide a countervailing view in the text to adjust the relative proportions of the main voice, either to corroborate or to qualify it. Distance is a problem for the reader, and certainty a big problem.

Defoe's own remarks on the nature and uses of irony corroborate

---

yet each turns out to exhibit the kinds of ambiguity that recent criticism of Defoe's novels has made familiar" ("Defoe as Ironic Impersonator," p. 159). Of one incident in *Moll Flanders* Zimmerman says "there are many possible views of this incident, none of them consistent" (*Defoe and the Novel*, p. 105).

[45] Quoted by Sutherland, *Defoe: A Critical Study*, p. 103.

[46] Sutherland, *Defoe: A Critical Study*, p. 12.

[47] James, *Voices*, esp. pp. 21, 93.

these suggestions. He says of his ironic tract on the Pretender that "being written Ironically, all the first Part, if taken asunder from the last Part, will read, *as in all Ironical speaking must be*, just contrary. . . . But taken complexly, taken Whole, and of a Piece, can leave no room to doubt, but that they are written to Ridicule and expose the very Notions of bringing in the Pretender. . . ."[48] "Taken complexly, taken Whole," can mean formal unity to modern readers accustomed to such values, but it can also mean a general thematic coherence that includes not only what is in the text but more importantly what is not in it: the views "just contrary" to those stated in the text. "It takes some perspective," Maximillian Novak observes, "to see that what is wrong with the speaker in *The Shortest Way with Dissenters* is his total lack of Charity, that he is very much of a priest and nothing of a Christian."[49] That critical perspective is provided by the reader, not the text.

With *The Shortest Way*, then, only the wholly detached or the foolish "could possibly not be offended,"[50] and taking offense—obviously the intended result—is a form of taking distance. This result seems so consistent in Defoe as to be attributable to some level of intention. "His generalizations in one field clash with his generalizations in another," a fact that "causes confusion and anomaly." But Defoe's consciousness of the instability of human motivation and commitment does not necessarily imply a cynical view of the possibilities of grounding motivation and commitment in something more stable. His tendency to write "on both sides or for causes he could not possibly have supported fully"[51] is not necessarily giving the devil his due, especially if the devil is represented by those who insist on finally choosing a side. Defoe's

---

[48] Quoted by Maximillian Novak, "Defoe's Use of Irony," in M. Novak and Herbert Davis, *Irony in Defoe and Swift* (Los Angeles: Clark Memorial Library, 1966), pp. 16-17. Novak's convincing essay establishes the importance of irony in Defoe's work, but others caution against making too much of irony in Defoe. See Starr, *Casuistry*; Price, *To the Palace of Wisdom*, p. 266; and Zimmerman, *Defoe and the Novel*, p. 17.

[49] Novak, "Irony," p. 37.

[50] Zimmerman, *Defoe and the Novel*, p. 16.

[51] Novak, "Irony," pp. 28-29.

resistance to uniformity in political, religious, or other views, his desire to accommodate variety, belongs to a spirit very congenial to realism; the fact that he did not fully imagine the social and psychological terms in which such a spirit might flourish may be testimony to the difficulty of doing so at the time he wrote.

> There is an inconsiderate temper which reigns in our minds, that hurries us down the stream of our affections by a kind of involuntary agency, and makes us do a thousand things, in the doing of which we propose nothing to ourselves but an immediate subjection to our will, that is to say, our passion, even without the concurrence of our understandings, and of which we can give very little account after 'tis done.[52]

How to accommodate this given without falling to the devil's party (i.e., one uniformity or another) is precisely the problem Defoe sets in *Robinson Crusoe* and, in seeking adequate accommodation, he thinks in terms of a cosmic context, not a social one.

Robinson Crusoe also presents problems of identity and consistency resembling those in *Pamela*. In one much-discussed passage Crusoe delivers a long apostrophe on the uselessness of gold, and then proceeds to carry it away with him.

> I smiled to my self at the sight of this money. "O drug!" said I aloud, "what art thou good for? Thou art not worth to me, no, not the taking off of the ground; one of those knives is worth all this heap; I have no manner of use for thee, e'en remain where thou art, and go to the bottom as a creature whose life is not worth saving." However, upon second thoughts, I took it away, and wrapping all this in a piece of canvas, I began to think of making another raft, but while I was preparing this, I found the sky over-cast, and the wind began to rise.
> . . .   (P. 75.)

There is no certain narrative clue how to take this. Is this a portrait of a man whose right hand does not know what his left

[52] Quoted by Martin Price, *Palace of Wisdom*, p. 267.

133

is doing? Does it suggest the value or the worthlessness of second thoughts? Even with the hindsight available to him Crusoe gives no hint in his narration that he even sees a problem of inconsistency. Crusoe's piety in general is a problem, especially the "identification in Crusoe's mind of the designs of Providence with pure self-interest."[53] He fires on the cannibals "in the name of God" (p. 234); he attributes to Providence his capture of the English mutineers; he attributes to Providence the escape of some of these very prisoners. Providence appears to make inconsistency consistent. For a writer as completely self-conscious as Defoe was about the uses of irony, such details as the body count of those killed in the name of God could not be without some ironic value. But in such cases, as when he associates providential design with self-interest, the problem of gauging his irony is complicated by the presence of modern notions, such as an association between providential design and self-sacrifice.

However this may be, it seems clear that, as Mark Kinkead-Weekes says, the style "seems oddly capable of holding apparent contradictions without discomfort. . . . There is this, and that, and also this; the style is essentially episodic and works by addition." All judgments depend on the situation, not on some prior constant. "*It all depends on the situation.* It is *our* assumption, that human beings ought to be consistent, that produces the 'irony!' "[54] Pamela doubts Mr. B's consistency; Mr. B doubts hers; but most of all the reader doubts both. Can the Mr. B who insults Mr. Andrews as an inferior really be considering him as a father-in-law? Can the Pamela who is so ready to wed Mr. B really be offended by his treatment? Can the Crusoe who keeps money really be believed when he scorns it? The behavior that inspires such questions can seem to be, in Leo Damrosch's phrase, a kind of "involuntary schizophrenia"[55]—at least to people accustomed to assuming the existence and value of a consistent self.

[53] James, *Voices*, p. 184.

[54] Kinkead-Weekes, *Samuel Richardson*, p. 477. Kinkead-Weekes describes *Robinson Crusoe* in these terms, but explicitly exempts *Pamela*; I am arguing that it applies to Richardson's novel as well.

[55] "Involuntary schizophrenia" is Leo Damrosch's phrase for the state apparently

In sum, while they resist both the oppositions and the corroborations of others, Robinson Crusoe and Pamela find no resting place in self. In the context of providential design, the proper attitude is humility, not self-reliance. Crusoe regards his attempts to determine his own life as mere "folly." When he discovers the dying goat that he had mistaken for an enemy, he recognizes that "there was nothing in this cave that was more frightful than myself" (p. 183). On the unregenerate level this can mean that there is nothing to fear, but it can also have the regenerate meaning that self is the most frightful thing: that there is "nothing but" self to fear. Like Crusoe, Pamela is often in terror of her enemies, but she manages somehow to defer all decisions to Providence. Her worst moment, one that brings her to the brink of suicide, comes when she attempts to take a hand in her own fate. By attempting to escape her persecutor she falls into the hands of "a worse enemy, myself" (p. 183). Self terrifies both protagonists almost as much as other people do.

The instability of their affairs teaches Pamela and Crusoe alike the limits of self-reliance. "When I was most disappointed, I was nearer my happiness" (p. 326) says Pamela; she has already learned "always [to] mistrust most when appearances look fairest" (p. 208). In a providential dispensation which, among other things, provides that the last shall be first, calculations of worldly probability can in an instant come to nothing. "My prison is become

---

recommended by Defoe in the *Complete Tradesman*, where the narrator discusses how a man "must be a *perfect complete* hypocrite if he will be a *complete tradesman*." In short, he must be a cringing cur below stairs and a wife-beater above. "What are we to make of this? . . . There is no hint that we are to disapprove of the Uriah Heep unctuousness" required for such a course ("Defoe as Ambiguous Impersonator," p. 158). The absence of a stable narrative viewpoint in the text is what gives modern readers difficulty. The text creates for readers a need to rouse themselves from moral passivity and to provide the stable controlling viewpoint themselves, a process associated more with satire than with realistic narration. Zimmerman discusses the close relation between Defoe's satiric and narrative methods. "Defoe's central achievement from *Robinson Crusoe* to *Roxana* is the same: with great power and some precision, he presents characters who have been taught to assume souls but have difficulty in finding them" (*Defoe and the Novel*, pp. 17-18).

135

my palace," says Pamela (p. 369). Who'd have thought it? Like Crusoe she can hold the line, but she cannot personally solve her problems. Mr. B's magical conversion, especially judging by the parallel example of Lovelace's failure, must owe something to Grace. Crusoe, too, makes much of being closest to salvation just when he thinks he's farthest away from it. And his "measures" serve him well sometimes and not so well at others. He is always facing the unexpected event. Even the habit of enclosure, which has made possible both physical and psychic survival, is the very same measure that, when he is attacked by wolves on the way to London, nearly gets him killed. Such reversal of worldly probability is often the surest sign of Grace.

Accommodating inconsistencies or incompatible differences in personality is not easy in these novels, and in both the accommodation is ultimately referred to social hierarchy. As a kind of structure that accommodates differences not by mediation but by subordination, hierarchy best suits the experience of a society defined by disjunction. The discontinuous time and territorial space represented in *Robinson Crusoe* and *Pamela* require some principle of coherence that accommodates and preserves difference, that saves the appearances. The difference between Pamela B and the original Pamela, like the difference between Pamela in two different suits of clothes, is an ontological difference. One "descends" or one rises, if one moves at all in her world (p. 447), and change involves a deeply significant alteration because it involves motion from one place to a *qualitatively* different one. Such hierarchy belongs not to a society conceived as a self-contained unity but to a society that belongs to a cosmic order. Pamela's final statement of obedience has Miltonic reverberations: "All the good I can do, is but a poor third-hand good; for my dearest master himself is but the second hand. God, the all-gracious, the all-good, the all-bountiful, the all-mighty, the all-merciful God, is the first: To him, therefore be all the glory!" (p. 528). This may seem a far cry from her earlier faith that, though the poor are despised by the proud and the rich, "yet we were all on a foot originally" (p. 271). But in *Pamela* religion proves no foe to degree. Pamela submits to Mr. B when (and

136

because) Mr. B conforms to Reason. The resulting distribution of powers does not entail inequality and does not require "command" or "obedience" because the differences between Pamela and Mr. B, like those between them and the rest of the population, have been accommodated by the hierarchical order (p. 473). Pamela is now "above" her former fellows in social degree as she has always been in virtue, and Mr. B finally achieves "heights of virtue" (p. 432) corresponding to his high social position. In virtue and in social degree both differ in kind from lower forms. Such differences, as Pamela reminds Lady Davers with some irony when the heat of argument reduces them to an equality (p. 404), must be preserved, not mediated and overcome.

In *Robinson Crusoe* hierarchy develops as soon as other people turn up on the island. And the more variety appears, the more we have of hierarchy, privilege, and exclusive definition. After a solitary footprint heralds the advent of other human beings, society increases in almost geometrical progression. Crusoe first regards the cannibals as subhuman and thus part of "meer" nature that he leaves to its ways. However, when the cannibals prepare to eat Europeans, Crusoe makes a distinction in order to save the human beings from the subhuman ones. When Englishmen appear next, Crusoe faces the more complex problem of distinguishing among Europeans, the former group being only Spaniards. Presented with the difference between Spaniards and English, and finally between good English (Captain and loyal crew) and bad English (mutineers), Crusoe has to make increasingly refined distinctions among human beings. In each case the differences are qualitative. At the end of this process Crusoe emerges as the "governor" or "*generalissimo*" at the top of a rigidly hierarchical order, one based on distinctions according to race, nationality, and social function. This hierarchy, however ironic Defoe's overtones may be, does correspond to the novel's general hierarchical vision of a universe that depends upon the "converse of spirits" up and down the ladder of nature. Whether hierarchy is separable from religion or not, it seems clear that absolute distinctions require absolute justification. Difference means more than mere difference: it means better or worse.

137

In his relation to this little world Crusoe stands outside it, like a providence: interested, involved, privileged. He functions like a kind of Grace for the English, as he himself says. He compares his first night on the island with theirs in an almost typological manner.

> As I knew nothing that night of the supply I was to receive by the providential driving of the ship nearer the land, by the storms and tide, by which I have since been so long nourished and supported; so these three poor desolate men knew nothing how certain of deliverance and supply they were, how near it was to them, and how effectually and really they were in a condition of safety, at the same time that they thought themselves lost, and their case desperate. (P. 250.)

Seen from his literal eminence, the new group of shipwrecked men is interpreted not in terms of their situation in time and place but in terms of another event, one widely separated from it in time and one that does not invite reflections about past causes or sequential development. Without thinking it incongruous, Crusoe interprets *their* present in terms of *his* past, and both in terms of an understanding that reverses the probabilities of the situation rather than developing from them. Crusoe's view of their situation, one that differs from their own, is not a partial, contributing glimpse of truth; it is the right view and theirs is the wrong. Crusoe's relation to these men, like his relation to Friday (someone who falls at his feet and acknowledges him as "master") resembles the relation of king and country, God and creation. Such micro-macrocosmic comparisons are another way of bridging qualitative differences. Even when he thinks of his own past, Crusoe tends to treat it as a microcosm of relationships rather than as a series of related aspects. "I run over the whole history of my life in miniature, or by abridgement" (p. 37), effectually detaching it from any homogeneous field in which relative measurement makes sense. Crusoe takes distance, but not in order to mediate a consensus.

Defoe, in fact, seems to see mediation as a fruitless occupation that is mainly destructive to the mediator. Describing his own

138

attempts to mediate disputes, Defoe locates the mediator not at a distance, coordinating the various differing viewpoints invisibly from a safe vantage-point, but smack in the middle of a lethal conflict: "I have been like a man that runs in between two duellers to part them, and who to prevent them losing their lives, loses his own; the furious gladiators run both their swords into him that would part them, and he falls a sacrifice to his own zeal."[56] This passage reflects a general sense that the mediator's role is an honorable course, but not a safe one; it involves preventing conflict rather than fostering agreement. In terms relevant to narrative perspective, Defoe sees that different viewpoints disagree (murderously, in fact), and that where they intersect is not where the mediator should be but outside them, like Crusoe, where they little suspect his presence and where he can muster his power invisibly. In this he exhibits the detachment, even the disembodied detachment, of later fictional narrators. He delegates his authority as "governour" and never appears in his own person within the group he governs. "I kept my self and one more out of sight, for reasons of state" (p. 265). This witty formulation acknowledges the importance of invisibility to governing power, and even the importance of disguise and subterfuge.[57]

Interestingly, Defoe dramatizes these relationships rather than incorporating them into the forms of realistic narration where they might function easily through the narrator. Crusoe, like Moll, is a character who only takes up that distance occasionally, and inconsistently overall. In trying to combine the roles of spectator and participant Crusoe attempts the impossible. As a narrator, he is like the man who keeps getting caught in cross-fire,

[56] Defoe's comment is quoted by Peter Earle in *The World of Daniel Defoe* (New York: Athenaeum, 1977), p. 13, from one of the last numbers of Defoe's *Review* (1713). Hans Andersen discusses Defoe's ability to "take either side without even mentioning the other," in "The Paradox of Trade and Morality in Defoe," *Modern Philology*, 38 (1941), 23-46.

[57] "When I showed my self to the two hostages it was with the captain, who told them I was the person the governour had ordered to look after them and that it was the governour's pleasure they should not stir . . . so I now appeared as another person, and spoke of the governour, the garrison, the castle, and the like, upon all occasions" (p. 267).

rather than one who maintains consistent identity and position. He lives in two different media at once, being both an actor, with his salvation to win or lose, and a providential agent co-ordinating the salvation of others. For someone thus attempting to cross the threshold between time and eternity, the image of a man caught in cross-fire is especially apt. It suggests the contradictoriness of a position both inside and outside of the picture.

Both *Pamela* and *Robinson Crusoe* provide fascinating examples of realistic techniques and values qualified and distanced by being put into unexpected frames. In the second part of each novel, when the character reenters society from solitude, the individual character that has appeared to develop in partially realistic ways disappears into exemplitude. The second half of *Pamela*, for example, sees the publication of the heroine: the complete explication of her meaning, value, thoughts, gestures, and past. Her journal and letters are circulated. Her reunion with her father is witnessed by the entire neighborhood as a kind of *demonstratio* (p. 308). There is no suspicion by the novel's end that some opacity in Pamela remains, some anomalous quality or individualizing quirk that will prove inconvenient for those interpretations of her dependable nature made by "all the world." Pamela has been published, along with her documents, and there's no lingering over the text, no reading for depths. After her apotheosis as Mrs. B, when she trades the power of resistance for the "godlike power . . . of doing good" (p. 329) Pamela confirms an exemplary career by studiously avoiding equality. There is nothing held in reserve, no secrets to save up for future need, and this is the way it should have been all along. Pamela unbeleaguered and in her rightful place can undertake the primal duty, which is praise, not self-improvement.

Defoe's treatment of Crusoe's experience as a social creature, in particular his becoming exemplary, is analogous to Richardson's, but wittier. Parallel to the publication of Pamela is the conversion of Crusoe into a sign or cypher. All the activity of his solitude—all the construction, stockpiling, and record-keeping—can be regarded as an attempt to objectify himself. No one else is present to see him, and he cannot see himself; but he can see his productions. His restless activity, which begins after one

140

night's sleep in a tree and continues for a quarter century, is a way of keeping track of himself: all various kinds of a journal. But these particular objectifiers, precisely because they are signs of his activity, involve him in a circularity by referring him back to himself. His constructions are only traces of himself. Even the footprint is equivocal. Whose is it? The question is never definitively answered, any more than the parrot's question is definitively answered. "It came into my thought one day, that all this might be a meer chimera of my own, and that this foot might be the print of my own foot . . ." (p. 165). Poor Crusoe, looking for objectifiers, keeps running into himself.[58] The reader shares his perplexity. Crusoe *says* he's tracing the footprints of Providence in his history, but we find ourselves tracing *his* footprints, his productions, his documents, his recollection. With all this displacement, the irreducible ambiguity of all signs becomes profoundly unsettling and makes reliance on Providence all the more imperative.

The appearance of other human beings, which in a realistic narrative might have been expected to end the anxious circularity of solitary experience, only intensifies it. Once an indefatigable maker of signs, Crusoe himself now becomes a sign to others. Once a reader of signs, now he is read. He maintains himself as "governour" by becoming a representation. Never showing himself directly to his subjects, he appears as "another person" representing himself. "I kept myself and one more out of sight, for reasons of state" (p. 265). The consensus that gives him power is based on a hoax and supported by the godlessness of other human beings who seem to prefer surrogate providences to the real thing. Being a sign to others does nothing to secure his sense of stable identity; on the contrary, he is as much alone as ever, his identity once more displaced.

Crusoe's discovery of the footprint and Pamela's marriage project them out of one kind of solitude into another, but the terms of their experience remain unchanged. Decoded by her peers,

[58] See Homer Brown's discussion of Crusoe's island as an "extension of himself" which "has dark areas Robinson has never explored; he is constantly startled by versions of himself, the voice of the parrot, the dying goat" ("Displaced Self," p. 573).

141

Pamela becomes an exemplary guide for her neighbors. Crusoe chooses to remain undecoded, closeted, invisible. But despite their differing responses to social contact, they find in society no new possibilities.

The absence of continuous time in *Robinson Crusoe* and *Pamela* means that the medium of experience, both for individuals and for groups of individuals, fosters mechanical conceptions of unity. Like the style of both novels—"there is this, and that, and also this"—both personality and society tend to remain collections of attributes rather than entities with organic internal relationships. The fascinating thing about both these novels is their inconstant flirtation with the techniques (and therefore with the premises) of realism, their invocation of the problems of history. But they stop short of history. Different experiences in time can be mutually informative, that is to say, they can share common properties and problems and opportunities only if they exist in a common medium. The disjunctive medium in each novel attenuates those possibilities for realistic development. An hierarchical order finally accommodates and preserves unreconcilable differences in both psyche and society.

The conception of society as an entity that develops in fiction later transforms the moral problems that face Crusoe and Pamela. The problem of maintaining proper alignment with Providence, for example, is in Jane Austen no longer the solitary responsibility of one soul, but one distributed throughout the social group. Authority and responsibility both are delegated to the group as a whole, so that society acts as a kind of buffer between the solitary individual and the divine. The soul wrestling with God becomes the self negotiating with other similar selves. In such relative contexts consistency has more value; one must be recognizable to others. The erratic soul becomes the consistent self in society, a fact that suggests the symbiotic relationship between the very ideas of self and society.

The idea of self has much more dignity in relation to other people than it has in relation to God. If Crusoe and Pamela could adjust their difficulties in terms of a social entity, every difficulty would be easier because it would be qualified. Like Boswell they

142

would never be delivered, but they would never be defeated, either.[59] The important liminal moments would be human and historical; the important threshold would be nothing more frightening than the difference between one self and another or between one's past and present experiences. Such liminal moments can even be postponed or otherwise controlled, even if only partially. The steps required for those transitions may be more or less frightening than the steps required to meet God or to obey the "secret dictates" of the "converse of spirits"; but they are decidedly different steps, involving different problems and rewards.

For Crusoe and Pamela, however, the important liminal moments are sacred and atemporal, the important thresholds those between God and man, between the spiritual order and the visible world. Such liminal moments are absolute and omnipresent. Any moment can be a supreme moment; properly conceived, every moment *is* a liminal moment. In such circumstances, to know where they are—that is, to answer the parrot's automatic question—does not involve a consensus among partial perspectives but rather a militant standpoint of the soul apart from time and space altogether. The presence of other viewpoints is not helpful, not mutually informative. In arriving at his conclusions about the shape and meaning of his personal history, Crusoe is not offered the possibility of consensus; nobody is looking at the "same" world as he is, either before or after other people land on his solitary island. Pamela fares somewhat better in that her virtue is praised from the start by the servants, who do so long before the gentry get around to it. But this is insignificant and uncertain corroboration at best. The virtuous Mrs. Jervis keeps silence rather than risk offending Mr. B by defending Pamela; and the praise of her social betters merely puts Pamela into new difficulties resisting the dangers of success. Like worldly opposition, even worldly confirmation must be resisted.

[59] See John Morris, *Versions of the Self* (New York: Columbia University Press, 1966), p. 221, on Boswell: "Never delivered, never defeated, Boswell worked at the very modern project of defining and creating himself."

143

CHAPTER FIVE

Jane Austen's
Critique of Distance

J ane Austen capitalizes more than Defoe and Richardson on the powers of the narrator. Her past-tense tellers represent a step back from "the moment" and a move toward the depersonalized consciousness of more fully realistic narrators. But only a step. Her novels still reflect the attention to social hierarchy, the suspicion of self, the rhetorical use of detail that characterize *Robinson Crusoe* and *Pamela*, and consequently the process of detachment whereby the narrator becomes "nobody" develops modestly in her novels, up until the last one. The differences between *Emma* and *Persuasion* offer striking evidence of a shift in social and personal values and a parallel shift in the management of narrative perspective toward consensus and realism. The marriage of Emma and Mr. Knightley resembles the social celebration of Pamela's more than it resembles the separate peace of Anne Elliot and Captain Wentworth. Anne Elliot dramatizes the strains of being "nobody," and the narrator in *Persuasion* assumes the role of neutral observer more decidedly than do earlier Austen narrators.

In *Emma* and the novels preceding it, the sign of personal integrity, as Francis Hart observes, "is measured motion, and timed or measured speech. Persuasion is always a threat; stasis—constancy and quiet—must be the norm, and deviations must be justified. Otherwise, in Jane Austen's social world, one has only noise or unquiet spirits, public persons, false intimacies, domestic and emotional and verbal clutter, and the restlessness that is a sign of inauthenticity."[1] But in *Persuasion* restlessness, the itinerant life of quick alarm, is not the sign of inauthenticity it is in *Emma*; rather it is a given condition of the world where the hereditary master of Kellynch Hall has abandoned his estate and moved to Bath. In the securely ordered society of *Emma* the heroine's detachment is dangerous and correctable, but in *Persuasion* detachment is a necessary condition of consciousness which cannot be avoided.

In such different worlds the values of realism have very different weight. Take, for example, the role of memory and projection in each. Emma is an imaginist, "on fire with speculation and foresight."[2] Not only is she chastened for this error, but the scourge is memory. For Emma, as for Frank Churchill and Jane Fairfax, recollection is "mortifying" (III: viii, xiv, xviii). For Anne Elliot, on the other hand, a good and faithful memory has the first importance. Her loyalty to the past, her sense of its importance, her ability to see validity in the conflicting claims of both Captain Wentworth and Lady Russell give Anne her power—a power that is even connected with her chief virtue, the ability to anticipate the feelings and needs of others. In *Emma* the character whose predicament most clearly resembles Anne Elliot's is Jane Fairfax, not the central heroine.[3]

This difference in social vision directly influences the management of narrative perspective. In *Emma*, which demonstrates the importance of social place and accommodates differences, the narrator functions mainly as a corrective to the heroine, appearing most clearly when she is making a palpable mistake. The narrator of *Emma* acts as a pivot from which the heroine's viewpoint

[1] Francis Hart, "The Spaces of Privacy: Jane Austen," *Nineteenth-Century Fiction*, 30, no. 3 (December 1975), 333. Susan Morgan argues that Austen associates such disorder with realism (*In the Meantime* [Chicago: University of Chicago Press, 1980], p. 11).

[2] *Emma*, Riverside edition (Boston: Houghton Mifflin, 1957), III, iii, 261. All subsequent references will be to this edition and will be included parenthetically in the text.

[3] Alistair Duckworth makes this point in *The Improvement of the Estate* (Baltimore: The Johns Hopkins University Press, 1971), p. 178.

145

diverges, first with slight risk and then more dangerously. The two viewpoints do not agree, they jar; the corrective function of the narrator drives a wedge between Emma's erring viewpoint and the correct one.[4] This novel especially cherishes the "counterfeit connection" that Mary Lascelles finds characteristic of Austen.[5] The connection Mrs. Elton makes on the last page between satin and seriousness is such a counterfeit; so is Harriet's exclamation to Emma, "Nobody is equal to you!" (II, xiii), a comment that proliferates conflicting meanings at a considerable rate. Distance is never neutral in *Emma*; it is always moral distance.

In *Persuasion*, on the other hand, a novel that deals with a social world in confusion and with consciousness sustaining itself apart from social place, the narrator functions more as a corroborator of the heroine's mind, extending and confirming rather than correcting it. The narrator is less distinct and acts more as a medium between minds. It is a less distinct and more supervisory narrator that describes the beach at Lyme and oversees the reunion between a present and a past life. In *Persuasion* the narrator steps back from silliness and, rather than accommodating it, acts more as a neutral medium between minds. By doing so this narrator takes a step toward fuller realism. Between *Emma* and *Persuasion*, then, the balance shifts from a narrative of correction, one that challenges and reaffirms a social order, to a narrative of corroboration and consensus, one that validates the heroine's reliance on memory and her radical separation from a social order that no longer functions properly.[6]

---

[4] In this the narrator is close to the traditional function of satire. See John Lawlor, "Radial Satire and the Realistic Novel," *Essays and Studies*, n.s. 8 (1955), 64.

[5] Mary Lascelles, *Jane Austen and Her Art* (Oxford: Oxford University Press, 1939), p. 145.

[6] Making a similar point, Alistair Duckworth places Austen "between what may be briefly termed the 'providential' fiction of Fielding, Richardson, and other eighteenth-century novelists, and the 'contingent' fiction of the Victorians" (*Improvement of the Estate*, p. xi); David Miller discusses, in somewhat different terms, the "pathos of unending narratability" in *Persuasion* (*Narrative and Its Discontents* [Princeton: Princeton University Press, 1981], p. 106).

Narrative Correction in *Emma*

Emma's social bias brings with it a whole cosmological view. Various critics have commented on this fact, though they often speak of all the novels and do not distinguish *Persuasion*. Alistair Duckworth states the point as follows: "Secure in the knowledge that the world is essentially ordered, the individual is also confident that it will—after much personal tribulation and a difficult process of education perhaps—provide him with a place." Though he finds the "controlling theological framework" of eighteenth-century fiction to have evaporated somewhat in Austen, still her social world has a "given structure" that is "ultimately founded in religious principle," even though it must constantly be distinguished "from its frequently corrupted form." The plots of novels in such a universe reflect a Christian vision of universal experience and are "evidently based to a quite explicit degree on the myth of the fall"—an old typological motif that, having had a salient role in novels like *Robinson Crusoe* and *Pamela*, becomes embedded in many nineteenth-century novels.[7] In *Emma* the case for social interconnectedness is still informed by this vision of the universe, one that severely restricts the importance of viewpoint and of temporal continuity. Austen, according to Marilyn Butler, "masters the subjective insights which help to make the nineteenth century novel what it is, and denies them validity."[8]

Emma thus validates a conception of social order that remains at odds with historical continuity; this means that the novel constantly maintains a competitive tension between its method and its moral. The leveling potential of the past tense, its tend-

---

[7] Duckworth, *Improvement of the Estate*, pp. 23, 12, 25, and 28. Variants of this view of Jane Austen's conservative, Christian outlook can be found in Bernard Paris ("The major unvarying element in Jane Austen's fiction is a code of values and conduct that serves as the norm by which all deviations are satirized and judged"), *Character and Conflict in Jane Austen's Novels: A Psychological Approach* (Detroit: Wayne State University Press, 1978), p. 170; and, more subtly, in Marilyn Butler (the crux of Austen plots is the struggle of individuals toward "a fixed and permanent truth"), *Jane Austen and the War of Ideas* (Oxford: The Clarendon Press, 1975), p. 260.

[8] Butler, *War of Ideas*, p. 274.

ency to equalize relations, constantly tilts (just as Emma unwit-
tingly does) against an hierarchical order resistant to it. For example, a fully realistic treatment of the relationship between
Emma and Miss Bates would emphasize what Emma has in common with the older woman (she was once young and handsome)
and would suggest that, but for her more fortunate circumstances,
Emma might easily share the same fate. But in Austen this is not
to be. This theme is sounded feebly, but the essential differences
between Emma and Miss Bates are much more important than
the circumstantial similarities between them. They are differences
of a sort that are not substantially modifiable by circumstances.
Emma bears out Mary Lascelles' observation that one of the things
Austen excludes is that "collective humanity" that mainly in-
terests those novelists intent upon temporal, linear, historical
relations.[9] Emma must learn the necessity for recognizing and
accommodating these differences, and the error of disregarding
them because of half-baked and vaguely romantic notions about
the nature of social intercourse.

The important differences between Emma and Miss Bates are
more than financial; they are ontological. Miss Bates is the medium of news, performing the function of circuit-maker in Highbury between one "family circle" and another. Miss Bates thus
reinforces mutual awareness among members of the community
in a way that requires no closer agreement among parties than is
possible given the differences in their natures. Even in her conversation, a barely articulated outpouring of facts and impressions—almost a model of discontinuity—she performs an important choral function. In planning the ball at the Crown, Miss
Bates is not wanted for any important decisions. "As a counsellor
she was not wanted; but as an approver (a much safer character),
she was truly welcome" (II, xi, 197-98). As a counsellor Miss
Bates is not wanted; as an approver Emma could not be wanted.
Both are required. As channel and as celebrant, Miss Bates has

---

[9] Lascelles, *Jane Austen and Her Art*, pp. 129-30, 132. David Miller comments
on "the equivocation of Jane Austen's form—its tendency to disown at an ideological level what it embraces at a constructional one" (*Narrative and Its Discontents*, p. 54, also p. 8).

an important role in the group. Emma must learn to acknowledge this, and, by extension, she must also acknowledge her own general dependence on the group for the important terms of her experience. This truth is what Emma denies at Box Hill.

When Emma insults Miss Bates, Mr. Knightley directly provides corrective pressure. The fact that he steps forward with direct correction, rather than leaving it to the indirect pressure of the narrator and community as a whole, gauges the seriousness of Emma's offense. His language calls attention not to Miss Bates's personal qualities but primarily to her place.

> Were she a woman of fortune, I would leave every harmless absurdity to take its chance, I would not quarrel with you for any liberties of manner. Were she your equal in situation— but, Emma, consider how far this is from being the case. She is poor; she has sunk from the comforts she was born to; and, if she live to old age, must probably sink more. Her *situation* should secure your compassion.
>
> (III, vii, 294; italics mine.)

Mr. Knightley's language of decline ("she has sunk . . . must probably sink more") suggests an ominous slippage affecting who and what Miss Bates is, and implying Emma's responsibility in supporting her. It is the kind of responsibility that she discharges properly with her father; and what John Bayley says of Emma's responsibility in that quarter also applies, though Emma has to learn it, with Miss Bates:

> Emma and her father cannot understand one another, but this is no bar to their affection. Harmony, even intimacy, can exist in a community without mutual understanding—indeed must do, for we must live as we can. And this acceptance of mis-understanding is surely the keynote of *Emma*, rather than—as has often been said—the confrontation of reality with a series of self-deceptions and misapprehensions.[10]

[10] John Bayley, "The 'Irresponsibility' of Jane Austen," in B. C. Southam, ed., *Critical Essays on Jane Austen* (New York: Barnes and Noble, 1960), p. 7.

The constant "vocabulary of separation" in *Emma* implies that "union" is a problem;[11] but the unification takes place by accommodating these distinctions, not erasing them.

Social harmony, that is, does not and cannot depend upon consensus because the points of view differ so absolutely as to make agreement in substantive matters impossible. What Mrs. Elton sees as a proper wedding Emma would regard with contempt; the reverse is also clearly the case. When Mrs. Elton proposes to Emma a joint musical project—"If *we* exert ourselves, I think we shall not be long in want of allies" (II, xiv, 214)—that "we" is a manifest impossibility so far as common ground is concerned. The only possibilities for two people learning to "think alike" (I, xii, 76) appear between pairs in marriage: Knightley and Emma, Jane and Frank, Harriet and Robert Martin, Mrs. Elton and her *caro sposo*. But between Harriet and either Elton or Churchill there is no significant basis for agreement, and trying to marry her to the one or the other is like trying to unite things as incompatible as a middle C and a shrub. Everyone agrees that "elegance" is a good, but this by no means constitutes a consensus. People differ in what they mean by this word, radically enough in some cases to make any possible agreement trivial. No mediation is possible. Some other kind of adjustment is needed between the various circles of Highbury.

The scene at the end of *Emma*, where the entire cast assembles at the Westons to view the new baby, provides an interesting case of harmony without agreement. Frank and Emma converse in a spirit of mutual reconciliation, and they do so, furthermore, in a retrospective mode, coming to agreement about the past. But the harmony here does not depend on a meeting of minds. In this collective moment, the incompleteness of their mutual understanding is most evident, especially on the question of decorum. Fortunately the group absorbs their differences in its timeless concerns: anxiety over the health of a first-born infant, the premature inclination to call the doctor—these have nothing new in them and are not the result of the narrated events.

[11] Duckworth, *Improvement of the Estate*, p. 151.

Social harmony, like musical harmony, depends upon carefully maintained intervals. In her various acts of dissociation—from the Coles, from Jane, from Mrs. Elton, from Robert Martin— Emma makes the crucial mistake of supposing that inequality prohibits relationship. The novel demonstrates her error by demonstrating that the differences among members of the group are not accidental to what they have in common but essential. The kind of privilege Emma tries to exercise leads her to treat differences as insignificant, whereas the true exercise of privilege, as Knightley shows when he dances with Harriet Smith, comes with a participation based upon acknowledgment and acceptance of those differences.

Jane Austen's intensity about social norms in *Emma* turns the linear properties of her narrative to special uses. Serial development is put to use not for developing character but for developing attributes, for discrimination concerning such attributes as "elegant," "amiable," "odd," "equal," "reasonable." These words are repeated in the mouths of almost everybody, but always with a different slant of intention, a different degree of irony or earnestness. In the process *they* accumulate depth.[12] It is almost as if the language and the characters have changed places, with individual words becoming the object of representation and characters part of the medium. Character becomes an occasion for the development of certain qualities, rather than the qualities being occasions for the development of character. "Indeed," says Howard Babb, "in Jane Austen's style such concepts are the real actors."[13] These "intensive" words run through the novel, accumulating resonance far beyond their meaning in any one syntactical arrangement.

The part of the novel most directly associated with temporal development and projected futures is the secret intrigue between Frank Churchill and Jane Fairfax, and their "wild speculation on

[12] See Stuart Tave's discussion of "delicacy" in *Mansfield Park*, what he calls an "intensive word" (*Some Words of Jane Austen* [Chicago: University of Chicago Press, 1973], p. 220).

[13] Howard Babb, *Jane Austen's Novels: The Fabric of Dialogue* (Columbus, Ohio: Ohio State University Press, 1967), p. 9.

the future" (III, xvii, 368). Both come to Highbury from else-where, and both resist assimilation into the group. By contrast with the "fixed" relationships of Highbury, Frank and Jane's relationship is associated with mobility and distance: with hasty trips to London and back; with unstable expectations as to their eventual financial circumstances and social place; with uncertain family relationships. The main awareness of linear time in the novel comes from the delays involving Frank and Jane. Frank is going to come to Highbury, but then he does not; Jane is going to go, but then she stays. Time hangs heavy when attention is thus focused on unfulfilled expectations and future events like these arrivals and departures. The ball that does not take place is one small instance of the instability introduced by Frank and Jane into the social setting. Frank's fondness for anagrams and other "deep" cryptic messages testifies to his perverse delight in shuffling the alphabet of existence.

Such things the novel decidedly rejects. Mr. Knightley, as usual, sums it up: "Mystery; Finesse—how they pervert the understanding! My Emma, does not everything serve to prove more and more the beauty of truth and sincerity in all our dealings with each other?" (III, xv, 350). Despite her faults, one sign of Emma's superiority is the accessibility of her mind, the fact that her character survives the open scrutiny it bears through most of the book. By comparison with Jane, whose interest derives mainly from her inaccessibility and insubstantiality, Emma's character, though self-deceived, is decided and open.

Time does not produce the really significant changes in the novel; far from being consequences of temporal delay and development, these changes are "the work of the moment" (III, xiii, 339), like Mr. Knightley's proposal. Emma's discovery of Elton's attachment to herself, the news of Elton's marriage, the discovery of the secret engagement all come to light by a shift of circumstances that seems arbitrary and sudden. A shift in the balance between Emma and Knightley, for example, revolution-izes the situation.

152

Within half an hour, he had passed from a thoroughly distressed state of mind, to something so like perfect happiness, that it could bear no other name.

Her change was equal.—This one half hour had given to each the same precious certainty of being beloved, had cleared from each the same degree of ignorance, jealousy, or distrust.

(P. 339.)

These developments confirm preferences that had nevertheless been present in their essentials from the start. "How long had Mr. Knightley been so dear to her, as every feeling now declared him to be?" (III, xi, 323). Emma cannot remember. There is in *Emma* a strong hint that time could begin to make a difference if Emma were to persist in her error. The threats in her behavior are real. But reason prevails, and Mrs. Elton remains impervious, Frank Churchill careless, and Emma basically charming.

Along with linear time *Emma* devalues mobility. There is no sense that the solution to thorny problems lies in increase of speed, number of acquaintances, or amount of white satin. The moral universe exists everywhere the same, and does not require the delays and departures, the gaps and absences of realistic plots to uncover it. Quality is quality, in Hartfield or in London (it does not much matter which). Mr. Woodhouse's fear of change is comic, but the bad opinion of radical change is not confined to him. The narrator seems to equate "real" with "long standing," and to find in the longevity of Mr. Knightley's establishment an important clue to its superiority. Furthermore, Frank Churchill's restlessness, his being continually "on the move" (III, ii, 249) trying to get himself into an advantageous position, is universally disapproved of. The potential for change in Jane Fairfax's situation threatens loss and diminishment as much as anything hopeful. The treatment of her marriage emphasizes the risk and the almost prohibitive difficulty it entails. Life is mobile, more mobile than Mr. Woodhouse will allow or than Emma's drawing can capture (her best portraits being of a sleeping child and a sofa), but the measured motion validated in the novel is a far cry from

153

the mobility required of characters in *Our Mutual Friend* or *Middlemarch*, or even *Persuasion*.

Linear history, the one associated with Frank and Jane's secret engagement, comes to an end in *Emma*, or at least to a pause significant enough to imply a break in continuity. The kind of time associated with delay and disorder does end, and gives way to another kind of time and to another valuation of sequence that is cyclic, not linear, closed, not open-ended, and belongs to a stable, hierarchical universe of values cutting across temporal continuities. In this *Emma* seems more typical of Austen's quiet calm than *Persuasion*. The distance from historical turmoil that has interested her critics suggests a position somehow not time-bound or time-dependent; her carefully patterned, often cyclical, temporal sequences seem to close upon themselves rather than to open on infinity. Because the unbridgeable gaps between minds like Emma's and Mrs. Elton's do not narrow with time, the narrator needs no long, open-ended temporal sequences to brood over. The time of health and reason is not linear, but cyclic, its forms not chronological but ritual.

Equilibrium restored, the action of *Emma* moves into a seasonal time, the time evident at Donwell. The slow, rhythmic temporal processes that produce the venerability evident at Donwell belong to the rhythms of nature—an orderly cosmos—and are best left to themselves. The whole estate is the product of aging and not of laborious effort. "Time, you may be very sure, will make one or the other of us think differently, and in the meanwhile, we need not talk much on the subject" says Knightley to Emma on the subject of Harriet's marriage (I, vii, 37). That "meanwhile" has no ominous quality. It is as good as done. "Time passed on," begins the penultimate chapter, with a confidence that no surprises are in store. The time that confirms, the time that simply passes on without bringing news, is not the linear time of disorder and delay: it is the cyclic time that moves, as it does in the novel, from marriage to marriage, that observes the natural cycle from marriage to childbirth, and that records Emma's passage to adulthood.

154

This is the periodic time of *Robinson Crusoe* and *Pamela*, the time appropriate to the conception of a cosmos where influences do not depend on time. It is a rhythmic time, the time of a dance. While these observations are not news to Austen scholars, their application in terms of realism does cast some new light on the narrative rhythms of *Emma*, rhythms that appear not only in the periodic structure of the novel but also in the narrator's remarkable minuet with the heroine.

Social harmony as it is conceived in *Emma* is a kind of counterpoint, the object of which is to maintain the equilibrium of the whole. At various levels the style of the novel confirms a state of equipoise. The plot is a series of disturbances to equilibrium that require corrective measures: Miss Taylor's marriage, Elton's defection from Harriet, Frank and Jane's deepening trouble, Emma's insult to Miss Bates, Harriet's romantic interest in Mr. Knightley.[14] The novel ends on a note of carefully balanced relationships: "The latest couple engaged of the three, were the first to be married," the first engaged were the last married, and Emma and Mr. Knightley take their place between, surrounded by two counterbalancing resolutions.

The rhythmic collection and dispersal so characteristic of this novel as a whole is obvious in the passage that precedes the spelling-party at Hartfield.

> He [Knightley] had walked up one day after dinner, as he very often did, to spend his evening at Hartfield. Emma and Harriet were going to walk; he joined them; and, on returning, they fell in with a larger party, who, like themselves, judged it wisest to take their exercise early, as the weather threatened rain; Mr. and Mrs. Weston and their son, Miss Bates and her niece, who had accidentally met. They all united; and, on reaching Hartfield gates, Emma, who knew it was exactly the sort of visiting that would be welcome to her father, pressed them all

[14] See E. F. Shannon's interesting summary of the rhythmic structure of *Emma*, in "*Emma*: Character and Construction," *PMLA*, 71, no. 4 (September 1956), 637-50. Cited in David Lodge, ed., *Emma, A Casebook* (London: Macmillan, 1969), pp. 130-47.

to go in and drink tea with him. The Randalls' party agreed to it immediately; and after a pretty long speech from Miss Bates, which few persons listened to, she also found it possible to accept dear Miss Woodhouse's most obliging invitation.

(III, v, 269)

On this as on other occasions we are conscious of an activity of joining and parting not unlike the development of line in a dance. These modulations of rhythm recur with increasing frequency as the novel progresses and as the lines of play, initially separated, join more together in mutual influence.[15]

The moral importance of such rhythms takes us close to the heart of this novel. Austen engages us in an almost constant attention to numbers in the sense of proportion or harmony. Emma's seating arrangement for her dinner party is an especially interesting example because of its echo of the scene in *Pamela* where the seating arrangement has equal importance, but for different reasons. In *Emma* who shall make the eighth is a problem first resolved, then undone with the unexpected appearance of Mr. John Knightley ("here would be a ninth"), and finally resolved again to the favorable number by Mr. Weston's unexpected defection. "Jane Austen's model of a comfortable society," Francis Hart comments, "appears always to be measurable in terms of the right number of people for the right size of room."[16] Just proportion is also a matter engaging considerable attention in planning the ball at the Crown, and the discussion reflects in its own shifts in balance and direction the very matter under discussion. One consideration tips the balance in one direction and then another shifts it back, the conversation moving back and forth, the passage itself imitating the rhythms of a dance (III, xi, 191-92).

[15] The pattern of meeting and withdrawal characterizes all the social interactions of the novel as well as the management of the narrative viewpoint. Walton Litz writes that "the characteristic rhythm of *Emma* is one of approach and withdrawal, an external confrontation of wills followed by personal reassessment" (*Jane Austen: A Study of Her Artistic Development* [New York: Oxford University Press, 1965], p. 147).

[16] Hart, "Spaces," p. 316.

Dancing creates its own kind of time, disturbing the neutrality and chronological succession and pulling its flow into uneven and arbitrary patterns. This effect characterizes the narrative style of *Emma*. There is a kinetic sense of rhythm in the treatment of individual chapters, each with a decided pause at the end giving the impression of forward motion contained.

Emma could not forgive her. (II, ii, 129)

It must be done, or what would become of Harriet?
(II, iv, 142)

Brother and sister! no, indeed. (III, ii, 258)

Oh! if you knew how much I love everything that is decided and open! Goodbye, goodbye. (III, xvi, 362)

Some chapters end by calling attention to unexplained circumstances like Frank's control of his visits (I, xiv, 95), or Harriet kissing Emma's hand (III, v, 268), or Emma's extraordinary tears (III, vii, 295). Each chapter (with a single exception) develops a single episode and ends with an extra terseness that punctuates the gathering momentum and redirects it.

This rhythmic pulse destabilizes the narrative perspective. The apparently reliable narrator has an unsettling habit of abandoning us to uncertainty by unexpected shifts in perspective, so that we are alternately abandoned to Emma's folly and then caught short by a narrative comment that clarifies the error. Such shifts occur all the time in this novel and to characterize them as "irony" is to some extent to beg important questions about their function. An example is the passage treating Emma's reflections about Harriet's visit with the Martins, a visit Emma has engineered.

Fourteen minutes to be given to those with whom she had thankfully passed six weeks not six months ago! Emma could not but picture it all, and feel how justly they might resent, how naturally Harriet must suffer. It was a bad business. She would have given a great deal or endured a great deal, to have had the Martins in a higher rank of life. (II, v, 143)

157

Everything up to the last phrase is commendable. It *was* a bad business and Emma rightly feels the obligation to relinquish something. But the inadequacy lies with Emma's imagination and not, as she implies, with the Martins' rank. She would do better to sustain the self-doubt that flickers and then goes out. Up until that final phrase ("to have had the Martins in a higher rank of life") no markers in the narrative distinguish Emma's mind from the narrator's, although the implied difference is, as always, shadowing the proceedings. With the final phrase there is a shift in balance, and a doubleness intrudes into the narrative perspective. Emma's thoughts seem to be sailing in the right direction, but somehow they arrive at the wrong destination or at least not the one we expected. Only this implicit correction of her error distinguishes the presence of the narrator.

This point is sufficiently important to justify another example. Reflecting on Harriet's accidental meeting with the Martins in town, Emma thinks, "The young man's conduct, and his sisters', seemed the result of real feeling, and she could not but pity them" (II, iii, 137). All is well up to the word "pity," an inappropriate word, at least inappropriate when applied to the Martins. We sense strongly the wrongness of the word and of the attitude it reflects, feeling that it might better be replaced by some other, for example *respect*. We sense that the substitution of one word would alter the balance, a fact which dramatizes the power of speech. In supplying the corrective, we align ourselves with the implicit narrator and thereby make a distinction that Emma herself blurs.[17]

This uneasiness and shifting in the narrative perspective accounts for a very significant part of *Emma*'s liveliness. The simple progression of the sentence suddenly exfoliates, a flicker of doubleness glides by. These rhythmic divergences between the implied narrator and Emma thread through the novel, creating an

---

[17] See Marilyn Butler on narrative style and the moral importance of language. The real sign of danger in *Emma* is the increasing discrepancy between words and truth. Although nothing "happens," there is an illusion of "vigorous movement" because its "conflicts are translated more fully than any of the other novels into the medium of language" (*War of Ideas*, p. 260).

increasing tension. One track becomes two, and then one again, as in a dance. Emma's mind can only appear as distinct when it diverges from clarity. As her errors increase, so does the tension between her view and the appropriate one, until it explodes for the heroine at Box Hill. While occasionally commenting on the interesting situations of young persons or on the irresistibility of dancing, the narrator does not consistently focus the narrative, and Jane Austen purposefully makes difficult the task of maintaining the correct awareness by the lack of markers telling whose consciousness is whose.

When Frank, for example, returns to Miss Bates's reluctantly but "with the hope of Hartfield to reward him" (II, ix, 181), the statement has some of the multivocality of eighteenth-century narrative language. We know this statement reflects Emma's thought, we know she is wrong, we know she has no inkling she is wrong, we know that Frank prefers the company at Miss Bates's, and we know that Frank is in a false position. Often things are less clear. "Emma was not required, by any subsequent discovery, to retract her ill opinion of Mrs. Elton. Her observation had been pretty correct" (II, xv, 217). This statement proves reliable, or at least it is not subsequently challenged; but it must be taken warily. There is always the possibility that this is only Emma's view and another of her mistakes. Clear markers are infrequent. We are always aware in reading this novel of the alternative point of view shadowing Emma's own, and with it the possibility of a radical shift at any moment, even in mid-sentence.[18] The narrative perspective thus has a mobility, a potential instability, that is felt almost as a kinetic experience. Even slight divergences give a sense of an enormous shift in distance. When Emma turns out to be wrong, she is wholly wrong: there is no justification for her error, she is not partially correct, her viewpoint cannot be joined

[18] "The written novel contains its unwritten twin whose shape is known only by the shadow it casts" (W. J. Harvey, "The Plot of Emma," Essays in Criticism, 17, no. 1 [January 1967], p. 55). While this point differs from the one I am making here, his metaphor aptly suggests the importance in reading of our sense of a presence never directly apprehensible.

in consensus with the narrator's (or anyone else's) as a different but complementary view of the same world.

Another way of saying this is that in *Emma* Jane Austen does not exploit the temporal function of her narrative perspective. Even though the existence of a past-tense narrator does consistently imply a distance from Emma's mistakes, time does not significantly function either in creating those mistakes or in correcting them. The differentiation between the narrator's mind and Emma's is not the quantitative distance between past and present but rather a qualitative distance between mind and mind; one that is not necessarily mediated by passing time. We know the precise nature of Emma's mistakes as she makes them, and the readiness and finality with which the correct view is available undermines any continuity between events in time, between the virtual present of Emma's experience and some more mature point of view attainable in the future. The gap between minds is always there and is fundamental to appreciating the novel even when we are not explicitly conscious of it. So even though the past-tense narrative signals that the correct view is a future view, it is a future that is fully available at every moment. What is needed to unfold it is not time, or at least not much time, but rather a shift in mental equilibrium that can be the "work of the moment." Distance, far from being a given condition of consciousness, is only a momentary necessity, something to be taken when correction is needed.

This kind of narrator—one that does not maintain a consistent distance—is appropriate in a novel that treats detachment harshly. Among the characters only Mr. Knightley becomes a spectator with the same corrective intention as the narrator, and he does so only once, during the spelling game. Sitting outside the circle, he attempts to decipher the coded messages being passed by Frank Churchill to different members of the group; "it was his object to see as much as he could, with as little apparent observation" (III, v, 272). His unobtrusiveness, like that of the ideal Jamesian narrator, is essential to clear sight; but it is a necessity of the moment, a response to subterfuge. There is no need for such detachment at Donwell Abbey because there are no subterfuges to uncover; the physical estate, arranged with "all the old neglect of prospect," has no secrets to disclose; "it was just what it ought to be, and it looked what it was" (III, vi, 280).

Emma, however, is keen on detachment, and the results do not recommend the enterprise. Because she refuses to see herself in the picture, Emma misguides Harriet, neglects Jane, and betrays Miss Bates.[19] In her desire to escape the fixity she detests Emma imagines herself detached, until she realizes that she has something personal at stake. When Harriet discloses her interest in Mr. Knightley, Emma experiences the perturbing "developement of self" (III, xi, 321) that reminds her of her place. The fact that she associates this "developement" with "confusion" and "threatening evil" underscores the implication that she has been a spectator out of fear. Yet the distance she has traveled from Robinson Crusoe and Pamela, who also shudder at self, is evident in the connection between this "developement" and Emma's growth.

As with Emma's misguided attempts at detachment, Jane and Frank's similar attempts directly threaten the equilibrium of the social group itself. There are many reasons for the disaster at the Box Hill picnic, including the fact that it is superfluous. But the languor and "want of union" is traceable chiefly to the (secret) rupture between Frank and Jane. Jane Austen insists on the metaphors of division—"want of union," "separated too much into parties," "tried in vain to harmonize," "principle of separation"— so that Emma's lack of control on this occasion takes place against a background of confusion generated by the hidden plot. Frank "said nothing worth hearing—looked without seeing—admired

---

[19] Mark Kinkead-Weekes discusses the analogy between this behavior and that of narrators ("This Old Maid: Jane Austen replies to Charlotte Bronte and D. H. Lawrence," *Nineteenth-Century Fiction*, 30, no. 3 [December 1975], 412-13). Darrel Mansell discusses Emma's interest in being "above 'sober facts' " (*The Novels of Jane Austen, An Interpretation* [London: Macmillan, 1973], p. 147); Howard Babb speaks of "Emma's compulsion to assert herself, indeed to prove herself unique" (*Jane Austen's Novels*, p. 177); Marvin Mudrick sees that "though Emma can imagine everything else, she cannot imagine her own commitment" and that "Emma is moved to play God" (*Jane Austen: Irony as Defense and Discovery* [Berkeley: University of California Press, 1968], pp. 188, 194).

without intelligence—listened without knowing what she said" (III, vii, 298-99). Being out of control, he inspires an uneasiness that mounts to suppressed hysteria, as he puts words into Emma's mouth and assumes her voice; when the coherence of the group degenerates so do Emma's manners. When Frank gets her to support questions about other people's private thoughts, Mrs. Elton is quite right to object. " 'It is a sort of thing,' cried Mrs. Elton, 'which I should not have thought myself privileged to inquire into' " (p. 289). The privilege exercised by minds de-tached from their circumstances has only destructive effects. Even Mrs. Elton can see that.

"Very seldom does complete truth belong to any human dis-closure" says the narrator of *Emma* (III, xiii, 339). This truth can cut two ways. In *Emma* the conclusion may be that one should not wait upon disclosure. In *Persuasion*, with its fuller realism, everything depends upon waiting. In her last finished novel, Austen shifts away from the paced harmonies of *Emma* and takes up the problem of detachment in a new way and with quite different results. She takes fuller advantage of the past-tense narrator, a difference not as slight as it may first appear. In *Emma* the recollective narrator appears fitfully, in *Persuasion* more con-sistently as the narrative of correction gives way to the narrative of corroboration and consent.

Narrative Perspective in *Persuasion*

Persuasion replaces the daily cycles of *Emma* with the sweep of years. Continuity has utmost importance in this last novel, and gaps in time and space take on a new value. There is a new importance to silence, to the empty expanse of beach and sea, to the empty years between Wentworth's departure and his return. These new values correspond to a more pessimistic view of social order. In *Emma* social hierarchy works and is the basis for clarity: but in *Persuasion* the group is considerably less coherent, and from that fact follow significant alterations. Where Emma chooses her detachment, Anne Elliot's is forced on her by the conditions of her existence. The negative, undesirable side of this detachment is evident in its association with powerlessness and ill health, but at the same time Anne's disengagement is an inescapable consequence of the social state of affairs. Her way back to health takes her permanently away from the stable hierarchies available to earlier Austen heroines and requires her literally to go to sea: to cast herself adrift on that familiar symbol of flux and mobility without benefit of social hierarchy or a providential setting. These changes, in turn, have significant influence on the nature of the heroine's experience and on her relation to the narrator.[20]

Separation, confusion, incompletion, irresolution characterize the social portraits in *Persuasion*. There is much idle chat and comparatively little of the brilliant conversation familiar from *Pride and Prejudice* or even *Emma*. The planning of excursions involves extensive difficulties with even the smallest details, such as who is going to ride in the carriage and who must walk, who is going to remain at Lyme and who will stay, who is or is not going to the play, who will sit beside whom at the concert. In Anne's experience during the novel moving is a way of life, but rather than moving like Elizabeth Bennet does, deliberately within a single world, Anne moves between worlds.[21] As she moves from Kellynch to Uppercross to Bath, Anne learns each time "another

---

[20] That *Persuasion* defines "a new outlook in Jane Austen's work" seems generally acknowledged. Alistair Duckworth summarizes the critics who notice the change in *Persuasion*, and notes that by comparison with the late work where "an attitude of detachment seems necessary . . . in earlier novels, the role of *spectator ab extra* had been criticized" (*Improvement of the Estate*, pp. 181, 221-22). Despite disagreement about the extent of the change, there is wide agreement that *Persuasion* conveys a new pessimism about the possibility of social order. Litz, *Development*, pp. 153-54; Kenneth Moler, *Jane Austen's Art of Allusion* [Lincoln, Nebraska: University of Nebraska Press, 1968), pp. 191, 203, 223; and Walton Litz, "*Persuasion*: Forms of Estrangement," in John Halperin, ed., *Jane Austen: Bicentennary Essays* (Cambridge: Cambridge University Press, 1975), p. 228.

[21] For good discussions of the new sense of disorder in *Persuasion*, see Hart, "Spaces," 331; Lascelles, *Jane Austen*, p. 185; Paul Zeitlow, "Luck and Fortuitous Circumstance in *Persuasion*," *ELH*, 37 (June 1965), esp. 189-95; and Mark Kinkead-Weekes, "This Old Maid," pp. 415-16: "The worlds of the Park and of Highbury are stable. They contain potential disorder, but once it has been diagnosed and dealt with, the good future for the community can be promised in the present. But *Persuasion* is Jane Austen's Mutabilitie Canto. Its world is one of flux, change, decay, and possibly, but by no means certainly, of renewal."

lesson, in the art of knowing our own nothingness beyond our own circle." Even *within* her own circle Anne is always "transplanted" and without a place of her own. She acknowledges it to be "very fitting that every little social commonwealth should dictate its own matters of discourse." But Anne, being "nobody with either father or sister," belongs to no discourse. "Her word had no weight; her convenience was always to give way;—she was only Anne."[22]

Because of the discords and discontinuities in her social world, Anne is often "caught" in the vectors of other people's shifting inclinations. One sample of this experience is the early passage describing the walking excursion to Winthrop. The entire event resembles an accident. Anne has settled indoors with Mary and the gentlemen have gone hunting when the Musgroves appear, wanting Anne but not Mary for company, ostensibly because

> . . . they were going to take a *long* walk, and, therefore, concluded Mary could not like to go with them; and when Mary immediately replied, with some jealousy, at not being supposed a good walker, "Oh, yes, I should like to join you very much, I am fond of a long walk," Anne felt persuaded, by the looks of the two girls, that it was precisely what they did not wish. . . . She tried to dissuade Mary from going, but in vain; and that being the case, thought it best to accept the Miss Musgroves' much more cordial invitation to herself to go likewise, as she might be useful in turning back with her sister, and lessening the interference in any plan of their own. . . .
>
> Just as they were setting off, the gentlemen returned. They had taken out a young dog, who had spoilt their sport, and sent them back early. Their time and strength, and spirits, were, therefore, exactly ready for this walk, and they entered into it with pleasure. Could Anne have foreseen such a junction, she would have staid at home; but, from some feelings of interest and curiosity, she fancied now that it was too late

[22] *Persuasion*, Riverside edition (Boston: Houghton Mifflin, 1965), p. 33 (I, vi); p. 5 (I, i). All subsequent references will be to this edition and will be included parenthetically in the text.

to retract, and the whole six set forward together in the direction chosen by the Miss Musgroves, who evidently considered the walk as under their guidance.

Anne's object was, not to be in the way of any body, and where the narrow paths across the fields made many separations necessary, to keep with her brother and sister.   (I, x, 65)

In its manner of joining together this group could scarcely differ more from the group that joins Emma during a walk through Highbury (the one resulting in the spelling game). Here the exact nature and size of the group shifts back and forth, as does its apparent destination: an irresolution compounded by Mary's inattention and the accident with the young dog. The plan changes maddeningly and, in trying to act deliberately, Anne finds herself (as she says on another occasion) "caught" (II, vi, 136).

Austen stresses the ontological consequences for her heroine of such confusion. Anne's instinct, when facing such contradictory circumstances, is to step aside: a gesture of high emblematic value for my purposes because it makes Anne into a spectator. Forced to it by circumstances, she sets herself aside and becomes a mediator, considering mainly how she "might be useful" or at least how she might avoid being "in the way of any body." Her circumstances thus impose upon her the necessity of preserving the continuity of her own consciousness by being "nobody." When Wentworth first is mentioned, she responds by dissociating herself from her own emotions in order to answer "as she ought." Initially "electrified" by the thought that *her* Wentworth was the man in question, Anne then discovers he is not; then, correcting her equilibrium again, she must hear with apparent indifference of *her* Wentworth. She then retreats from notice quietly, gratefully, and, this time at least, successfully. The bloom of her life over, Anne seems to stand outside her own experience as a spectator and to participate, to the extent she does, only as a mediator in the small affairs of others.

In this role as perpetual spectator Anne very much resembles a narrator: close to a variety of individual minds, yet always detached; capable of powerful insight, but burdened with a kind

165

of "deadness" all the same.[23] She is "too much in the secret complaints of each house" and treated with "too much confidence of all parties" (I, vi, 35): "How was Anne to set all these matters to rights? She could do little more than listen patiently, soften every grievance, and excuse each to the other; give them all hints of the forbearance necessary between such near neighbors . . ." (p. 36). As such a mediator Anne occupies the position between inharmonious parties that Defoe pronounced lethal. As Stuart Tave characterizes it, "Anne's position in the novel, again and again, is to stand between opposed forces, neither understanding her and both putting pressure on her, without losing her ability to judge."[24] In the midst of this confusion Anne maintains her private self-consciousness in solitude, quietly sustaining herself on the powerful "secret of the past" (I, iv, 24).

Reading *Persuasion* is almost like following a dialogue of Anne's mind with itself, so allied with her mental reflexes does the narrative remain. It is not so much that the narrator shadows Anne's mind as that hers approximates the narrator's, both remaining at a distance from events and sustaining a private conversation of consciousness by recourse to memory. Anne's mind does not need correction, as Emma's does; Anne can correct herself and frequently must. The unresolved tension between parties that costs Emma so much at Box Hill is a tension sustained for Anne Elliot through most of her life. "Anne longed for the power of representing to them all what they were about, and of pointing out some of the evils they were exposing themselves to" (I, x, 64). But this clarity also entails powerlessness. She longs to tell them but cannot; she can be electrified but cannot electrify in return. In becoming "inured" she has become detached from personal exercise. It is not until the end of the novel that she departs from this detachment, relinquishes her role as "nobody," and disap-

[23] Bernard Paris speaks of "the inner deadness which has been the price of her tranquility" (*Character and Conflict*, p. 165).

[24] Tave, *Words*, p. 274. Howard Babb puts this in terms more suggestive of negative capability: "Anne's special quality . . . is precisely this ability to live with, to assimilate, the contrarieties of experience without seeking impatiently to dissolve the tensions engendered by them" *Jane Austen's Novels*, p. 237). Both suggest the strenuous nature of Anne's role as connecting medium.

pears into the crowd. The function of "nobody" is too strenuous for a single person to sustain.

While Anne leads her invisible life what is most evident about it is its terrible strain, a strain that accounts in good measure for her loss of bloom. Austen insists in various ways upon the heroic nature of Anne's solitary efforts. Anne learns to "dissociate" consciousness from position, emotion from place, and she learns to preserve a balance between the private and public lives that are thus differentiated.[25] Her exertion is as heroic as any naval officer's, without the magnitude of physical expression. In the process, however, Anne pays a heavy price. Too much can be made of the "balanced integrity of her feelings and exertions," and too little of the pain, even anguish, and loss of health entailed by that heroic behavior. The fact that "she has no physical vigor to spare" should alert readers to the debilitating nature of her exertions.[26] Anne does a great deal of silent physical and psychic work of a kind that brings her no rewards in mutual consciousness and mutual recognition. Her frail health suggests to what extent her long-sustained, long-unrecognized effort is merely strenuous and crushing. When she hears that Wentworth has found her altered, her reflection that it "must make her happier" has a grim fortitude in it that suggests a state of bare necessity. Until Wentworth returns her feelings and confirms her consciousness, she sustains them completely alone. For much of the novel even he is too "bewitched" by the attentions of others to "see or hear" Anne; it is only when he starts "striving to catch sounds" from Anne's direction (II, x) that there is some hope.[27]

[25] Valerie Shaw, "Jane Austen's Subdued Heroines," *Nineteenth-Century Fiction*, 30, no. 3 (December 1975), p. 300. "Dissociate" is her word, not Austen's. Francis Hart discusses the developing need for privacy ("Spaces," pp. 319 and 312) but does not consider the anguish associated with it.

[26] Tave, *Words*, p. 284; see also p. 287. It is true that "her submission is coordinate with her strength" (p. 271), but it is also coordinate with her failing health. While I disagree frequently with the extrapolations Bernard Paris draws from his central hypothesis, I think he rightly cautions against glorifying "the defenses which the heroines develop in response to being abused" (*Character and Conflict*, p. 167).

[27] Tave, *Words*, p. 263. "He has the closed, foolish mind that only a clever man can have" (p. 258).

The difficulty of sustaining her consciousness without support and of bridging even the bridgeable gaps makes Anne's story an epic of consciousness. It is a heroic action of the inner life, what Anne calls "loving longest, when existence or when hope is gone" (II, xi, 186). Anne demonstrates her power of loving in her power to remember, to see that despite the wear of time Wentworth is "the same." Whether or not Jane Austen has Homer in mind, the epic undertones in *Persuasion* reinforce the idea of conscious life as heroic life. The novel pattern limns an epic pattern of return and recognition (in fact delayed return and delayed recognition), and uses recognition as a test of integrity and an ontological confirmation. Anne is not only Wentworth's Penelope, waiting at home, she is also "nobody" in her own private Odyssey of psychic survival. It is a drama of exertion so extreme that the toll has become visible. Wentworth's ability to meet her mind finally rescues her from the need any longer to sustain her consciousness alone. *Persuasion* gradually provides Anne with recognition, agreement, *mutual* consent, and the more Anne is recognized in the same terms she understands herself the more she becomes liberated from her detachment and the more she leaves that function for the narrator alone.

The sea, rather than the drawing room, is the background metaphor of *Persuasion*, and the mobility associated with the navy and the life of "quick alarm" is the one link with health, vigor, and success. Mrs. Croft, a woman who would rather be overturned traveling with her husband than safe on a sofa with Mrs. Musgrove, makes the explicit connection between health and mobility.

"I have always been blessed with excellent health, and no climate disagrees with me. . . . The only time that I ever really suffered in body or mind, the only time that I ever fancied myself unwell, or had any ideas of danger, was the winter that I passed by myself at Deal, when the Admiral (*Captain* Croft then) was in the North Seas. I lived in perpetual fright at that time, and had all manner of imaginary complaints from not knowing what to do with myself or when I should hear from him next; but as long as we could be together, nothing ever ailed me, and I never met with the smallest inconvenience."

(I, viii, 55-56)

The comparison is clear between Mrs. Croft's robust health and Anne Elliot's pale decline. Anne's "transplanted" existence demonstrates that, for her, there is no alternative to mobility. Mrs. Croft's example confirms the portable nature of what is valuable. By itself memory cannot support a full existence either for Mrs. Croft or for Anne. On departing from Uppercross she thinks characteristically that she "left it all behind her" once again— "all but the recollection that such things had been" (II, i, 97). Both women (by implication anyone sensible) get sick stuck on shore and living by memory alone.

The more Anne is drawn into participation—that is, the more she becomes an object of attention—the more she endures those dizzying losses of perspective that increasingly punctuate her history, beginning with the time she first sees Wentworth again. Here a buzz of confusion ("the room seemed full—full of persons and voices") disturbs her detachment and literally her perceptions of spatial proportion and relationships (I, vii, 47). The next such moment comes with the discovery that Captain Wentworth has shown her the distinct attention of interfering between her and an annoyance: "Her sensations of the discovery made her perfectly speechless. She could not even thank him. She could only hang over little Charles, with most disordered feelings. . . . and it required a long application of solitude and reflection to recover her" (I, ix, 64). At the end of the first volume Wentworth hands her into the carriage with this effect:

Yes,—he had done it. She was in the carriage, and felt that he had placed her there, that his will and his hands had done it. . . . Her answers to the kindness and the remarks of her companions were at first unconsciously given. They had travelled half their way along the rough lane, before she was quite awake to what they said. (Pp. 71-72.)

169

Here the momentary loss of perspective intensifies to the border of solipsism, producing a dissociation from her companions and surroundings in which her emotions block her other senses. She is described as conscious only of herself, and her companions have to settle for whatever is "unconsciously" given.

These episodes contribute to a dissociation under way in Anne's mind. As the tension increases, Austen becomes explicit about this division in the scene where "inclination" wins out over the "wiser" Anne Elliot.

> For a few minutes she saw nothing before her. It was all con-
> fusion. She was lost; and when she had scolded back her sense,
> she found the others still waiting for the carriage. . . . She
> now felt a great inclination to go to the outer door. . . . Cap-
> tain Wentworth must be out of sight. She left her seat, she
> would go, one half of her should not be always so much wiser
> than the other half, or always suspecting the other of being
> worse than it was.   (II, vii, 138-39)

Anne departs from her own "inured" mind into more immediate engagement and exercise. In the process she endangers the clarity that her former distance gave her. The extremity of Anne's re-sponse in these episodes needs accounting for. Beyond surprise, there is the unaccustomed fact that Anne has been the explicit object of attention, attention she values, and attention that fully, as Henry James might say, takes her in. Meeting Wentworth's eye triggers a profound response, the profound circumstance of finding herself in mutual agreement where she most cares to agree. Her departure from her accustomed "wiser" distance reanimates Anne's feelings. Having for so long dimmed the impression from her own feelings, in order to adjust to her fate as "nobody," Anne finds her feelings make strong claims, momentarily dimming those impressions from outside herself that used mainly to occupy her. This is more than an altercation between reason and feeling. It amounts to the transformation of a spectator into a participant. It is a heady and even potentially dangerous experience.

Being drawn into activity increases her liveliness and bloom.

170

Even her father notices her being " 'less thin in her person, in her cheeks; her skin, her complexion, greatly improved—clearer, fresher. Had she been using anything in particular?' " (II, iv, 114). Anne the spectator needed exercise, and the more active she becomes, the more she gets it. On the beach at Lyme, "having the bloom and freshness of youth restored by the fine wind," she catches the eye and the "earnest admiration" of a passing gentleman (I, xii, 82). Anne not only looks, people look back, and with direct regard. Accustomed to her role as spectator, she finds herself increasingly the object of attention and even (as at the concert) of competitive attention. When the personal stakes are higher, however, as they are in the case of Wentworth, Anne experiences not just a pleasant increase of circulation but a vertiginous loss of perspective that Austen explicitly associates with a loss of consciousness and clarity.

When Anne and Wentworth depart into private life, taking their places in the crowd, the entire mediating labor of consciousness is left to the narrator. Up until the end the narrative remains close to Anne's mind—seems almost a reflex of it, with the exception of the early passage that briefly threads into Wentworth's mind. At the end Anne seems almost to give up on detachment altogether. She departs from her "wiser" half, leaving her vantage-point for the narrator to fill. In *Persuasion* uncertainty about the social bases for individual life generates the necessity for distance, and hence for private understandings and for preference of mutual consciousness over social behavior. It generates, in short, the opportunity of the nineteenth-century narrator, one that arises from the apparently unredeemable disorder of society.[28]

In one remarkable passage especially Anne separates from the detached lucidity that has shadowed her through the novel and that has been so closely associated, even in her unstable moments, with her own mind. She and the narrator conspicuously part company in this passage.

[28] Walton Litz reasonably concludes that Anne's "despair is that of the modern 'personality,' forced to live within itself" and that [therefore] "the familiar world of the nineteenth century novel is at hand" (*Jane Austen*, pp. 154-55).

In half a minute, Charles was at the bottom of Union-street again, and the other two proceeding together; and soon words enough had passed between them to decide their direction towards the comparatively quiet and retired gravel-walk, where the power of conversation would make the present hour a blessing indeed; and prepare it for all the immortality which the happiest recollections of their own future lives could bestow. There they exchanged again those feelings and those promises which had once before seemed to secure every thing, but which had been followed by so many, many years of division and estrangement. There they returned again into the past, more exquisitely happy, perhaps, in their re-union, than when it had been first projected; more tender, more tried, more fixed in a knowledge of each other's character, truth, and attachment; more equal to act, more justified in acting. And there, as they slowly paced the gradual ascent, heedless of every group around them, seeing neither sauntering politicians, bustling housekeepers, flirting girls, nor nursery-maids and children, they could indulge in those retrospections and acknowledgements, and especially in those explanations of what had directly preceded the present moment, which were so poignant and so ceaseless in interest. All the little variations of the last week were gone through; and of yesterday and to-day there could scarcely be an end. (II, xi, 191)

In comparison with Jane Austen's other reunions—Emma and Knightley in the garden at Hartfield, or Elizabeth and Darcy in the garden at Longbourne—this moment differs in its treatment of time. This immortalizing conversation takes place in an odd time-warp. Just when immediate feeling presses with most intense interest, the narrative skips out of the present into the future, from which projected vantage-point the narrator reflects back on "the present hour." The whole novel has built toward this point of contact, the moment of "conversation" between the two main figures, but when this moment is reached it is presented as a hypothetical recollection: the narrator's, not Anne's. The narrator explicitly calls attention to the temporal vantage-point from which the whole past-tense narrative has been told: a future vantage-point, furthermore, which confers upon the proceedings of the moment an "immortality" in recollection.

The "division and estrangement" between past and present are healed; the "little variations" of "yesterday and today" will have their resolution in time. This establishing of temporal continuity is the more striking by contrast with the discontinuity represented in the social scene. Anne and Wentworth make their "ascent" among a jostle of different "groups" whose want of union implies that the condition at Box Hill has become permanent. The quiet manner of their progress through this undifferentiated crowd suggests comparison with the ending of *Little Dorrit*, where Amy and Clennam "quietly" assert the stability of domestic love while chaotic humanity "made their usual uproar." Anne and Wentworth are in harmony, but what surrounds them is not. Whether their implicit task is to subdue it, or to ignore it and live apart, their separation is distinctly etched. Their social relationship is not given, as in *Emma*, but problematic. The medium for their resolution is the continuities of time and consciousness, not the responsibilities of social place.

The silent conversation of consciousness discussed in Chapter Three is a central subject in *Persuasion*. Austen's last novel demonstrates the personal costs as well as the power of detachment, and dramatizes with great explicitness the invisible consensus forming between minds and sustaining them amidst social confusion. Communication or mutual consciousness is not conceived here, as it was formerly, in terms of language, but instead in terms of silent, private transactions.[29] In Anne's love story the secret correspondence, the significant glance—things that in *Emma* are highly suspect—have a new validity. Visual recognition often suggests this silent communication in *Persuasion*. The occasions when Anne is recognized, when another's gaze actually meets her own, have a surprising quality, even an erotic eclat, for the character inured to invisibility.

[29] The truth reaches Wentworth by "means outside of reason, or indeed of language, the prime rational system" (Duckworth, *Improvement*, p. 204; see also p. 206).

Two important scenes demonstrate the nature of such moments, both near the novel's end. One is the scene at the concert where Anne, surrounded by a crowd typically preoccupied with confused jockeying for position, sits apart, on the lookout for Wentworth.

> He did not come however. Anne sometimes fancied she discerned him at a distance, but he never came. The anxious interval wore away unproductively. The others returned, the room filled again, benches were reclaimed and re-possessed.
> . . .
> In re-settling themselves, there were now many changes.
> . . . and by some other removals, and a little scheming of her own, Anne was enabled to place herself much nearer the end of the bench than she had been before, more within reach of a passer-by. She could not do so, without comparing herself with Miss Larolles, the inimitable Miss Larolles,—but still she did it. . . . After an early abdication in her next neighbours, she found herself at the very end of the bench before the concert closed.
> Such was her situation, with a vacant space at hand, when Captain Wentworth was again in sight. She saw him not far off. He saw her too; yet he looked grave, and seemed irresolute, and only by very slow degrees came at last near enough to speak to her. . . . They talked . . . he even looked down towards the bench, as if he saw a place on it well worth occupying; when, at that moment, a touch on her shoulder obliged Anne to turn around.—It came from Mr. Elliot.
>
> (II, viii, 150-51)

Anne is a stable eye in a shifting scene. When she finally catches Wentworth's gaze, the connection has an importance sufficient to still the restlessness around her and to occupy her completely. When the social context abruptly reasserts itself, it does so not in support of their further communication but as an obstacle to it. The obstacle, furthermore, is Mr. Elliot, the man who looked pointedly at Anne on the beach at Lyme in a way that involved a recognition of her attraction if not her name. His interference

breaks the connection between Anne and Wentworth and re-
generates anxiety about bridging the remaining gap between them.
Correctly attributing Wentworth's departure to jealousy, Anne
thinks like a realist—in terms that recognize the gap to be bridged.
"How was such jealousy to be quieted? How was the truth to
reach him?"

The other scene is the penultimate scene at the White Hart,
one like the concert scene also characterized by clatter and confusion. Anne and Wentworth are again in the same room, but
occupied in different tasks, he writing a letter for Captain Harville
and she talking to the Captain about the constancy of affection.
For all their physical proximity they do not occupy the same
space, so emblematically involved are they in separate tasks.
Composed of subgroups apparently oblivious of each other's activity, this scene dramatizes social separations. The narrative style
itself has an inharmoniousness, even an awkwardness, that reinforces the sense of general disorder. In this setting Anne and
Wentworth's mutual consciousness of one another—mutual but
unavailable to discourse—does establish a common awareness,
but one at odds with the rest of the scene. The physical separations
and the intensifying mutual consciousness increase tension to a
pitch relieved only by Wentworth's stumbling letter of proposal,
awkwardly written and awkwardly delivered. His departure produces "momentary vexation" at the incompleteness of their reunion, now so imminent, but also a flood of "full sensation" and
a confidence finally in her "power to send an intelligible sentence"
(II, xi, 188-89). The general description presents a situation in
which the gestures are inarticulate and awkward, the social context has almost no importance, and the silent communication
between these two has utmost importance. The meeting of minds
is like an invisible filament of consciousness connecting two points
and making possible a luminousness that creates amidst the uncertain definition of the background a unified and secure space.

Both this and the concert scene valorize distance as the condition of clarity and meaningful connection. Taken together with
the general development of the story, they underscore the importance of reserve as a condition of power. The privately main-

175

tained mutual consciousness that was so disruptive a force in *Emma* is the main source of stability in *Persuasion*.

For a novel where so much finally depends upon the "power of conversation," there is very little of it represented. "How was the truth to reach him?" How will Anne muster "the power to send an intelligible sentence"? The language suggests the stress of maintaining between minds those continuities that are so difficult even to establish. They are not maintained verbally. Few words pass between Anne and Wentworth during the entire novel, and none that are especially significant. "They had no conversation together, no intercourse but what the commonest civility required. Once so much to each other! Now nothing! There *had* been a time . . ." (I, viii, 49). That last phrase suggests the silent conversation that Anne has carried on in her mind, invisible and apart from her gestures and speech for "so many, many years." Her consciousness is precisely a silent conversation, a way of maintaining a coherent view of things by inward means even when outward experience contradicts it.[30] The epic of consciousness is heroic but silent, both in Anne's mind and even in her most crucial contacts with Wentworth. Their mutual awareness, after he has quietly lifted the child from her back (Charles talking all the while) or after he unexpectedly hands her into the carriage, exists silently. Even when Wentworth finally addresses her with a second proposal, he does not speak. He "seized a sheet of paper, and poured out his feelings" (II, vi, 191). The silence of these conversations does not detract from their power, and the "power of conversation" mentioned by the narrator has more to do in this novel with mutual consciousness than with actual speech.

In *Emma* the differentials of character and social place eclipse the importance of time and consensus; in *Persuasion*, however, where no stable social matrix remains, mediating power becomes more important, both in the character of Anne Elliot and in the narrator; both look toward the possibilities of a silent conversation

---

[30] Yasmine Gooneratne observes that "Anne's ability to provide, without notice, an accurate account of Wentworth's brother-in-law's career illuminates for a moment the mental activity that goes on in the privacy of her calm silence" (*Jane Austen* [Cambridge: Cambridge University Press, 1970], p. 177).

of consciousness based upon mutual agreements and temporal continuity. But even in *Persuasion*, the most realistic of Austen's novels, the narrator's distance is a contracted and relatively unstable one by comparison with narrators in Dickens and George Eliot. Even Austen's last novel reminds the reader of the precariousness of those continuities that bind together separate minds and separate moments. Only at the end is the narrator's presence felt to be conclusively distant from Anne and Wentworth.

Still, Anne's story, by confirming the two apparently opposed values of detachment and involvement, dramatizes the opportunity of the fully realistic narrator. Anne's detachment, despite its numbing effect on her bloom, has considerable social value, especially when we compare Anne's calm clearness with the muddle around her. Yet the marriage to Wentworth clearly means an end to the state of detachment in which we first find her and a new beginning of health and vitality. Both Anne's "wiser" half and her active, blooming, responsive half appear important and even essential to a fully balanced existence. This division is not really solved, nor can it be. The division between public and private life in *Persuasion* suggests permanent need to shift back and forth between the imperatives of the one and the claims of the other.

RECOLLECTION
AND CONSENT

CHAPTER SIX

Mutual Friendship and the Identity of Things in Dickens

The past-tense narrator, the mediating Nobody of realism, is a rich and powerful instrument capable of many variations. This section and the Epilogue describe some of these powers as they appear in the work of three central novelists, Dickens, George Eliot, and James. The increasing importance of the narrator's mediating function corresponds to an increased emphasis on the values of history and memory as the basis for social and personal definition. The more society is conceived as a self-contained entity rather than as part of a cosmic hierarchy, the more differences in temporal and spatial position are treated as quantitative rather than qualitative differences. We become interested in relative distinctions between private and public claims, rather than in the more absolute distinctions between the claims of temporal experience and those of eternity; explanations are more sequential, less typological; duty is conceived in terms of improvement, not praise; experience in terms of mobility, not stasis; and identity in terms of a consistent self, not an erratic soul. These important shifts in emphasis are coterminous with the asssumption of continuous time as a homogeneous, neutral medium of common experience and with the entire view of consciousness entailed by it.

The investigation of depth in Dickens's novels generally takes place on a scale much larger than that of individual psychology. Certainly Dickens is aware that psychological estrangement is a

181

condition of social existence, and he pays special attention to the psychic liabilities of social conditioning. "Nobody" frequently appears as a character in his novels, usually a victim of class privilege. But on the whole Dickens's overriding concern lies with the individual psyche as a part of the system that conditions it, even as a reflex of that system. In Dickens it is the world entire that is intelligible, not merely individual character. The patterns of mutual informativeness coordinated in his novels by structural parallels and commanding metaphors all confirm the unitary nature of society. It is the identity or "depth" of this entity that his novels chiefly unfold.

Problems of Articulation

Dickens's commitment to social intelligibility has certain consequences for his conception of character, consequences which, from his day onward, have been interpreted as signs that Dickens was incapable of portraying inner life. George Eliot's complaint that he does not develop inward life and E. M. Forster's observation that his characters are "flat" have been often cited, and it is certainly true that Dickens's characters do yield their abstractions easily and seem even to *be* abstractions, lacking the variety of aspects common, say, in George Eliot. Dickens's characters "reiterate" an identity that "remains exactly the same" time after time, without apparent ability to move on.

In *Bleak House*, for example, the Dedlocks' marriage has other aspects than the one reiterated, and both characters are described as having capacities for fidelity and love; but little of this variety is apparent. Variable aspects of both individuals fall away silently, and we are left with iterative attention to the lady's coldness and her secret, her husband's mouldering estate and mouldering life. As representatives of a class, the Dedlocks yield their identities easily, while any depths of personal feeling or idiosyncrasy remain unavailable and barely suggested. On the opposite side, characters who resist such reduction often struggle with split personalities. In *Bleak House* George Rouncewell, falsely accused of murder,

182

develops more than one "self" simply in order to cope, and can be found talking to himself as if he were somebody else. " 'I don't see how an innocent man is to make up his mind to this kind of thing without knocking his head against the walls,' " he says, " 'unless he takes it in that point of view.' " Society creates another "guilty" self, a partner of his "innocent" self, and the two Rouncewells then have a severe problem of mutual recognition.[1]

Such psychic splits—the enforced division of the self into private and public aspects—are, as *Great Expectations* shows, the inevitable result of social life. This novel begins with the birth of perspective. Self-consciousness begins for Pip with the psychic division brought on by complicity with a nameless convict. When Magwitch turns him upside down in the first chapter, Pip first learns "the identity of things." Like the first Adam, he learns at this moment of separation the names of things that before had none, especially his own name and his own separateness: "that the small bundle of shivers growing afraid of it all and beginning to cry, was Pip." In this crucial moment of self-consciousness Pip first perceives that there is more than one way to view things, including his own identity, an experience that produces a state of divided allegiance in which he continues and which causes him endless suffering. As he moves from one context to another, his consciousness of self grows with his consciousness of estrangement; he is a "traitor" to Joe, a "common labouring boy" to Estella, and, much later, a victim of his own childish fantasies of supremacy and triumph carried into adult life. With the commencement of his first private friendship, even though its mutuality remains to be confirmed, Pip becomes an outlaw: a person hiding a guilty secret, leading a double life. As his double life increases in complexity, a variety of doubles appear as carriers of qualities that he finds too difficult to imagine or to accept in himself, especially the libidinal energy of Orlick and the snobbish

[1] *Bleak House*, Riverside edition (Boston: Houghton Mifflin, 1967), ch. 52, p. 533. All subsequent references in the text will be to this edition.

cruelty of Bentley Drummle: characters linked in Pip's own consciousness to his private hopes and fears.

This parceling out of one psychic energy among several characters creates problems of articulation for individuals that cannot be solved by them because these problems stem from general problems of articulation in the society as a whole. Dickens's curiosities—characters like Quilp or Wemmick—take on emblematic value in ways that distort the sense of ordinary relations central to realistic agreements. His compounding use of details like the prison in *Little Dorrit* or Chancery in *Bleak House* also has such emblematic function. These effects are not inconsistent with realism. With characters like Quilp the curiosity is that so little distance appears between consciousness and behavior; and this lack of distance is precisely what divides the social entity and threatens its agreements. The almost mechanical inwardness of such characters is most often a sign of the impoverishment Dickens wishes to counteract by concentrating on the social entity as a whole. Presiding over a multitude of such aggressively self-limiting apparitions, Dickens's narrator stresses the unitary nature of consciousness and the common forms of experience seen from the margins; this narrator focuses not on the depths of personality but on the depth of the social world taken as a whole. His work thus demonstrates the flexibility of realistic conventions. So long as the past-tense narrator sustains the consensus whereby the available viewpoints in the text converge upon the same world, the convention can accommodate emblematic details to a degree not allowed for by discussions of realism that do not look beyond details to the comprehensive management of formal relations.

The forces of society in Dickens exert tremendous pressure on individual life, a pressure so great that the private power of resistance staggers with the burden. The deeply fractured personality in Dickens's novels is an effect traceable to social institutions that, having developed a life of their own, destroy the creative tension between private sense and public role. As D. W. Jefferson observes of Dickens's characters, "to say that 'they don't develop,' in the sense used by E. M. Forster, is meaningless. Their very role involves a halting of development," and what we see are their efforts to adapt their role to circumstances.[2]

When the inconsistencies between personal and social position are acute, the multiplication of selves can even have value because it makes possible a kind of freedom. This is why temporary anonymity or role-playing has special importance in Dickens. The mask can be misused, but it can also allow a saving fracture between the apparent identity, derived from some restrictive norm like social class, and the more flexible, variable person. By becoming "nobody," a character can preserve personal integrity by hiding out from social enforcements—sometimes, as in George Rouncewell's case, law enforcement.

The development of "nobodies" in response to such oppositions is especially overt in *Little Dorrit*, where the inconsistencies between Poverty and Riches, prisoners and travelers, past and present are focused in the difficulties of the hero, Arthur Clennam. In his double roles as detective and suspect, spectator and participant, "nobody" and somebody, Clennam seems like someone whose one half scarcely knows what the other is doing. What can be said for the "identity" of someone who in the affairs of others resolutely pursues justice and revelation but who in his own affairs has "no will"?[3] The original title of the novel, *Nobody's Fault*, suggests a theme still present with reference particularly to Arthur's failures in love (see, for example, the chapters titled "Nobody's Weakness," I, 16; "Nobody's Rival," I, 17; "Nobody's State of Mind," I, 26; "Nobody's Disappearance," I, 28).[4]

Though Clennam is the chief he is not the only example in *Little Dorrit* of "nobody." The novel moves by a capillary action that implicates the whole social body in every private defeat and triumph and that reiterates the multiple identity of "nobody." J. G. Schippers' analysis of the novel directs attention to the

[2] D. W. Jefferson, "The Artistry of *Bleak House*," *Essays and Studies*, 1974 (London: John Murray), p. 44.

[3] Peter Garrett makes this point in *The Victorian Multiplot Novel: Studies in Dialogical Form* (New Haven: Yale University Press, 1980), p. 73.

[4] John Butt and Kathleen Tillotson, *Dickens at Work* (London: Methuen & Co. Ltd., 1957), p. 223.

185

schizoid nature of a society that separates vision from action, and particularly to the "vicious circle of *nobody* and *I*." At the same time as Pancks claims to be Amy Dorrit's "fortune teller" he says, "I am nobody."[5] The emphatic "I" of Rigaud or Miss Wade or Tattycoram is the reverse aspect of Clennam's paralyzed will. Both extremes of self-assertion and passivity "amount to the same thing": Miss Wade is merely "Nobody speaking in the Imperative Mood." As Schippers argues, Dickens shows how "nobody" is the "essence of man in a commercial society," a truth that he anchors even in the linguistic habits of various characters like Old Nandy, Mr. Plornish, Casby, Mr. Dorrit, Mrs. General, Tattycoram, Miss Wade.[6]

Dickens explicitly associates the function of Nobody in *Little Dorrit* with the end of personal time. The good characters in *Little Dorrit* have an accurate sense of clock time and history, and the bad characters are those who try to evade time by waiting for what Mike Hollington calls a "private apocalypse." In particular "clock time," as something objective and shared, is vigorously and ominously repudiated by characters like Mrs. Clennam or Mr. Dorrit in favor of a "subjective time" that Hollington calls the "time of dreams." Instead of going "inch by inch" like Amy Dorrit, most characters deflect the continuities of time and responsibility by means of various "nobodies" like Society, Fate, Precedent, or the Fatality of My Character—nobodies that reduce the necessity for personal change and patience.[7] When the gentle-

[5] *Little Dorrit* (Baltimore and London: Penguin, 1967), pp. 336-37. All subsequent references in the text will be to this edition.

[6] J. G. Schippers, "So Many Characters, So Many Words: Some Aspects of the Language of *Little Dorrit*," *Dutch Quarterly Review of Anglo-American Letters*, 8, no. 4 (1978), esp. 256, 263, 265. For discussion of alter egos in *Little Dorrit* see Elaine Showalter, "Guilt, Authority, and the Shadows of *Little Dorrit*," *Nineteenth-Century Fiction*, 34, no. 1 (June 1979), esp. 37.

[7] Mike Hollington, "Time in *Little Dorrit*," in George Goodin, ed., *The English Novel in the Nineteenth Century: Essays on the Literary Mediation of Human Values* (Urbana: University of Illinois Press, 1972), esp. pp. 111-15. It is not so much the road, he argues, as its "wonderful divergences" that gives *Little Dorrit* its particular quality. "Indeed, time is not really felt primarily as an abstract theme in the novel at all. We are conscious of time, first and foremost in the *texture* of

man learns to acknowledge his common cause with a mere debt-
or's daughter, when he abandons his high unenvious course for
the "vanishing point" (*Dorrit*, II, 27, 801) of love, only then
does he find the key to taking his place as a unified integrated
personality.

The social context in Dickens is what provides the commentary
and the connections. Florence Dombey's constant love is, as
Dickens said, her father's "bitterest reproach";[8] so Amy Dorrit's
should be to her father. This context can widen beyond a single
work.[9] Both Amy Dorrit in *Little Dorrit* and Lady Dedlock in
Bleak House meditate on the view from their windows; both successful lovers in *Bleak House* and doomed ones in *Little Dorrit* pass
from sun to shadow as they recede into the distance; the distant
shaft of sunlight finds Jo sweeping his crossing in *Bleak House*,
finds Little Dorrit in prison, finds Magwitch in court. These are

---

the novel: in the extraordinary *swiftness* of Dickens's imagination, in its quick
and deft linking of incongruities. . . . Only the energies of the imagination are
capable of challenging static inertia in *Little Dorrit*, and of setting the world in
motion again." What Hollington calls "Dickens's" imagination I prefer to reserve
to the narrator, that "nobody" whose place and power the reader is so often
invited to assume in Dickens. For discussion of time in Dickens, see also K. J.
Fielding, "Dickens and the Past," in Roy Harvey Pearce, ed., *Experience in the
Novel* (New York: Columbia University Press, 1968).

[8] Quoted by Fred Boege, "Point of View in Dickens," *PMLA*, 65, no. 2 (March
1950), 92.

[9] A. E. Dyson suggests that the whole of Dickens's writing series is an extended
context for particular characters and problems; see *The Inimitable Dickens: A
Reading of the Novels* (London: Macmillan, St. Martin's Press, 1970), p. 255.
This characteristic recourse in Dickens to universal gesture and structure explains
why his books refer so willingly to contexts outside fiction. See Norman Feltes's
discussion of the vision of community expressed in Bleeding Hearts Yard in relation
to the economic vision of limited liability, "Community and the Limits of Liability
in Two Mid-Victorian Novels," *Victorian Studies*, 17, no. 4 (June 1974), 360.

The odd continuum is something Dickens explores in every conceivable way
in his attempts to extend his meaning. The continuity between people and
furniture is an obvious example; another is the opening hallucinations in *The
Mystery of Edwin Drood* that create, in Peter Garrett's words, a "magical perspective, available to no actual spectator but only to the imagination, in which
places or events widely separated in space or time can be grasped syntoptically"
(*Victorian Multiplot Novel*, p. 24).

guarantees and reminders of homogeneity in the human world. Everybody sees the same sun. Various kinds of rhymes and echoes between settings and vocabulary encourage the search in imagination for underlying connections. "When collected," as Dickens says of the serial publication of *Pickwick Papers*, they "form one tolerably harmonious whole."[10]

By literalizing the metaphor of psychic splits Dickens threatens his realism, but his most grotesque effects generally create only local disturbances or warps in the general project, which is to refer individual idiosyncrasy to social context. Dickens's most powerful arguments in favor of mobility and connectedness are his casualties: characters who have been brought to a stop or whose motion takes them nowhere new; those whose experience is not a series of cases but (like the Jarndyce suit) one "endless case." However much it may be disguised or ignored, the unity of the social world, the reality that exists between persons, is the ultimate source of personal wholeness or fracture in Dickens and the source of his realism.

On the larger scale Dickens's dual structures enable him to experiment with the problems of consensus and community. From the first novel to the last he experiments with opposed structural modes; from the converging worlds of *Pickwick Papers* to the complementary metaphors of *Our Mutual Friend*, he characteristically plays with lines of development that do not develop, convergences that do not converge, in order to trace to their origins the deep fractures in the identity of things that threaten discontinuity and confusion. For all the familiarity of their furniture, however, the novels are not repetitive because of the deep ontological importance of these issues and because of the variety

[10] Cited in Raymond Williams, *The English Novel from Dickens to Lawrence* (New York: Oxford University Press, 1970), p. 33. The object of representation in Dickens, he says, is "the system" (p. 51). See the analysis of how Dickens imports various voices or "languages" into a single sentence in Bakhtin's *Dialogic Imagination* (trans. Michael Holquist and Caryl Emerson [Austin: University of Texas Press, 1981]), in the discussion of "Discourse in the Novel," esp. p. 303. His terms in this chapter apply suggestively (but always with caution) to George Eliot, though he does not mention her.

188

of ways they find expression. The split psyche, dual structures, and opposing metaphors are Dickens's ways of exploring the premises of his social faith.[11]

The split narration in *Bleak House* brings to the forefront the problem of consensus in time, separating the two functions that ordinarily work together in realism, overview and recollection. The ideal of social harmony is articulated in this novel most explicitly by the character least qualified to understand its nature. "I take it," says Skimpole, "that my business in the social system is to be agreeable; I take it that everybody's business in the social system is to be agreeable. It's a system of harmony, in short" (ch. 18, p. 192). The split narration implicitly questions such optimism. Alternating between the anonymous present-tense narration, with its fragmentary discontinuous syntax and attention, and Esther's past-tense narrative, with its demonstrably subjective coherences, the split narration implicitly questions the power of overview to hold things together and the power of memory to be

---

[11] Several commentators have described the dual tensions as "centripetal" and "centrifugal"—terms that seem especially appropriate because of their kinaesthetic value. Most notable is Jerome Beaty's discussion of continuity between this life and another, "The 'Soothing Songs' of *Little Dorrit*," in Clyde de L. Ryals et al., eds., *Nineteenth-Century Literary Perspectives* (Durham, North Carolina: Duke University Press, 1974), pp. 219-37. For centripetal-centrifugal elements see also J. Hillis Miller, "The Fiction of Realism: *Sketches by Boz, Oliver Twist,* and Cruikshank's illustrations," in Ada Nisbet and Blake Nevious, eds., *Dickens Centennial Essays* (Berkeley and Los Angeles: University of California Press, 1971), pp. 85-154; and John Henry Raleigh, "Dickens and the Sense of Time," in his *Time, Place, and Idea: Essays on the Novel* (Carbondale, Illinois: Southern Illinois University Press, 1968), esp. p. 133. John Carey sees violence and order as the two poles (*The Violent Effigy* [London: Faber & Faber, 1973]); Edwin Eigner sees a "combination of positivist and visionary strains" as a central problematic in Dickens (*The Metaphysical Novel in England and America* [Berkeley and Los Angeles: University of California Press, 1978], p. 7); George Ford discusses the "two poles of public and private" ("Dickens and the Voices of Time," *Nineteenth-Century Fiction*, 24, no. 4 [March 1969], 433); Northrop Frye in similar terms compares the public with the green worlds ("Dickens and the Comedy of Humours," in Pearce, *Experience in the Novel*); Christopher Herbert discusses the opposed idyllic and gothic modes in *Pickwick* ("Converging Worlds in *Pickwick Papers*," *Nineteenth-Century Fiction*, 27, no. 1 [June 1972], 1-20).

189

objective. The split narration thus cuts across this novel's "pattern of convergences," creating a problem of temporal reconciliation.

W. J. Harvey's reading of this dual narrative sums up much that has been said about it: that Esther's narrative provides "stability, a point of rest in a flickering and bewildering world," and that though she is passive and insipid she is at least consistent, and provides "a brake, controlling the impulse to episodic intensification" that characterizes the narrator's "mobility" and "swooping" panoramic view.[12] The problem with this description is that the two narratives do not look at the "same" world. The present tense itself clearly constitutes a different vision from Esther's, and occupies itself mainly (though not exclusively) with different events. Esther records her personal "progress," while the present-tense narrator deals with the discontinuities of Fashion and Chancery, which together resemble the vicious circle of "nobody and I" of *Little Dorrit*, Fashion being just the voice of chaos in the Imperative Mood. The present-tense narrative destroys the continuities established by Esther, interrupting her story every few chapters with its grim reminders.

Given this deadlock in the narrative perspective, we have an opportunity in Inspector Bucket, the all-seeing, omnipresent detective, and several readers have made much of him. Albert Hutter's excellent discussion reminds us how much Bucket has in common with the traditional "omniscient" narrator. At his first appearance he is introduced as "nothing" and "a third person" (ch. 22), and he appears through the novel in various guises that suggest omnipresence and arbitrariness.[13] Both Mr. Hutter and Ian Ousby connect Inspector Bucket with the narrative perspective that exceeds even the anonymous present-tense narrator's vision. "He mounts a high tower in his mind," says the narrator, "and looks out far and wide" (ch. 56, p. 581), showing that, according to Mr. Ousby, Bucket "can transcend the partial view-

[12] W. J. Harvey, "Chance and Design in *Bleak House*," in Martin Price, ed., *Dickens: Twentieth-Century Views* (Englewood Cliffs, N.J.: Prentice Hall, 1967), pp. 137-41.

[13] Albert D. Hutter, "The High Tower of His Mind: Psychoanalysis and the Reader of *Bleak House*," *Criticism*, 19, no. 4 (Fall 1977), esp. 300, 302, 304.

point to which most of the characters are limited to see the world from a god-like eminence like that enjoyed by the third-person narrator."[14] Mr. Hutter agrees that "by the time Bucket has 'mounted the high tower in his mind,' reader, omniscient narrator, and detective all seem to share a common perspective and, for the moment at least, a common identity."[15] While these interpretations are very suggestive, Inspector Bucket appears in only half of the narration during most of the novel, and his elevated perspective is, as Mr. Hutter says, "for the moment" only.

The searching eye of intuition reaches only so far in *Bleak House*. The two narratives finally converge on the trail of Lady Dedlock, that is to say, the track of the past. Inspector Bucket, who has belonged chiefly to the anonymous present-tense account, comes to Esther for help in tracing the lost lady, and for the first time both narratives come together with the same objective, and with some mutual consciousness formerly impossible. But these separate narrative lines converge just short of the Burying Ground. Inspector Bucket continues bailing out the universe with information, but what is needed is a miracle. *Bleak House* uncovers mysteries of betrayal too deep even for the ubiquitous inspector. He has been on the trail from early in the novel, investigating Nemo the "no name" key to coherence and connection, tracking Jo to get information for Tulkinghorn. But Inspector Bucket's trails all end in death: first Nemo, then Tulkinghorn, then Jo, then Lady Dedlock. Even to find Lady Dedlock he needs Esther's help, and though he pursues his lost lady to the "brink of the void" he arrives, as people always do in this novel, too late. Death is the vanishing-point in *Bleak House* and, with few exceptions, no satisfactory reconciliations or understandings take place this side of the grave, especially not Esther's improbable marriage. The heart of Lady Dedlock is the lynchpin that fails, but hers is only one case of a general condition of fracture and disconnection that the novel maintains to the end.

[14] Ian Ousby, "The Broken Glass: Vision and Comprehension in *Bleak House*," *Nineteenth-Century Fiction*, 29, no. 4 (March 1975), 392. What's more, Bucket intuits Lady Dedlock's course and the wishes of a speechless Sir Leicester.

[15] Hutter, "High Tower of His Mind," 304.

The important connections between worlds in *Bleak House* are left up to readers; the mutual relatedness of things is not demonstrated by any promising successes in the story:

> What connexion can there be [the anonymous narrator asks the reader], between the place in Lincolnshire, the house in town, the Mercury in powder, and the whereabout of Jo the outlaw with the broom, who had that distant ray of light upon him when he swept the churchyard step? What connexion can there have been between many people in the innumerable histories of this world, who, from opposite sides of great gulfs, have, nevertheless, been very curiously brought together!
>
> Jo sweeps his crossing all day long, unconscious of the link, if any link there be. (Ch. 16, p. 167.)

The fragmented patterns of coincidence and convergence suggest an unassembled jigsaw puzzle, and even the joint collaborative efforts of readers and narrators produce at best a vision uneasily unified.

Despite occasional direct addresses to the reader, Dickens's narrator generally delegates commentary to his structural parallels and iterating metaphors, letting one part of the world comment on another through similitude. The narrative consciousness is most like a medium in Dickens, and least like an individual character itself. His narrating consciousness is transparent, not opaque; it is more like a still sad music of humanity rising from every object and event in his fictional world, an all-pervasive medium that is closely identified with all presences and not individualized at all. The sense of performance that Robert Garis describes in Dickens does not personalize the narrator. Notwithstanding the occasional passages of direct address and the heavily evaluative descriptions of agencies like the Circumlocution Office, the Dickens narrator keeps a low profile by comparison with George Eliot's brooding, reflective narrator, or Fielding's gentlemanly literary narrator, or even Thackeray's puppeteer. These narrators inch toward personification in ways Dickens's narrator does not. The possible range of voices available to Dickens's past-tense narrator is small by comparison with the wide-ranging, many-voiced community of consciousness that the narrative perspective sustains.

In Dickens the narrator seems almost to become the characters, each in turn, and to leave to the reader the considerable work of coordinating that variety. In discussing the workings of this narrator, Taylor Stoehr provides invaluable clues from Dickens's Memoranda book. Dickens not only *saw* his characters, Stoehr argues, he *was* them. "I do not mean merely that he identified with them, took sides, and so on; his projection . . . was much more complete than that. A glance at the 'Memoranda' book in which he recorded ideas for stories during his later years will indicate just how total that identification was." In his selections, from which I have taken a few samples, Stoehr emphasizes the way Dickens speaks of each character as if each were a role he temporarily assumes:

"Bedridden (or room-ridden) twenty—five and twenty—years; any length of time. As to most things, kept at a standstill all the while. Thinking of altered streets as the old streets—changed things as the unchanged things—the youth or girl I quarreled with all those years ago, as the same youth or girl now. Brought out of doors by an unexpected exercise of my latent strength of character, and then how strange!

Done in Mrs. Clennam"

"I affect to believe that I would do anything myself for a Ten Pound note, and that anybody else would. I affect to be always book-keeping in every man's case and posting up a little account of good and evil with everyone. . . . While I affect to be finding good in most men, I am in reality decrying it where it really is, and setting it up where it is not.

Done in Dorrit [Henry Gowan]"

"I stand by my friends and acquaintances; —not for their sakes, but because they are *my* friends and acquaintances. *I* know them, *I* have licensed them, they have taken out *my* certificate. Ergo, I champion them as myself.

[Podsnap]"

193

" 'If they were great things, I, the untrustworthy man in little things, would do them Earnestly'—But O No, I wouldn't!

[Eugene]"

Though all such entries are not couched in the first person, Stoehr quotes these and others like them "to show the variety of points of view with which Dickens was able to identify . . . even despicable ones. . . . In this sense at least, Dickens seems to be *in* all his characters, to feel and identify with them, regardless of the formal perspective finally adopted for their presentation in the novels. This identification with all the characters is especially important because it seems to prevent his taking any one role and identifying himself deeply with it." This disappearing narrator, in other words, projects into the entire world, and lets its physical attributes speak. "Pushed to its extremes, this is the opposite of dehumanization; it is animism, another basically metonymic device in its dependence on the contiguity of characters and the objects which surround them."[16] The narrator, and by extension the reader, becomes the world, in order to confirm not an individual identity but a social one: the identity of things; the mutually related and ultimately unitary nature of human society.

These glimpses of the Memoranda book help to account for the reader's sense that the consciousness represented is all part of the same consciousness, and yet one for the most part inaccessible to personification. The social entity exists everywhere and nowhere, invisibly, between the various characters and events and only partially located in each. Stoehr cites two more passages that, brought together, sum up this sense of projected consciousness: the first from the Memoranda book; the second from John Forster.

Open a story by bringing two strongly contrasted places and strongly contrasted sets of people, into the connexion necessary for the story, by means of an electric message—*be* the message—flashing along through space—over the earth, and under the sea.

[16] Taylor Stoehr, *Dickens: The Dreamer's Stance* (Ithaca: Cornell University Press, 1965), pp. 41-57.

No man had ever so surprising a faculty as Dickens of be-coming himself what he was representing; and of entering into mental phases and processes so absolutely, in conditions of life the most varied, as to reproduce them completely in dialogue without the need of an explanatory word.

"Electric messages" without an "explanatory word": a good de-scription of the way Dickens manages his narrative perspective.

The absence of the explanatory word and the confinement to enactment require a great deal of readers. Each moment is suc-ceeded by another, what appears momentous can turn out insig-nificant. Quilp looms evilly at the beginning of The Old Curiosity Shop but dwindles in importance and power; the mysterious Dou-ble of Flintwitch in Little Dorrit proves to have less significance than we anticipated. Proportions shift in this way, from big to small, threatening the stability of the controlling perspective and engaging the reader considerably more immediately than those novels where the narrator is more comfortably, more comfortingly tangible. The entire world is galvanized by a consciousness com-mon to all times and all places: electric messages without an explanatory word.

The anticlimax is a particularly effective Dickensian device for enlarging the arena of conscious possibility by depreciating single solutions and single causalities. The anticlimax works by sug-gesting that there is more than one point of view concerning any event. In Little Dorrit, for example, all Arthur Clennam's research only leads him in a circle to himself; the Clennam will that ostensibly motivates much of the plot and contains clues for sorting out the legal relationships is burnt; and even though William Dorrit's fondest daydreams come true—magical inher-itance, release from restraint into new life—it changes little. [17] Similarly, in Great Expectations the dark secret turns out to be Compeyson, who betrayed both Magwitch and also Miss Hav-isham, but Compeyson matters much less than Pip's betrayal of

[17] Peter Garrett comments on the hollowness of these climaxes and the con-sequent "sense of ironic disproportion between effects and their supposed cause" (Multiplot Novel, p. 15).

Magwitch. The melodramatic plot-resolutions are frequently off center, sometimes perversely, as when Magwitch is delivered to the bar of "justice." The "happy" endings—the cheery jingle of Esther's hope or the married burbles of Bella Wilfer—do not mask the deep and consciously articulated problems remaining for those characters at the end of their novels. Only the simple-minded look for simple solutions, often in terms of ready cash. Many factors make up the general truth, and only the characters who recognize the need to bridge the gaps between its aspects can discover the identity of things. These are the characters who can, consequently, sustain their own identities and thus contribute to the social fund of saving instances. The shifts in form and meaning in Dickens are like the seismic shifts of inner life, and much depends upon the reader's capacity, unaided by explicit narrative comment, to "read" an entire cumulatively modified sequence.

The tension between restless motion and fixed position finds enactment in so many ways in Dickens's novels that it becomes a property of the world, a general gesture of form in the nature of things which individuals only participate in. These are the "laws" of the Dickens world. His novels enact versions of a single struggle between centripetal and centrifugal energies. The force and uniqueness of his scenes deflect attention repeatedly, creating separate enclaves that recapitulate similar problems without mutual reference. But gradually, as a denizen from one neighborhood or household meets another, the very process of deflection turns up clues that eventually reveal a commanding structure of significance, uniting various worlds of experience into one. Dickens's metaphors are especially powerful in this process. His symbols work, as John Holloway says, not by augmenting but by transmuting the meaning. "The symbolism is rather a dimension than an ingredient. What it does is to modify literality until the work as a whole stands in a new perspective."[18] The development of these resonances gives Dickens's novels their depth. The commanding structure comes into view slowly, emerging from all parts

[18] John Holloway, "Dickens and the Symbol," in Michael Slater, ed., *Dickens 1970* (London: Chapman and Hall, 1970), p. 64.

of the world and grounded in them. Each point is a relay for the electric messages that connect them.

What Dickens understood intuitively and from the beginning was the systematic nature of his own realism, and while he pushes the limits of that system to a level of explicitness that threatens to show it to be a convention, he does not depart from it. Dickens's vast, dark, social amphitheater is populated by smaller-than-life-size figures that resemble reflexes of a single organic group. From the anonymity and randomness of the street his novels recover those hidden relationships that confirm the existence of a social entity, and in so doing, as Raymond Williams says, Dickens forces the reality of this community "into consciousness. This creation of consciousness—of recognition and relationships—seems to me indeed to be the purpose of Dickens' developed fiction."[19]

Consensus in *Our Mutual Friend*

Dickens's last completed novel sublimely recapitulates those forms and conceptions, evident through all his work, that lie at the heart of the realistic value-system. The two central metaphors especially, the river and the dust mounds, are emblems for the linear flow of time and the disconnected heaps of rubbish produced by it. These two metaphors, among other devices in the novel, raise the question: what of essential value survives the linear flow of time? What, either of individual identity or of social coherence, can be salvaged from circumstances? What form-of-the-whole finally stands revealed? Through the entire novel these two allusive metaphors reinforce the central struggle between continuity and discontinuity.

The river Thames, a continuous, common medium of life and death in *Our Mutual Friend*, stands for many things. For Lizzie Hexam it is time. She looks downstream into a future that reveals "the vast blank misery of a life suspected, and fallen away from

[19] Raymond Williams, *The English Novel from Dickens to Lawrence* (New York: Oxford University Press, 1970), p. 33.

by good and bad . . . stretching away to the great ocean, Death."[20]
Being the medium in the novel where everyone from Riderhood
to Veneering dives for a living, the river explicitly connects time
and depth. But the river's most allusive property is its linearity.
All literal and figurative rivers become tributaries of the same
stream, the common stream of time that everyone inhabits, however different their fates.

The endangered characters are those who cannot keep to a
linear track. An especially eloquent case is the drunken Mr. Dolls,
trying to cross the street.

> Over and over again, when the course was perfectly clear, he
> set out, got halfway, described a loop, turned and went back
> again, when he might have crossed and recrossed half-a-dozen
> times. Then he would stand shivering on the edge of the pave-
> ment, looking up the street and looking down, while scores of
> people jostled him, and crossed, and went on.
>
> (III, x, 506)

Failing to get into the stream he is washed up, like waste, on the
side. He dies soon afterwards. But Mr. Dolls is one case of a more
general problem. John Harmon struggles against the same pattern
when he first attempts to track the path of his fatal night.

> He tried a new direction, but made nothing of it; walls, dark
> doorways, flights of stairs and rooms, were too abundant. And,
> like most people puzzled, he again and again described a circle,
> and found himself at the point from which he had begun. "This
> is like what I have read in narratives of escape from prison,"
> said he, "where the little track of the fugitives in the night
> always seems to take the shape of the great round world on
> which they wander; as if it were a secret law."
>
> (II, xiii, 356)

His relation to his own track has the same ontological importance
as it does for Mr. Dolls. Though Harmon has more success, he

---

[20] *Our Mutual Friend* (New York: E. P. Dutton & Co., 1907), I, vi, 66. All
subsequent references will be to this edition and will be included parenthetically
in the text.

must cope with similar gaps in consciousness, tracking himself through a drugged state: "sick and deranged impressions; they are so strong that I rely on them; but there are spaces between them that I know nothing about, and they are not pervaded by any idea of time." He determinedly thinks it out "straight": "Don't evade it, John Harmon; don't evade it; think it out!" When he does slip momentarily into the present tense, he stops himself short immediately. " 'But this is not thinking it out; this is making a leap to the present time,' " and " 'again I ramble away from thinking it out to the end. It is not so far to the end that I need be tempted to break off. Now, on straight!' " This drama literally enacts the problem of realism, as Harmon tries to recover his identity by reconstructing sequence.

The strain of maintaining an independent consciousness, victorious over unconsciousness, circularity, and confusion reverberates in this passage as it does throughout the novel. It is a strain that the weak cannot support. Bradley Headstone, tracking Eugene, finds himself doubled back upon by his subtle prey; Gaffer Hexam dies tangled in his own lines. By contrast with those who cannot make connections, Harmon's telling himself his own story in his mind, becoming his own narrator and his own objectifier, is a wonderful metaphor for consciousness perilously sustaining itself in the absence of other corroboration. In his conversation with himself, John Harmon proves equal to the challenge of keeping on the track of his own personal truth.

If the river suggests time's flow, dust suggests time's effluvia: the accumulated refuse of human living, a heap of curiosities and shards without articulation and, therefore, without intelligibility. The Boffin Mounds are a gigantic image of discontinuity, echoing in the novel with the "human, warious" of Venus's bone shop, and with Shares. The stream of mutual consciousness, of mutual friendship, that Harmon and others labor to maintain competes continually with the forms of dust and death. Old Harmon bequeaths dust to his children, and turns their prospects to dust. His daughter hinted that the marriage he sells her into "would make Dust of her heart and Dust of her life—in short, would set her up, on a very extensive scale, in her father's business" (p.

199

13). She dies offstage and her brother survives by escaping into oblivion. Dust-shoveling, in fact, is a national occupation, as the narrator remarks in describing proud poverty's flight from Charity.

> My Lords, and gentlemen, and honorable boards, when you in the course of your dust-shovelling and cinder-raking have piled up a mountain of pretentious failure; you must off with your honorable coats for the removal of it, and fall to the work with the power of all the queen's horses and all the queen's men, or it will come rushing down and bury us alive.
>
> (III, viii, 477)

An allusion to Humpty Dumpty seems especially appropriate in a novel about putting the pieces of identity back together again. Pieces, leftovers, effluvia, dust, in short, "human, warious"—all can be turned into cyphers of value and substituted for living realities. Eugene's father appears only as cyphers "M.R.F."; the cyphers "L.S.D." fascinate Fledgby not as what "they stand for," but only "the three dry letters" (II, v, 256), and as cyphers for Pounds, Shillings, Pence they stand for a complex contention between Bella on the one hand and, on the other, herself, the Boffins, and Rokesmith (III, xv, 562). The mutual metaphors of dust and the river in the novel variously amplify the general tension between dispersal and reunion, differentiation and harmony, surface and depth.

Both dust and the river, in the subtle wit of this novel, have more aspects than one. The dust contains golden opportunity, as Boffin's nickname, the Golden Dustman, suggests, and the mounds can be put into a train of carts and carried off to be converted. Waste can be reclaimed in *Our Mutual Friend*, largely because of mutual friendship spreading among the Boffins, Bella, Harmon, then Wrayburn, Lizzie, and others. Like the mounds, the river is turned to use at the locks on the upper track of the Thames. Compared to its destructive potential downstream, here the river submits to the hand of man. The milldam that turns the mill's wheel, or the series of locks on the river, compartmentalizes and tames the energy, backing up the water into a placid pool or converting the controlled flow into useable energy.

The locks even permit travelers to move on the river in a direction opposite to its current. Together these human instruments control the stream and give it a different aspect. "The great serene mirror of the river seemed as if it might have reproduced all it had ever reflected between those placid banks, and brought nothing to the light save what was peaceful, pastoral, and blooming" (III, ix, 495). Human intervention subdues the river to human use and produces a reflective calm. The variety of usage for these two metaphors, like other forms of allusiveness in the novel (various "disappearances," forms of poverty, articulation, dead-men's money, etc.), act as carriers of mutual meaning, confirming the potential for mutual consciousness.[21]

The double plot in *Our Mutual Friend*, another fracture needing recovery, poses the central problem of the novel. During their parallel but separate histories, both John Harmon and Eugene Wrayburn face the problem of putting together a consistent personal identity from fragmented experience, and how these parallel lines converge provides the clue to the chief mystery of the novel, the deep, unifying identity of things to be rescued from discreteness and disconnection. The parallels between their histories are more obvious than their unifying connection. Both learn to become somebody by being nobody, both endure an identity crisis because of constricting, univocal social forms, and both achieve moral regeneration. They are separate cases of one truth, and yet these connections between their two plots can seem somewhat arbitrary unless we grasp the more profound connection. The recovery of John Harmon from his series of aliases depends not on his private solutions alone—they are all in place well before

[21] Harmon "disappears" into Radfoot, Radfoot into Handford, Handford into Rokesmith, and Rokesmith back into Harmon; Eugene's "disappearances" begin the night he meets Lizzie (p. 168) and continue to worry Mortimer (p. 269); Bella's "disappearances" into her husband's embrace take on a figurative ominousness. There are many forms of poverty, including the independent Betty's total lack of cash and the social creature Lightwood's repose on credit. Articulation takes place in Venus's shop, in Harmon's personality, and in various compositions of dust, for good or ill. The power of dead men's money is felt differently by Lizzie, Harmon, Wrayburn, and Betty Higden. These are the patterns, developed from the linear series, that confirm the identity of things.

the end—but on the confirmation Eugene Wrayburn's case provides, by the mutual friendship of another like himself. Alone, their experiences remain eccentric, but these two converging lives—like the two converging sight-lines in pictorial realism—together objectify a world and thus reclaim unity from discontinuity and confusion.

When John Harmon returns to England, he attempts to solve his initial problem—the separation over an indefinite gap of years between the boy he was and the man he has become—by taking on an alias. But this gesture of separation from himself, one that acknowledges the rift between his private identity and his roles as son and legatee, only compounds his problems and clinches his separation from the legal entity "John Harmon." The murderous attack by the man who assumed his clothes and aspired to his money dissociates life, consciousness, and name:

> "I could not have said that my name was John Harmon—I could not have thought it—I didn't know it—but when I heard the blows, I thought of the wood-cutter and his axe, and had some dead idea that I was lying in a forest. . . . I cannot possibly express it to myself without using the word I. But it was not I. There was no such thing as I, within my knowledge.
>
> "It was only after a downward slide through something like a tube, and then a great noise and a sparkling and a crackling as of fires, that the consciousness came upon me, 'This is John Harmon drowning! John Harmon, struggle for your life.' "
>
> (II, xiii, 350)

The novel is about his deliberate journey back from "not I" to "I," but not before circumstances have encouraged him to develop more and more aliases; "George Radfoot" survives the river only to become "Julius Handford," who disappears in turn into "John Rokesmith" and later into an anonymous sailor.

Uniting these various aliases in one identity is difficult because of the society he lives in. In social terms his identity problem becomes vastly more significant than he first anticipates. His private sense of identity depends upon *avoiding* the social roles set up for him to play—son, brother, legatee, lover, secretary, witness—but though they save his private self-consciousness from his social roles, his masks proliferate, projecting him into an elaborate game of lost and found. "I am lost," he says, when he views the body that has been drowned in John Harmon's clothes. What makes for identity, clearly, is not the "body found" but something more complex. The crucial question in his monologue is, "Should John Harmon come to life?" So long as the question of resurrection concerns not the private man who survives under aliases but his social roles, "John Harmon is dead." When he becomes Mr. Boffin's "Secretary," Harmon takes up residence in his own life under an alias, and lives apart from himself, a double life in which he is a "living-dead man" (II, xiii, 352-53). He tells Mr. Boffin, with a Homeric touch, "I am nobody . . . and not likely to be known" (I, viii, 89). His disguise, like Odysseus's in Ithaca, is necessary to save him from certain extinction at the hands of parasites, yet to be fully himself he must learn to assume once again his proper role at his own hearth. "Unrecognized" is as good as dead, in all but private terms, and dead he wants to stay until he can have his life back on his own terms, for his "own sake."

In this dissociated state he functions as a "ghost" in his dealings with others, operating in absentia in order to avoid the problem of existing simultaneously in two conflicting identities. For example, as the Secretary he persuades Riderhood to write a confession restoring Hexam's good name, but he cannot deliver the document himself without risk of meeting Charles Hexam, who knows him as Julius Handford. So long as he has no clue to the whole truth he hesitates at partial revelation and chooses to preserve his separate identities disarticulated. The tensions of the split between his past and present selves become most strenuous in the presence of Bella Wilfer, the fiancée indicated for him by his father's will. With Bella "the present John Rokesmith, far removed from the late John Harmon, remained standing at a distance. A little distance in respect of space, but a great distance in respect of separation" (II, xiv, 364-65).

Being "nobody" at Mr. Boffin's gives the Secretary enormous power in the administration of other lives. He intercedes for Betty

Higden when the Boffins' kindness threatens her independence; he invents a plot to improve Bella's character; he assists the Boffins' search for an orphan to replace himself as the new "John Harmon"; he finds a trade for Sloppy and clears Gaffer Hexam's name; in short, he acts as mediator, and usually as invisible mediator, for nearly everyone. At the same time he can never act directly, never declare himself. He both is and is not dead, he is both engaged in action and watching himself at the same time. As Boffin's Secretary he is a sort of deputy providence, disposing and proposing anonymously without personal responsibility or personal reward. Even when he marries Bella he marries as John Rokesmith and not as John Harmon.[22]

Eugene Wrayburn's case has obvious similarities with Harmon's. Like Harmon, he shrinks from fulfilling his father's will and inhabits his life without really living it, though much less deliberately in both instances. Like Harmon, he receives a blow to consciousness that forces him through a ritual death and finally achieves a new life through the power of love. Even his crisis takes place in the same river and is described in the same imagery of sparkling, crackling fires and watery struggle.

> In an instant, with a dreadful crash, the reflected night turned crooked, flames shot jaggedly across the air, and the moon and stars came bursting from the sky.
> Was he struck by lightning? . . . After dragging at the as-

---

[22] The Secretary's explicit role as "nobody," the nature of his influence as an administrator that aligns him with the role of the past-tense narrator, is nothing new in Dickens. The authority-figure withdrawn from sight but not from influence is the role of Old Martin Chuzzlewit, and both Chuzzlewit and Harmon probably owe their existence to Shakespearean characters like the Duke in *Measure for Measure*. Certainly it is misleading to read into *Our Mutual Friend* (as Jonathan Arac does in *Commissioned Spirits: The Shaping of Social Motion in Dickens, Carlyle, Melville and Hawthorne* [New Brunswick: Rutgers University Press, 1979]), a rejection of overview ("overview and synecdoche" in fact), an "end of a fiction of 'social motion,'" and a move toward the inward and "private" (p. 12). More than any Dickens novel the last demonstrates that the "private" is not the same as "inward" but rather half of the crucial distinction between "private" and "public," and that both halves exist in symbiotic connection.

sailant, he fell on the bank with him, and then there was another great crash, and then a splash, and all was done.

(IV, vi, 662)

This description, as well as the other parallels, aligns Eugene Wrayburn's struggle for fully human survival with Harmon's, and together they reveal the predicament, the legal and social predicament of the English gentleman.

But where Harmon maintains his private, irreducible center of consciousness apart from his circumstances, Eugene scarcely has one. His legal vocation is a "fiction." He is only a "gentleman" by birth—something that involves neither work nor love nor self-understanding. He is wholly a creature of circumstance, especially class distinctions, and this strange existence is characterized by an insurmountable lassitude. He has none of the power that John Harmon finds in detachment. Harmon needs masks because he has something to cover, a constant identity to protect; Eugene is dangerously close to having nothing to hide. No spectacle of need moves him to action. In response to Jenny Wren's grief for a drunkard father, for instance, "Eugene Wrayburn saw the tears exude from between the little creature's fingers as she kept her hand before her eyes. He was sorry, but his sympathy did not move his carelessness to do anything but feel sorry" (III, x, 505). For his own ends he even bribes her alcoholic father with alcohol, watches his tipsy, unsuccessful struggle to cross the street, saunters home, and sleeps lightly (p. 516).[23] He peers at Lizzie through her window, regarding her distantly as a "sad, solitary spectacle" (I, xiii, 154). By the time his crisis literally hits him the reader, treated to his insolence, feels he deserves everything he gets. If, as realism supposes, human truth is deep and hidden, Eugene's humanity appears to be permanently lost, so detached has he become from any fellowship.

[23] For a discussion of an "historical shift in the perception of time" that casts some light on Eugene's characteristic saunter, see Norman Feltes's connection between sauntering and a certain view of time, "To Saunter, To Hurry: Dickens, Time, and Industrial Capitalism," *Victorian Studies*, 20, no. 3 (Spring 1977), 245-67.

The height of his life-crisis is a literal struggle to get into the present and to stay there. During the long illness succeeding his crisis, his consciousness wanders "at an immense distance." He pleads to his friend, "Keep me here . . . if you know the harassing anxiety that gnaws and wears me when I am wandering" (pp. 698-99). The emotional detachment he enjoyed previously has overtaken him with a vengeance; he is a "drowning man" rising and disappearing into "the deep" (p. 701), and the violence required to blast him into life suggests the magnitude of his problem. The effort to recollect himself is so terrific that he needs Jenny Wren to think of the word that will save him, and he needs Mortimer to pronounce it (IV, x, 703-704).

Such identity problems are not confined to Harmon and Wrayburn only, a fact that directly influences their respective powers to cope with their own identity problems. In various ways other characters recapitulate and generalize the identity problems central to the double plot. The extreme case of a split personality incapable of recovery is Bradley Headstone. Bradley lives and dies making obsessive clutches at things, a characteristic dissociation in his gestures that suggests the presence of completely unregulated and unsynchronized forces in his personality. He is volatile and yet slow to react; he leads two distinct lives, as schoolmaster to growing minds and as Eugene Wrayburn's night-prowling double, and yet he claims to "avoid reservations or concealment." His blood even seems to circulate in batches, alternately rendering him heated and "deadly white" (II, xi, 324-27). He communicates by satellite, his referents dangle, his abruptness continually gives the impression of barely suppressed rage, unarticulated, uncontrollable. His insistent proposals to Lizzie are terrifying exercises in dissociation, including arbitrary definitions of space and the separation between his verbal address to her and his physical address to a nearby stone. He insists on another interview "under more favorable circumstances, before the whole case can be submitted," but it is precisely the "whole case" that eludes him, especially since it involves her point of view. His hopeless disarticulation is the psychic analogue for the physical hiatuses of Silas Wegg.

Bradley's extreme case of internal fracture, however hopeless from a therapeutic viewpoint, at least gives him two options, something an unregenerate man like Rogue Riderhood can only clutch at when he faces death. His "Alfred David" giving witness against his friend requires only, so Rogue understands it, his own word. He does not see the need for a corroborating point of view. He, too, falls into the river, and after he is fished out his acquaintances briefly see "the same respected friend in more aspects than one." The closer he comes to death the more evident his humanity becomes. "Neither Riderhood in this world, nor Riderhood in the other, could draw tears from them; but a striving human soul between the two can do it easily." Unlike the gentlemen, however, Riderhood comes back unbaptized. "The short-lived delusion begins to fade. The low, bad, unimpressive face is coming up from the depths of the river, or what other depths, to the surface again. As he grows warm, the doctor and the four men cool. As his lineaments soften with life, their faces and their hearts harden to him" (III, iii, 421-23). His mortality links him in momentary mutual friendship before his individualizing features return to isolate him and to return him to the one aspect in which he is known.

For the development of depth through various aspects the most interesting character in the novel is Bella Wilfer. She has a density and depth, before she declines into a wife, because of her self-consciousness about her own inconsistencies and her ability to "war with herself." Because she knows her own variety, she can integrate it (unlike Headstone). Her better self can come into ascendancy over her worse (unlike Riderhood), because she is capable of taking various, even conflicting positions. The Boffin subterfuge, forcing Bella's better self into play, has the calculated effect because she has power over her own variety. By agreeing with her worst voice, " 'You are right, go in for money, my love. Money's the article' " (III, v, 448, 441), Mr. Boffin confirms only part of her mind, and a part she dislikes. Bella's contradictory nature is most realistic, that is, has most depth, when she is giving herself penitential pokes, and it is a pity she has to lose her depth and interest in order to succeed, as it appears she does in the episodes after marriage. Once wrestling with "contradictory" (II, viii, 305) impulses, Bella suddenly seems lobotomized, no longer thinking of a self or even appearing to have one. Her "disappearances" into husbandly embraces at the end are really no joke, since they mark the disappearance of the variety that gave her personality its depth and interest.

This proliferation of identity problems alone, however, without some other connection between them, would be repetitive and essentially discontinuous. The problem of the "identity of things" is so general a problem in *Our Mutual Friend* that it does not depend, as it does in *Great Expectations*, on the personal recollective intuition alone. The opening chapters develop images of people preying on other people—both the "birds of prey" like Hexam and Riderhood and the gossips of society; these images ring through the book almost endless changes on carrion, cannibal, prey, dust, disarticulation, scavengers. The dancing partner, with one eye screwed up to extinction, looks down on the heiress Miss Podsnap like a hawk on prey, as if he descried her "at the bottom of some perpendicular shaft, brought her to the surface, and ambled off with her" (I, xi, 132). The cannibal theme becomes explicit in the final scene, with Tippins's empty cleverness concerning Eugene's marriage to a "horrid female waterman."

> "Long-banished Robinson Crusoe," says the charmer, exchanging salutations, "how did you leave the Island?"
>
> "Thank you," says Lightwood, "It made no complaint of being in pain anywhere."
>
> "Say, how did you leave the savages?" asks Lady Tippins.
>
> "They were becoming civilized when I left Juan Fernandez," says Lightwood. "At least they were eating one another, which looked like it."   (IV, Chapter the Last, 773)

Not just personal coherence but the coherence of the social group is a matter of life and death in *Our Mutual Friend*, and it is a problem that not even John Harmon can solve alone.

Without the personal confirmation of Bella's affection, John Rokesmith buries John Harmon "under a whole Alpine range. . . .

The ghost should look on for a little while longer at the state of existence out of which it had departed, and then should for ever cease to haunt the scenes in which it had no place." The threat of disarticulation is explicit. "He had lapsed into the condition in which he found himself, as many a man lapses into many a condition, without perceiving the accumulative power of its sep-arate circumstances" (II, xiii-xiv, 358-59). But this private con-sensus is not enough. Bella's heart proves reliable and she marries the penniless John Rokesmith, but still John Harmon does not declare himself alive. His purely personal solution as John Rokesmith remains a separate peace.

This impasse indicates the importance to Harmon of Eugene Wrayburn's private history. Eugene finally discovers in himself that same power to live independent of circumstance and social role that John Harmon discovered at the beginning. Like Bella, Eugene repudiates Shares in favor of mutual friendship and love, and in so doing gives consent to John Harmon's view of the world, a view that has been heretofore a single, unconfirmed, ontologically insecure view. Though their separate plots meet only twice—once at the beginning when a messenger opens the "circle" of Society with word of the Harmon murder, and once at the end when Wrayburn and Harmon meet, as married men, for the first time—Eugene's personal solution confirms Harmon's and converts it from a social freak into a general possibility.

John Rokesmith is "harmonized," to invoke Dickens's pun on Harmon's name, by the corroboration and mutual friendship Eu-gene's recovery makes possible. It is a life-and-death struggle for both, despite the differences in their circumstances and vantage-points. Eugene's commitment to a "human" world, which is the same for him and Lizzie regardless of differences in social class, confirms his consent to live in common with humanity as one. The implicit agreement between Harmon and Wrayburn, made possible by the personal risks they have taken, has deeply on-tological consequences both for them and for the remains of a hierarchical society that has cluttered their paths with dead forms. John Harmon wants Bella, but he also needs Eugene; wife and

209

friend together make the world safe for John Harmon's full return to himself.

Dickens fully allows for the difficulty of establishing such a mutual friendship, both in the strain of connection between the two plots, and in the implications for a society far removed from the stream of life. The strain is evident in Eugene at the end. "Sadly wan and worn was the once gallant Eugene, and walked resting on his wife's arm, and leaning heavily upon a stick. But he was daily growing stronger and better, and it was declared by the medical attendants that he might not be much disfigured by-and-bye" (IV, xvi, 769). The strain of the consciousness in its battle against mortality becomes visible in Eugene, but it is a strain maintained by the novel from beginning to end. The fact that the two plots have so little explicit connection, despite the deep implicit similarities between them, dramatizes the fact that the saving mutual consciousness that sustains the human world exists, as it must exist, transcendently invisible, independent of immediate circumstances. The saving power of independent consciousness in John Harmon that continuously overcomes the separations among the different moments of his existence—separations acted out in various aliases—can also overcome the separations between himself and the others who can attempt, from their different positions, to meet him. The power of becoming anonymous, of being "nobody," frees Eugene, as it freed Harmon, from the limiting definitions of circumstance.

This is something other characters manage in milder ways. Boffin's virtue lies in his ability to remain the same, apart from his wildly fluctuating fortunes.[24] When Lizzie becomes too involved with contradictory commitments to her brother and to Eugene, Riah helps manage a saving "disappearance" for her. " 'I placed her,' said the old man, 'at a distance' " (III, i, 408). When

[24] Masao Miyoshi considers Boffin's ability to remain "the same," dust or no dust, in "Resolution of Identity in *Our Mutual Friend*," *Victorian Newsletter*, no. 26 (Fall 1964), 509; W. J. Harvey comments that "greed and avarice hover around the fringes of the benevolent Boffin as a possibility which gives the character unusual depth and resonance" (*Character and the Novel* [Ithaca: Cornell University Press, 1965], pp. 126-27).

she first reappears in the novel in the brief episode describing Betty Higden's death, Lizzie reappears as a voice, without embodiment or name. It is the moment of mutual consciousness most transcendent in the novel, least dependent upon material and closest to the boundaries of mortality.[25]

The lineaments of life are restless and mobile, like the elements in *Our Mutual Friend*: full of "tumults" and "disorder," but containing clues. "The voice of the falling water, like the voices of the sea and the wind, was an outer memory to a contemplative listener" (IV, 1, 596). Like the images in Lizzie Hexam's fire, the restless, shifting forms of life flicker, and a penetrating soul like Lizzie can see the past in them and tell the future. Mrs. Boffin recognizes Harmon through intuitive connection with her memory of old Harmon's face and the faces of his children. When she shuts her eyes, she sees "the old man's face, and it gets younger. The two children's faces, and they get older. A face that I don't know. And then all the faces" (I, 16, 181). Even Mrs. Lammle, capable of a similar saving intuition, learns the secret identity of Twemlow's persecutor by the same means. " 'How do you know it?' " Twemlow asks, " 'I scarcely know how I know it,' " she answers; " 'the whole train of circumstances seemed to take fire at once, and show it to me' " (III, 17, 588-90). Twemlow wants "proof" (how like a man, she says), but her intuition is a more powerful tool of discovery in a universe of shifting and potentially infinite sequences.

This demand on intuitive grasp exercises the memory, as Mrs. Lammle and Mrs. Boffin suggest. One must observe and recall in order for the train of circumstances to take fire at once and reveal their hidden form. Dickens does not neglect his readers' exercise in this regard. The style and structure of this novel challenge the reader's ordinary intuitions and force a search for the hidden affinity, the clue to form.

---

[25] U. C. Knoepflmacher remarks on the "immateriality" of the physical location in this scene (it is pure dialogue and with one anonymous persona), although he attributes this effect to Lizzie's presence rather than to the mutual consciousness of the two women (*Laughter and Despair* [Berkeley and Los Angeles: University of California Press, 1971], p. 160).

He had no net, hook, or line, and he could not be a fisherman; his boat had no cushion for a sitter, no paint, no inscription, no appliance beyond a rusty boat-hook and a coil of rope, and he could not be a waterman; his boat was too crazy and too small to take in a cargo for delivery, and he could not be a lightman or river-carrier; there was no clue to what he looked for, but he looked for something, with a most intent and searching gaze. (I, i, 1)

No name dispels the mystery of Gaffer Hexam's occupation. It is "a living" both like and not like familiar things. Such descriptions shock recognition and force attention toward renewed grasp of meaning. Another instance, perhaps the most exaggerated, is the description of Wegg's errand at Venus's shop, and exaggeration carried out in the whole Wegg-Venus subplot. Eugene's struggle for the word that will save him—not "Lizzie," which he repeats "millions of times," but "wife"—is another instance giving importance to the power of grasping the right clue, the key that gives name and form to what has remained disconnected. Ordinary categories fail, the mind reaches for the clue that will unlock meaning. " 'These things happen so oddly sometimes,' said Bella with a steady countenance, 'that there seems to be a kind of fatality in them' " (IV, xi, 707).

The turnings of plot between Volumes Three and Four demonstrate these mysteries on a larger scale. When Betty Higden flees for her life from the Good Samaritan, the narrative takes up her point of view so that she becomes a temporary mediator, but one who makes the familiar world strange. The anonymous Deputy Lock who lets her escape, for a bribe, awakens an echo when he says "I'm an honest man as gets my living by the sweat of my brow" (III, viii, 483), but there are no other material clues sufficient to identify Riderhood. It takes the reader another hundred pages to ascertain with certainty that Deputy Lock is the "same" man as Riderhood. The anonymous voice that the dying Betty Higden hears uncertainly at a distance we recognize only when the name is pronounced, "Lizzie Hexam." The fact that Lizzie and Riderhood, whom we thought we had left behind down-

212

stream, come to meet us upstream gives an impression of strangeness that the recognitions only gradually dispel.

The shift upstream, where the river wears a different aspect,
requires a new effort of attention before the continuities with
previous experiences can be sustained. The translation opens new
opportunities and new dangers, ones that are too much for the
powers of Riderhood and Headstone and almost too much for
Eugene, and we are made to feel the difficulty of sustaining the
connections and the importance to those connections of a growing community of voices that have become partially dematerialized, detached from the particulars of life in London in a way
analogous to the detachment of the characters who have exchanged London for this new setting. This new turning of the
plot feels almost like the past coming to meet us: but transformed,
anonymous, dematerialized, belonging to a mental and auditory
world separate from the ordinary indicators of the familiar physical
setting where they originated. These experiments strain the consciousness of readers trying to grasp connections and locate common denominators between the two plots and between the two
locations on the river, one in London, the other upstream.

The corrupt "Social Chorus" is gradually drowned out by a
chorus of other human and natural voices, a chorus that seems
to arise from all parts of the world in *Our Mutual Friend* and to
justify a certain optimism concerning the possibilities for mutual
awareness. Various plot intersections and mutually supportive
meetings begin to confirm the mutual relatedness of things.

These human continuities, particularly those of time and consciousness, are nowhere so apparent as they are at the moments
when time stops, their value never more evident than when they
most clearly become impossible: at moments near death (Betty
Higden's or Riderhood's); or moments after death (Gaffer Hexam's); and always at the Veneerings. All these passages, some of
them quite extended, Dickens writes in the present tense. Time
stops literally for Gaffer Hexam's death, the past tense giving way
to a eulogy in the present.

Father, was that you calling me? Father! I thought I heard
you call me twice before! Words never to be answered, those,

213

upon the earth side of the grave. The wind sweeps jeeringly over Father, whips him with the frayed ends of his dress and his jagged hair, tries to turn him where he lies stark on his back, and force his face towards the rising sun, that he may be shamed the more. A lull, and the wind is secret and prying with him; lifts and lets fall a rag; hides palpitating under another rag; runs nimbly through his hair and beard. Then, in a rush, it cruelly taunts him. Father, was that you calling me? Was it you, the voiceless and the dead? (II, 14, 164)

A chorus of voices join to lament, indistinguishable between Lizzie and the wind. The voice of the human past joins the voices of physical reality and of the narrator to address dead Father in a ritual, incantatory way. The present tense stops time, distances the event, and sums it up in bare outline. ("Why not speak, Father? soaking into this filthy ground as you lie here, is your own shape. Did you never see such a shape soaked into your boat?") The Inspector's reconstruction of the death follows, also respectful, and the present tense manifestly confirms the fact that time has ended for Gaffer.

"Now see," said Mr. Inspector, "see how it works round upon him. It's a wild tempestuous evening when this man that was," stooping to wipe some hailstones out of his hair with an end of his own drowned jacket, "—there! Now he's more like himself, though he's badly bruised,—when this man that was, rows out upon the river on his usual lay. He carries with him this coil of rope."

Mr. Inspector, as he notices aloud, still addresses Gaffer as if he were an individual with identity. " 'I still call it *him*, you see' "; but time and identity end together for Gaffer. This passage is intense and brief, ending with the dawn, with the disappearance of Eugene, and with a reversion back into the past-tense narrative.

This death, however, is more than a local disturbance to time in the novel. Readers continue to feel the shock of Hexam's death even when the novel reverts to the past tense and time begins moving again. A compensatory spin of the reel takes place immediately after this eulogy, confirming the fact that something important has happened. Before the transition is assured back to the regular pace of the past-tense narrative, time speeds up and becomes distorted in the semi-conscious mind of the exhausted witness, Mortimer Lightwood. Still speaking in the collective "we" and in fragmentary syntax, Mortimer asks the Inspector, " 'Can we get something hot to drink?' We could [the narrator continues the collective style], and we did. In a public house with a large fire. We got hot brandy and water, and it revived us wonderfully." Then the narrator resumes its anonymous distance from Mortimer, but Mortimer's confusion continues.

As Mortimer Lightwood sat before the blazing fire, conscious of drinking brandy and water then and there in his sleep, and yet at one and the same time drinking burnt sherry at the Six Jolly Fellowships, and lying under the boat on the river shore, and sitting in the boat that Riderhood rowed, and listening to the lecture recently concluded, and having to dine in the Temple with an unknown man who described himself as M.R.F. Eugene Gaffer Harmon, and said he lived at Hailstorm,—as he passed through these curious vicissitudes of fatigue and slumber, arranged upon the scale of a dozen hours to the second, he became aware of answering aloud a communication of pressing importance that had never been made to him, and then turned it into a cough on beholding Mr. Inspector. For he felt, with some natural indignation, that that functionary might otherwise suspect him of having closed his eyes, or wandered in his attention.

"Here, just before us, you see," said Mr. Inspector.

"I see," said Lightwood, with dignity.

"And had hot brandy and water too, you see," said Mr. Inspector, "and then cut off at a great rate."

"Who?" said Lightwood.

"Your friend, you know."

"I know," he replied, again with dignity.

After hearing, in a mist through which Mr. Inspector loomed vague and large, that the officer took upon himself to prepare the dead man's daughter for what had befallen in the night, and generally that he took everything upon himself, Mortimer Lightwood stumbled in his sleep to a cab-stand, called a cab, and had entered the army and committed a capital military offence and been tried by court-martial and found guilty and had arranged his affairs and been marched out to be shot, before the door banged. (Pp. 166-67.)

This exploration of altered consciousness has special relevance to the novel's deepest themes. The slower his body goes, the faster his mind, until it is difficult to decide which of these dissociated parts constitutes Mortimer. His mental continuum is complex and lucidly arranged, and yet deranged in terms of simple, chronological time. The unevenness of pace here, immediately after Gaffer's death, connects the collective minds' watch over his end with Mortimer's still living but overstretched consciousness. The rupture with the serene continuity of the past tense is powerfully felt even after the event, like an experience of grief.

The continuities between unlike things especially fascinate Dickens, particularly where they open opportunities for enlarging the arena of consciousness. Besides the obvious play on continuities between human beings and furniture (Wegg and Twemlow, for example), there are various other surprising modes of connection or disconnection that use the continuities of space or time to build paradoxes concerning mutual relationship. Turning the corner, for example, becomes a disturbing moment of connection or disconnection that places special demands on awareness. The Lammles turn the corner and disappear almost as if from one state of existence. "In turning the street corner they might have turned out of this world, for anything Mr. and Mrs. Boffin ever saw of them to the contrary" (IV, iii, 616). Another interesting corner brings John Harmon suddenly to light. The more his existence as John Rokesmith has developed into love, marriage, and fatherhood, the more he has postponed full self-revelation and the farther he seems to drift from the need to manage it. He has successfully hidden his true identity by avoiding, among others, Mortimer Lightwood; but out walking one day with Mrs. Rokesmith chatting about baby Rokesmith everything changes. "They turned the corner and met Mr. Lightwood" (IV, xii, 717). The recognition unearths Rokesmith's other aliases and makes a whole train of circumstances take fire together. The tension and distortion in the succeeding episodes of self-revelation, especially in the scene where Harmon silently presents himself to the real murderers of the real George Radfoot, can be explained, I think, like Lightwood's altered state of consciousness after Gaffer's death, in terms of the extra stress associated with this revelation.

The other margin of consciousness where the novel lapses into the present tense appears in all the chapters dealing with the Veneerings; only unlike Gaffer's death, which was a real death and worth pity, these dead are still walking about and the tone differs considerably from that of his eulogy.[26] As their name suggests, what the Veneerings and company lack most noticeably is depth; and that lack, as we might expect in a novel so devoted to the premises of realism, appears most noticeably in their lack of a past.

Mr. and Mrs. Veneering were bran-new people in a bran-new house in a bran-new quarter of London. Everything about the

[26] The present-tense chapters punctuate the novel in important places. Each of the four volumes ends with a present-tense chapter (three of them about the Veneerings). Volume I ends in "A Dismal Swamp" with a chapter about various fortune-hunters collecting around the newly rich Boffins; Volume II ends with "An Anniversary Occasion" on which the Lammles celebrate their returns; Volume III ends with "A Social Chorus" about Lammle's bankruptcy; and Volume IV ends the novel with the same "Social Chorus." While there are one or two extended passages of present-tense narration, such as the one describing Gaffer's death, the present tense belongs mainly to nine separate chapters, six of them about Veneerings. All concern various villains, and their frequency decreases as the novel progresses toward resolution, reunion, marriage, and projects for the future.

VOL. I: Chapters 2, 7, 10, 17
VOL. II: Chapters 3, part of 14, 16
VOL. III: Chapters 3, 17
VOL. IV: Chapter 17.

> Veneerings was spick and span new. All their furniture was
> new, all their friends were new, all their servants were new,
> their plate was new . . . and if they had set up a great-grand-
> father, he would have come home in matting from the Pan-
> technicon, without a scratch upon him, French-polished to
> the crown of his head. (I, ii, 6)

All things at the Veneerings are "in a state of high varnish and
polish." They cultivate men like Podsnap, who has the "fatal
freshness" on him (p. 8). The past of their dear friends, the
Lammles, is invented and completely false. Their common element is not time and human mortality, but "shares." "Have no
antecedents, no established character, no cultivation, no ideas,
no manners; have Shares. . . . Where does he come from? Shares.
Where is he going to? Shares. What are his tastes? Shares. Has
he any principles? Shares" (p. 108; I, x). All time, all cause, all
purpose past and future reduced to a single common standard.
But, unlike time and consciousness, this medium and its votives
have a tendency to fade, as Mr. and Mrs. Lammle learn after
their Shares have faded away and they find their dear friends have
exhibited the same tendency. All is flat, insubstantial, reflecting
surface. In this environment only the living gestures are the fakes.
Sophronia and Alfred even have fake pasts, and the husband
values the wife's genuine expressions of affection to Georgiana
only because he takes them to be pretense.

The whole machinery of continuity supported by the past-tense
narration is brought to a grinding halt in the nine chapters about
Veneerings, reinforcing the message that they connect with no
past, no future, no meaning, no vital circulation of any kind.

> Eugene (who would seem to be in a gloomy state of sugges-
> tiveness) suggests, "Suppose you have no means and live be-
> yond them?"
> This is too insolvent a state of things for the Father to
> entertain. It is too insolvent a state of things for any one with
> any self-respect to entertain, and is universally scouted. But it
> is so amazing how any people can have come to a total smash,
> that everybody feels bound to account for it specially. One of

the Fathers says, "Gaming table." Another of the Fathers says, "Speculated without knowing that speculation is a science." Boots says, "Horses." Lady Tippins says to her fan, "Two es-tablishments." . . .

Eugene, leaning back in his chair, is observing Mr. Podsnap with an irreverent face, and may be about to offer a new suggestion, when the Analytical is beheld in collision with the Coachman; the Coachman manifesting a purpose of coming at the company with a silver salver, as though intent upon making a collection for his wife and family; the Analytical cutting him off at the sideboard. The superior stateliness, if not the superior generalship, of the Analytical, prevails over a man who is as nothing off the box; and the Coachman, yielding up his salver, retires defeated.

Then the Analytical, perusing a scrap of paper lying on the salver, with the air of a literary Censor, adjusts it, takes his time about going to the table with it, and presents it to Mr. Eugene Wrayburn. Whereupon the pleasant Tippins says aloud, "The Lord Chancellor has resigned!"   (III, 17, 593-94)

Clever, elliptical, empty. Discontinuity prevails at Veneerings. A simple gesture of delivering a note elaborates beyond recog-nition; repetitive speeches suggest a futility worthy of Bradley Headstone and twice as respectable; attention skips fashionably around; the retainer collides with the coachman: in all, a total achievement of collective interference. What is manifestly im-possible here is collective attention to a single point. Such scenes recall Earle Davis's remark that *Our Mutual Friend* was Dickens's *Inferno*.[27]

The emblematic side of *Our Mutual Friend* that is expressed in the Veneerings and all their crew appears as well in the fantastic characters like Jenny Wren, Mr. Riah, Wegg, and Venus. Al-though they are more integrated than the Veneerings into the past-tense narrative and are not turned into the present tense,

---

[27] See Earle Davis's valuable study, *The Flint and the Flame: The Artistry of Charles Dickens* (Columbia, Missouri: University of Missouri Press, 1963), pp. 281-82.

nevertheless, in their iterative aspect—their tendency to do one thing over again like a record with the needle stuck in one groove—*they* are forms of the present tense. They arrest development, repeating the same aspect rather than advancing from one to another. This arrest of the series is used to emphasize the importance of the serial to the connections so manifestly broken in society. In fact, these aggressively self-containing characters demonstrate especially clearly the need for the overview steadily present in the narrator.

Our Mutual Friend celebrates the anonymous power of a "nobody" in ways beyond those in *Bleak House* or *Little Dorrit*, which tend to minimize that power. The Secretary manages his estate in ways that resemble the anonymous activity of past-tense narrators; when he has resumed his place among the others, the responsibility for maintaining a human identity in things falls upon the powers of mutual friendship. In *Little Dorrit* and in *Great Expectations* the saving mediations take place apart from society, in personal and private life. In *Our Mutual Friend* various characters, like Harmon, Wrayburn, the Boffins, Lizzie, provide mediations that were formerly often left to the narrator or to the reader alone. By comparison with these earlier novels, the invisible community of consciousness here appears triumphant.

In most of Dickens that community remains grounded in particular embodiments, dependent upon its props. Dickens's readers are always aware how much consciousness there is in *things* and how great is their power to command. The ideal of consciousness as electric messages flashing between points in space and time remains an ideal even in the last novel. Much of the reader's effort there, as in Dickens's previous novels, is to free consciousness from that grounding—an enterprise important to the peculiar pleasure of reading his work. The common power is dispersed in the common medium and the act of recovery is an all-or-nothing proposition. The integrated personal identity of John Harmon depends upon a promise that Eugene Wrayburn's achievement finally confirms: the promise of mutual consciousness and mutual understanding that supports the world. Even more than Austen's last novel Dickens's portrays the strain of such an enterprise as well as the new importance it gives to romantic love and marriage as ontological confirmation. The private consent of Harmon and Wrayburn objectifies a world of hope held out against the dark alternatives. In *Our Mutual Friend* Harmon's consciousness, like the narrator's and readers' seeking the circuit of communication, most often finds itself grounded in this or that particular case. Fascinated absorption at intermediate stages of integration threatens the final recovery because the circuit of communion runs through the entire social world (dead spots like Veneerings excepted). Harmon's case is a recognition of the patience, and the strength of memory and will, required for the individual to sustain a continuing consciousness apart from particular claims. The threat of discontinuity in Dickens suggests the pressing need for an overview that can remain independent of particular cases. That seems an almost impossible goal because of his insistent holism. Unlike George Eliot, who is content to situate consciousness in the middle of the range of relevancies, Dickens attempts to situate the mind on the defining edge of an entire world, at the vanishing-points of love and death.

CHAPTER SEVEN

George Eliot's
Invisible Community

G eorge Eliot's invisible human community
is more provisional than Dickens's social whole and it cannot be
captured by means of metaphors like circumlocution or a mega-
losaurus in the mud. Her open-ended networks of influence cannot be grasped as a whole because they are dependent upon
individuals and therefore are constantly changing. This community need not be grasped as a whole, however, because it is
securely rooted in historical traditions. "Our sentiments may be
called organised traditions; and a large part of our actions gather
all their justification, all their attraction and aroma, from the
memory of the lives lived, of the actions done, before we were
born."[1] In focusing on the intimacy between individual consciousness and the traditions that sustain it, George Eliot exploits
the narrator's powers deliberately and fully. She employs two
complementary voices: a personalized voice familiar to her readers
for its epigrammatical wit, and a narrator that acts as nobody,
supervising the transmissions backwards and forwards between
past and present. In this general continuum, individual consciousness creates eddies and even tides in the stream of historical
continuity. Her novels focus on the transmissions from moment
to moment and from mind to mind because these points of contact

[1] "The Influence of Rationalism" (1865), in Thomas Pinney, ed., *Essays of
George Eliot* (New York: Columbia University Press, 1963), p. 409.

222

are where historical continuities, and the realistic agreements that support them, are made or broken.

In George Eliot's novels the institutions of a culture, its language, and its unspoken codes provide a matrix for individual consciousness, a system within which lies its only possibility of definition and outside of which is only inhuman darkness. One suggestive moment in her third novel, *Romola*, has special emblematic value for my general argument in this chapter and will serve as a preliminary statement of its central themes. *Romola* is George Eliot's tribute to the Renaissance and her scholar Baldassare Calvo is a tribute to the powers of that original period, particularly to the new learning and to an entire society's recovery of the past. The poignance of this recovery appears most forcefully at the moment Baldassare recovers his memory after long and crippling hardship. Staring helplessly at the pages of Pausanias's history, he first sees only unintelligible black marks, enigmatic as his own half-forgotten self and half-remembered past. But the shock of confrontation with his stepson awakens his sense at one stroke. The black marks become magical. "An hour or two ago he had been looking hopelessly at that page, and it had suggested no more meaning to him than if the letters had been black weather-marks on a wall; but at this moment they were once more the magic signs that conjure up a world." As the amnesia disappears, Baldassare assumes once more "that sense of mental empire" that tells him who he is and enables him to tell others.

> He was once more a man who knew cities, whose sense of vision was instructed with large experience, and who felt the keen delight of holding all things in the grasp of language. Names! Images! — his mind rushed through its wealth without pausing, like one who enters on a great inheritance. . . . All came back to him: the recognition of the page in Pausanias, the crowding resurgence of facts and names, the sudden wide prospect which had given him such a moment as that of the Maenad in the glorious amaze of her morning waking on the mountain top.

223

Disconnected from a syntax, the marks are unintelligible, like separate events that nevertheless make up a single history or like the sequentially perceived cases of a single form in realism. Recollection transforms meaningless marks into magical signs that conjure up a common world and with it a personal identity. He recovers simultaneously self-consciousness and the past, and with them the language that constitutes his "wealth."[2] His human power is at root a power to convert randomness into meaning. The fact of the illegible book underscores the magic of the legible one, a magic belonging to the rationalizing power itself. That magic, embedded in tradition and language, makes available to Baldassare the generative potential of a collective code; without access to that code his individual mind slips close to inhumanity.

Of the human experience presented by George Eliot here, two features have general importance in her work: first the intimacy between consciousness and time; second, the rootedness of both in particular expressions. George Eliot stresses that the basis for human connectedness is recognizing difference; difference recognized is difference overcome in her social scheme. In showing how difference is a basis for connection and how time functions in creating difference, George Eliot begins with a norm of embodied consciousness that must be understood if her complex treatment of time is to be fully apparent. For George Eliot, consciousness is inseparable from the objects in human experience. She shows a keen awareness of that reversible premise of realism discussed in Chapter Three, the premise that consciousness of an objective world is necessarily consciousness of human subjectivity because what is objective is the collective result of human agreements. These agreements are accessible through the particular forms, definitions, and other intentional objects that culture has produced. These efforts at incarnation are what create those important differences upon which human fellowship depends, so it

[2] *Romola*, Everyman edition (New York: E. P. Dutton, 1907), ch. 38, pp. 326-28. All subsequent references will be to this edition and will be included parenthetically in the text. Since the Clarendon edition of George Eliot's novels is not yet available for most of the works, I am generally using easily available texts.

is important to begin by giving a brief account of how George Eliot conceives the links between consciousness and objects.

Ideas and Things

The objects with which human beings must contend are intentional objects: not inert objects like rocks and stones and trees but ones informed by consciousness. "All actions men put a bit of thought into are ideas—say, sowing seed, or making a canoe, or baking clay; and such ideas as these work themselves into life and go on growing with it."[3] The complexity of coping with this intentional reality becomes evident when we consider that such objects include not just a loaf of bread but also a parliament, a prayer book, or that most living of cultural embodiments, a personality. The Feuerbachian notion of personality as form appears everywhere in the novels,[4] most explicitly in *Middlemarch* where Dorothea and Will are discussing poetry. Dodo has had the experience Will describes as poetic, but she is sure she could never produce a poem. "You *are* a poem," is the well-known reply.[5]

It is the presence of intentional objects, the presence of ideas, that distinguishes culture from nature in George Eliot's view. She makes a rigorous distinction between nature and culture. There is no message of love written in the heavens, as Romola and other characters discover, but only the indecipherable expanses of a material universe. Nature may be orderly or not; but ethically it is neutral. No idea informs it, except those that human beings project there. Natural objects do become colored by consciousness, so powerful is its creative capacity, but George Eliot is always clear that the meanings are projected on nature, not found there.

[3] *Daniel Deronda*, ed. Barbara Hardy (Harmondsworth: Penguin Books, 1967), p. 583. All subsequent references will be to this edition and will be included parenthetically in the text.

[4] Ludwig Feuerbach, *The Essence of Christianity*, trans. Mary Ann Evans (George Eliot) (New York: Harper and Row, 1957), p. 147.

[5] *Middlemarch*, ed. Gordon S. Haight, Riverside edition (Boston: Houghton Mifflin, 1956), p. 166. All subsequent references will be to this edition and will be included parenthetically in the text.

Her treatment of nature in *Adam Bede*, for example, shows a marked change as the human community undergoes its crisis. When Hetty passes from the world of light and speech into what is nearly a grave, she shakes the confidence of an entire community. Her objectless wandering in a dark nature outside Hayslope, her beauty gone with the security of Hall Farm, is a far cry from the opening passages in Adam's workshop filled with sunlight and his song of praise, or from the distinct and serene objects of Hall Farm before the fall. Humanity gives meaning to nature, not the other way around. Characters like Stephen Guest, who argue for a course of action because "it is natural," badly misunderstand human circumstances.

By separating nature and culture George Eliot humanizes all consciousness, giving it no recourse beyond the human. The radicalism of George Eliot's distinction has been insufficiently appreciated. By confining consciousness to the human realm, she separates nature and culture and, at the same time, joins ideas and things. The "severing *ideas* from *things*" she says, summarizing an argument she is reviewing,

> is the fundamental error of philosophy, and, from Parmenides downwards, has issued in nothing but the bewilderment of the human intellect. Kant's classification of Infinity and Universality as ideas *à priori*, and of Space and Time as purely subjective forms of the intelligence, is a further elaboration of this fundamental error. These abstract terms on which speculation has built its huge fabrics are simply the *x* and *y* by which we mark the boundary of our knowledge; they have no value except in connexion with the concrete. The abstract is derived from the concrete: what, then, can we expect from a philosophy the essence of which is the derivation of the concrete from the abstract?

To reunite ideas and things within the realm of culture means a new conception of relations between abstractions and concretes, one that goes against the drift of Western philosophy from Parmenides to Kant.[6]

[6] "The Future of German Philosophy" (1855), *Essays*, pp. 150-53.

226

Thus the objects of nature differ from those of culture, and so the scientist's object differs from the artist's. The natural object is severed from ideas where the cultural object is not. The material of science and culture resemble each other in that they contain regularities, not randomness, and hence a basis for law. But the presence of laws does not mean the presence of the same law. Science and art treat very different material, and this difference informs all the analogies between them that George Eliot employs to convey her idea of cultural life. The conception of "universal regular sequence," growing out of the patience and the silencing of preconceptions urged on the mind by physical science, substitutes for caprice and recommends itself as a model for culture; in both regularity substitutes for the "miraculous." But this does not mean that culture is the same as nature, or subject to the same laws.[7]

The inseparability of ideas and things within the cultural realm means that no systematic approach to culture is adequate. Its law is irreducibly diverse instead of single. In the Christian view both men and nature are part of a single reality informed by a single, divine law; in the naturalistic view man is inseparably part of nature and subject to its law. But in George Eliot's view the diverse objects of culture are irreducible to any absolute. They do not reveal transcendent laws, they *are* laws in themselves. Every object, from a personality to the prayer book and parliament, is a law in her sense of the word: an irreducible, determinate condition. Because these are intentional objects, they cannot be reduced to a single system. There are as many cultural laws as there are particular, cultural incarnations. Human knowledge is a reduction derived from a series of cases, but such knowledge cannot be grasped whole; it is mutable, fluid, often contradictory. No aerial perspective exists from which to resolve these laws once and for all into a single set, operating like divine or natural law beyond the particulars of human culture and controlling them. Control is dispersed among members of the human community who, by their choices taken collectively, constitute whatever

[7] "The Influence of Rationalism," *Essays*, p. 413, and "The Progress of the Intellect" (1851), *Essays*, p. 31.

reality exists. Dorothea is a poem; that is, she has made a syntax of her own out of the chance confusions of her surroundings, out of those laws of her existence that come in the form of rural England, books, Mr. Brooke, and the rest; and she in turn becomes a law influencing the lives of others. Like anything else people put a little thought into, personality is a thing inseparable from ideas.

Because they are inseparable from particulars, then, cultural laws, as distinct from natural laws, are irreducibly diverse. When George Eliot speaks of moral laws as "external Reason" she refers neither to a transcendent Reasoner nor to some transcendental collective mind abstracted from particulars. "External Reason" is rather the sum of particulars arising from diverse causes. Institutions and events, the increase of population and the behavior of the colonies, railways, electricity, paintings, personalities, and the simplest artifacts are all "part of the external Reason to which internal silliness has inevitably to accommodate itself." Perhaps the only accurate way to speak of moral law in the singular is to speak of the law of facticity, always recognizing that for George Eliot a fact is an incarnation.[8]

[8] "The Influence of Rationalism," *Essays*, p. 402. For a fuller discussion of these issues see Elizabeth Ermarth, "Incarnations: George Eliot's Conception of 'Undeviating Law,' " *Nineteenth-Century Fiction*, 29, no. 3 (December 1974), 273-86. For discussions of the importance of subjectivity to Eliot's realism see Rosemary Ashton, "The Intellectual Medium of Middlemarch," *Review of English Studies*, n.s., 30, no. 118 (May 1979), 154-68; Ian Adam, "The Structure of Realisms," *Nineteenth-Century Fiction*, 30, no. 2 (September 1975), 127-49; Edward Hurley, "Piero di Cosimo: An Alternate Analogy for George Eliot's Realism," Victorian Newsletter, no. 31 (Spring 1967), 54-56; and Darrel Mansell, "Ruskin and George Eliot's Realism," *Criticism*, 7, no. 3 (Summer 1965), 203-16 (this article also contains a good summary of the criticism on the subject to 1965). An interesting if ultimately unconvincing counterview to Mansell is Michael Y. Mason, "Middlemarch and Science: Problems of Life and Mind," *Review of English Studies*, n.s. 22, no. 86 (May 1971), 151-69. George Levine emphasizes the continuum that mind establishes in the otherwise "discontinuous" cosmos of experience in "George Eliot's Hypothesis of Reality, *Nineteenth-Century Fiction*, 35, no. 1 (June 1980), 1-28. Norman Feltes treats George Eliot's move toward uniting the dissociated sensibility in "George Eliot and the Unified Sensibility,"

This emphasis on incarnate consciousness has profound con-sequences for George Eliot's treatment of consensus. Her refusal to depart from the particular and limited manifestations of con-sciousness is close to Feuerbach's view of multiplicity as the "es-sence" of culture. In George Eliot's own translation: "Doubtless the essence of man is *one*, but this essence is infinite; its real existence is therefore an infinite, reciprocally compensating va-riety, which reveals the riches of this essence. Unity in essence is multiplicity in existence."[9] In other words, the unity of culture is the summation of everything that is. This is the law or essence revealed at last to Gwendolen Harleth when she finally becomes "dislodged from her supremacy in her own world" and discovers the vast array of determinate conditions that she had formerly ignored and that now inspire her with a "dreadful presentiment of mountainous travel" (*Deronda*, pp. 974-76). She is facing for the first time both her freedom to choose a particular course and the laws of her existence—those particular incarnations of human effort such as her ill-developed talent, her family's poverty, her strength of will, not to mention Zionism, that are "inevitable" in that they are actual and no magic can dismiss them. George Eliot is always harsh on the propensity to avoid the hard, un-accommodating actual: in characters like Deronda who become squeamish when ideas press upon them "as something warmly incarnate" (*Deronda*, pp. 113-14); in the poet Young's flight into bloodless abstractions; in Hetty's narcotic daydreams or Janet Dempster's alcoholic stupors. All these efforts at forgetfulness not

---

PMLA, 79 (March 1964), 130-36. Critics who find contradiction between the claims of realism and the presence of mind in George Eliot's work are Calvin Bedient, *Architects of the Self* (Berkeley: University of California Press, 1972); U. C. Knoepflmacher, *George Eliot's Early Novels* (Berkeley: University of California Press, 1968); and Bernard Paris, *Experiments in Life* (Detroit: Wayne State University Press, 1965). Missing George Eliot's acceptance of the abstract nature of convention has generated confusion about morality in her works. What is antithetical is not, as Bernard Paris suggests, realism *vs* moralism (*Experiments*, pp. 1-3), but both realism and moralism *vs* "the darkness of moral insensibility and incapacity," as Reva Stump argues in *Movement and Vision in George Eliot's Novels* (Seattle: University of Washington Press, 1959), p. 8.

[9] *Essence*, p. 158.

only cripple the individual consciousness by isolating it from its chief support but also create lesions in the human "essence" by refusing support to the collective enterprise.

It is precisely because of the self-reflexive nature of consciousness that incarnations take on such importance. If it is true that even "the most active perception gives us rather a reflex of what we think and feel, than the real sum of objects before us," then we are saved from solipsism by the inevitably social nature of consciousness, by the fact that even our sentiments are organized traditions and take their definition from common formulations.[10] The redemption from solipsism and its solitude lies with the entire human complex—its history, its languages, its traditions—but not the human complex as a whole because this abstraction is unperceivable. The otherness it represents becomes available through individuals and the other particular artifacts of culture. Within the realm of culture this otherness is infinite and self-sustaining. Outside it, nature offers no objectification except that of conceptual darkness and material death.

Difference and Form

The unsystematic diversity of culture baffles attempts to see it steadily and see it whole. Its nature cannot be defined because its limit cannot be reached by human powers, and there are no others. One must concentrate on a limited range of relevancies where particular incarnations take on considerable value because they are the means for establishing and maintaining mutual understandings. George Eliot stresses the importance of making or doing "not anything in general, but something in particular" (*Middlemarch*, p. 62) because the particular incarnation is what literally makes a difference: it creates a boundary, a definition, a determinate condition; it externalizes reason. Negotiating the boundaries between "differenced" things—between one mind and another or between one moment and the next—becomes the central problem in her fiction. These negotiations resemble the

[10] "Three Months in Weimar" (1855), *Essays*, p. 89.

form-giving effort of the artist and in fact, because of the intimacy between ideas and things, every human construction can be considered artistic. In her "Notes on Form in Art" she describes the importance of difference to creating form. "Form is unlikeness," and, consistent with this meaning, "every difference is form." This has obvious relevance to the minute articulations making up her own large books, but for the moment it is enough to linger over her descriptions of form for their relevance to problems of consensus and mutual consciousness. "Every difference is form"— that is, the beginning of connection. "Even taken in its derivative meaning of outline, what is form but the limit of that difference by which we discriminate one object from another?—a limit determined partly by the intrinsic relations or composition of the object, & partly by the extrinsic action of other bodies upon it." Thus form, as an element of human experience, "must begin with the perception of separateness." What is not distinct cannot be joined together. Perceiving the limit between separate things is the basis for establishing identity in George Eliot. The principle of separation is thus the first principle of connectedness.[11]

This fundamental perception of difference belongs to a rhythmic process of differentiation and combination by which particular incarnations become linked with others as parts of larger incarnations; different qualities or functions make up one individual, who in turn makes up a part of a community. The model is "the most varied group of relations bound together in a wholeness which again has the most varied relations with all other phenomena" ("Notes on Form in Art"). The repetitive pattern is part of a rhythmic persistence that selects, binding together into

---

[11] "Notes on Form in Art" (1868), *Essays*, pp. 432-36. In this essay she uses the term "consensus" for the homeostatic relations between functions of a system, although the organic analogy invoked here must be recognized as only a metaphor: "The word consensus expresses the fact that in a complex organism by which no part can suffer increase and diminution without a participation of all other parts in the effect produced & a consequent modification of the organism as a whole." The metaphor of an organism, while it finally is inadequate to the headless and footless networks of influence making up society in her novels, does suggest the intimate relation between individual parts and the system of relationships in which they have their function and definition.

231

common likeness and mutual dependence elements from a diversified field of conditions. Even with this abstract statement, it is possible to see how this process of differentiation and combination, in increasing complexity, suggests the way Eliot's narrative develops, alternating between repetition and diversification, likeness and difference. Her narrator presides over differences between individual minds and between separate events so as to call attention to the transitions between them and to the differences that make those transitions possible.

Before turning to her management of narrative perspective, however, I want to consider how her characters deal with difference. In her novels the inability to deal with difference is widespread, and it is a symptom of moral disorder because it preserves stasis. To recognize a boundary is to discover the need for mediation. With nothing to select from, there is only uniformity of the sort practiced by characters like the Rev. Stelling in *The Mill on the Floss*, who teaches his pupils "the right way—indeed, he knew no other" (II, i), or the purveyors of "rural opinion" in *Middlemarch*: "sane people did what their neighbors did, so that if any lunatics were at large, one might know and avoid them" (p. 7). As she says in "Notes on Form in Art," the "fundamental discrimination" of difference gives birth "in necessary antithesis [to] the sense of wholeness or unbroken connexion in space & time." This fundamental discrimination is a response to conditions involving a clear perception of an other (the "altro" of altruism). The difference between self and other is what defines both; they exist in mutual reciprocity. In any case, there can be no sympathy and no clear personal integrity either, without clear perception of fundamental differences. This is a lesson that most of her characters need to learn. The mutual acknowledgment of difference means that "every limit is a beginning as well as an ending." Thus begins the ending of *Middlemarch*, with a statement that applies not only to the form of that novel but also to the idea of social life it embodies.

This perception of difference is the key to sympathy, a much misunderstood term in George Eliot that does not imply giving up the self. Her novels are a good place to learn how extensively the very idea of self depends upon the idea of others present in the same social medium. Other-denying egoism is familiar enough to George Eliot's readers and requires no further discussion here; but self-denying altruism deserves some special attention. Dinah Morris's "total absence of self-consciousness" as a preacher, for example, extends unfortunately into her private life. "I seem to have no room in my soul for wants and fears of my own" she tells a suitor.[12] Her project of self-denial accounts in large measure for the impersonal inflections of her speech and for the woodenness of even her best behavior. For example, when she visits Hetty in the adjacent bedroom, Dinah does not grasp the difference between Hetty's actual state of mind and the forlorn lamb she envisions. Dinah is good at saying "we" to her brothers and sisters, but not very good at saying "I." This kind of self-denial runs through the novels, always with the same effect. Maggie Tulliver's produces a fatal weakness.[13] Daniel Deronda suffers from "a too reflective and discursive sympathy" that results from the "habit of seeing things as they probably appeared to others" and only entails "meditative numbness" (*Deronda*, pp. 414-15). Feeling "no influence that would justify partiality," he roams his social rounds like a "disembodied spirit." Altruism is bootless without ego, just like egoism without a sense of the other. Balancing the two is a high and difficult achievement, as Dorothea must learn and as Farebrother knows.

Dorothea is well known for her "fanaticism of sympathy." As Celia complains, she likes "giving up"; and like Dinah Morris she has an unpleasant habit of saying "we." "If we had lost our own chief good," she intones to Ladislaw, in pale resemblance to the narrator, "other people's good would remain, and that is worth trying for. Some can be happy" (*Middlemarch*, p. 593). This is all very well, preferable perhaps to the errors of egoism, but hardly consoling to a would-be lover, one from whom she is

[12] *Adam Bede*, ed. John Paterson, Riverside edition (Boston: Houghton Mifflin, 1968), ch. 3, p. 32. All subsequent references will be to this edition and will be included parenthetically in the text.

[13] See Elizabeth Ermarth, "Maggie Tulliver's 'Long Suicide,' " *Studies in English Literature*, 14, no. 4 (Fall 1974), 587-601.

about to part needlessly for the last time. She has already done this once before, and even then she knew that the "world of reasons" keeping them apart were false reasons. Dorothea at her most dreadful is Dorothea leaving Ladislaw in the dust, acting on a sense of duty that can only seem perverse. Under the circumstances, Ladislaw's reticence toward her is understandable (it is, after all, her money that stands between them) but her reticence seems an exaggerated withdrawal, a refusal to act in her own interest.

Dorothea's crucial lesson in the novel necessarily involves Rosamond and Lydgate because it is only through her jealousy of another woman that Dorothea learns the force of her own claims. In her night of crisis it is *her* anger and *her* pain she feels. Once she has put herself into the picture, she then can perform in a meaningful way the shift of perspective that acknowledges difference. "But why always Dorothea" is something Dorothea finally learns how to say meaningfully, not by relinquishing personal claims but by acknowledging them. "Was she alone in that scene? Was it her event only?" (p. 577) is a most meaningful question when Dorothea has something at stake.

When she returns to Rosamond, her language—faltering from "we" to "I"—registers the difference between her present and her former way of proceeding. Talking to Rosamond is not so easy as planning cottages. In this conversation she joins herself, so to speak, in the scene from which she has kept personally aloof.

> "Marriage is so unlike everything else. There is something even awful in the nearness it brings. Even if we loved someone else better than—than those we were married to, it would be no use"—poor Dorothea, in her palpitating anxiety, could only seize her language brokenly—"I mean, marriage drinks up all our power of giving. . . . And we are weak—I am weak—"
>
> The waves of her own sorrow, from out of which she was struggling to save another, rushed over Dorothea with conquering force.   (Pp. 583-84.)

Caught by the rhythm of her own emotion—her memory of marriage, her love for Ladislaw, her new sense of shame in having

234

loved him unawares, her jealousy—Dorothea lapses from a collective to a personal voice. The previous long night has taught her that perspective is not privilege and that she cannot escape to the position of "mere spectator" (p. 578).

Farebrother is the best example of a developed altruist, especially in the chapter where he goes to warn Fred against habits that are costing him Mary Garth's affection. Mr. Farebrother has already helped Fred in this way once before, and since he, too, loves Mary this gesture can seem sentimental. But far from giving up his own wishes for the sake of another's—a form of subjection that is the farthest thing from his or from George Eliot's mind—he acts precisely in his own self-interest.

> My prompting was to look and see you take the wrong turning, wear out Garth's patience, and lose the best opportunity of your life. . . . I have said to myself, "If there is a likelihood of that youngster doing himself harm, why should you interfere? Aren't you worth as much as he is, and don't your sixteen years over and above his, in which you have gone rather hungry, give you more right to satisfaction than he has? If there's a chance of his going to the dogs, let him—perhaps you could nohow hinder it—and do you take the benefit." . . . But I had once meant better than that, and I am come back to my old intention. I thought that I could hardly *secure myself* in it better, Fred, than by telling you just what had gone on in me.
> (Pp. 494-95.)

By waiting, keeping his knowledge to himself, and profiting from Fred's ruin, he has an opportunity to act as Bulstrode did with Mrs. Dunkirk's lost daughter. But Bulstrode's case demonstrates the dangers: how one inaction begets a whole series of more deliberate lies. Initially no action is performed yet the psychological state shifts, and eventually Bulstrode is beyond his own control. Farebrother, by acknowledging the difference within himself between one motive and another, acts to secure himself, *not* to eclipse himself for Fred's sake. As Farebrother's case makes clear, altruism begins at home in the mind's own divisions. By recognizing the presence in himself of two distinct motives, Fare-

235

brother is able to keep control of himself, literally to maintain his identity.

Bulstrode, with whom he is so pointedly compared in Book Seven, fares differently. Faced with alternative courses of silence or confession he tries to blur the difference between them, and that lie is the "moment of transition" into "two distinct lives" (p. 451). He has not one but several opportunities to secure himself (as Farebrother calls it), and each failure reinforces the split he refuses to acknowledge. This evasiveness characterizes some of George Eliot's most brilliant psychological portraits. Lydgate faces such moments of decision, so do Arthur Donnithorne and Tito Melema. It is careers like theirs that Farebrother rejects, because by confessing he throws away the means to act against himself. "A man vows," says the narrator of Bulstrode, "and yet will not cast away the means of breaking his vow. Is it that he distinctly means to break it? Not at all; but the desires which tend to break it are at work in him dimly, and make their way into his imagination, and relax his muscles in the very moments when he is telling himself over again the reasons for his vow" (p. 519). Farebrother secures himself by throwing away the means to undermine himself.

Confession has importance in George Eliot's work because it is a way of confirming a limit or even of creating one by giving particular statement to a consciousness that has remained general. It means accepting a place, relinquishing the pride of consciousness that remains potentially superior to all limitations. Confession confirms a mutual understanding by confirming a separation. Arthur Donnithorne, when he comes to the "brink of confession" and then shrinks away from the contact that would secure him, misses his chance to be something in particular. "The opportunity was gone. While Arthur was hesitating, the rope to which he might have clung had drifted away—he must trust now to his own swimming" (*Bede*, pp. 175-77). The language of this passage clarifies the ontological importance of such moments.

George Eliot's work suggests constantly the resemblance between these transactions within a single mind and those more dramatic transactions between individuals and groups that make or break consensus. Eliot's emphasis on particular incarnations of consciousness and on the precise differences between one mind and another means that her narrative focuses attention on the boundaries and the points of transition between one mind and another, between one event and another. She deliberately focuses on the crucial connections where consensus is made or broken. These transitions include not only those adjustments of sympathy between characters but also the formal transitions her novels force readers to undertake. In both, the achievement of consensus is a strenuous affair involving heroic mediations of consciousness. Distance is always provisional and difficult to maintain; time is less a categorical imperative than a Feuerbachian "essence," expressed and sustained only by the multiplicity of awarenesses that constitute it.

In the constellation of minds composing her narrative medium, George Eliot's narrator is a protean figure. As an intermittently personalized voice, part of the rhythmic element of her novels, the narrator inches toward personification; this presence, one who has a scientific friend, a limited range, and selective attention, demonstrates the incarnate nature of consciousness and its intimacy with the particular manifestation. As Nobody, the narrator is a kind of generalized historical awareness hardly distinguishable from our own, a power of transition between minds and moments, an implied awareness that makes the realistic series possible. It is a medium that includes the personalized narrative voice with other voices in a continuum of minds and voices that even extends beyond characters into the metaphors and tempo of the novels. Thus George Eliot's narrator shuttles between extremes of personalization and abstraction: now like Velasquez's second self, getting into his own picture; now generalized, a power of abstraction and of connection that belongs to a consensus of individual perceivers. From her earliest published efforts at fiction it is clear that George Eliot intended to focus her readers' attention not on character only, nor on the "vulgar coercion of conventional plot," but on the "medium" of presentation.[14]

[14] "Leaves from a Notebook," *Essays*, p. 446. My discussion here goes beyond

The management of narrative voices conveys the difference between minds at the same time as it conveys the sense of common awareness that depends upon those differences. Her novels all begin with a distinct, personalized narrative voice that dissolves into others during a slow shifting process, almost as if an orchestra were being tuned one instrument at a time. *Adam Bede* begins,

> With a single drop of ink for a mirror, the Egyptian sorcerer undertakes to reveal to any chance comer far-reaching visions of the past. This is what I undertake to do for you, reader. With this drop of ink at the end of my pen, I will show you the roomy workshop of Mr. Jonathan Burge, carpenter and builder, in the village of Hayslope, as it appeared on the eighteenth of June, in the year of our Lord 1799.

This distinctly personal voice introduces a past moment and then immediately retires behind a scene of dramatic roundness and distinct, serene detail, a scene where, because we have no knowledge of the particular context, we cannot identify the characters or interpret their actions. The narrative then shifts from an "elderly horseman" who watches Adam walking home, to Mr. Casson watching the elderly horseman approach Donnithorne Arms, back to the horseman as he rides away to hear Dinah speak, then to the narrator who delivers a literary quotation in connection with the rustic gathering before being effaced in a passage of dialogue. This procedure characterizes the opening of the other five novels, with more or less emphasis on the aerial perspective that sees the continuities in human time. The proem to *Romola* opens with such an overview:

> More than three centuries and a half ago, in the mid-springtime of 1492, we are sure that the angel of the dawn, as he travelled with broad slow wing from the Levant to the Pillars of Hercules . . . saw the same great mountain shadows on the same valleys

---

an earlier treatment of George Eliot's "medium" (as she frequently called it) where I dealt only with her personalized narrator and how it functions like a character ("Method and Moral in George Eliot's Narrative," *Victorian Newsletter*, no. 47 [Spring 1975], 4-8).

as he has seen today. . . . The great river courses which have shaped the lives of men have hardly changed; and those other streams, the life-currents that ebb and flow in human hearts, pulsate to the same great needs, the same great loves and terrors. As our thought follows close in the slow wake of the dawn, we are impressed with the broad sameness of the human lot, which never alters in the main headings of its history— hunger and labour, seedtime and harvest, love and death.

This proem, invoking the Renaissance, "dawn," and the course of "our thought" in one breath (not to mention 1492 and the discovery of the "new" world), gives way to a process of narrative metamorphosis in which the narration is handed from a spirit called the angel of the dawn, to "our imagination," to the shade of an old Florentine, and finally to an anonymous voice that ironically cautions the shade against descending to the disappointments of embodied existence.

The later novels have similar beginnings. *Felix Holt, The Radical* opens with a Fielding-like coach ride through the neighborhood of Treby Magna ("Five and thirty years ago the glory had not yet departed from the old coach-roads"), lapses into conversation with the coachman about the passing importance of Transome Court, and then shifts in the first chapter to the waiting woman and the coach arriving at her door: a modulation from one coach to another that suggests that the story about to commence is a tributary of a wider life. *Middlemarch* begins with a prologue about St. Theresa, and a first chapter full of rural "opinion" about Miss Brooke; *The Mill on the Floss* begins with a quasi-personal memory introducing a series of opinions about the education of girls and boys; *Daniel Deronda* begins with a question ("Was she beautiful or not beautiful?") and a leisurely, three-book development around the single point, a roulette wheel in Leubronn. In each of these opening developments the distinct voice of the personalized narrator becomes part of a constellation of voices, the single consciousness part of a constellation of minds accumulated around one or another point in time or space.

This clustering of minds is something George Eliot calls atten-

239

tion to at the beginnings of her novels, but it is something that is present in the texture of every scene. Collective events punctuate *Middlemarch* as they do *Emma*, but with the difference that George Eliot stresses the potential instability introduced by multiple perspectives. An instance is the wedding party for Dorothea given by her uncle for the local gentry, where all the talking is "done in duos and trios more or less inharmonious" (ch. 10, p. 65). Another instance is the episode where Sir James, Mrs. Cadwallader, and the Brookes stand together looking out the window at Featherstone's funeral, itself a collective event (ch. 34, p. 238). In the group at the window, everybody notices something different in the scene; and the group they view, hardly a uniform communion of grief, includes very mixed responses. In this scene we not only have various viewpoints on a common subject, but this situation doubled—one group observing another group that is in turn observing a common ritual.

Several viewpoints can even be imported into an event through the mind of one character. On one such occasion Dorothea goes to get Lydgate's medical opinion concerning Casaubon. She finds Lydgate not at home, but there she does stumble for the first time upon Rosamond and Ladislaw warbling together (ch. 43). Dorothea advances to greet Ladislaw "with unmistakeable pleasure" and then, having prepared to wait while a servant fetches Lydgate, her mind "flashed in a moment over many connected memories" and she abruptly changes her mind and decides to go to Lydgate herself, her mind "evidently arrested by some sudden thought." Dorothea's own, personal response is arrested by her sudden awareness that Casaubon might disapprove and, typically, she not only takes that other viewpoint into consideration, she assumes it. She even inadvertently confirms Casaubon's viewpoint by a further reflection: "She found herself thinking with some wonder that Will Ladislaw was passing his time with Mrs. Lydgate in her husband's absence. And then she could not help remembering that he had passed some time with her under like circumstances, so why should there by any unfitness in the fact?" (p. 317). Her deduction from her own innocence to Rosamond's leads from a doubly false premise, as we know. In the first place,

Rosamond's interest in Will is not wholly innocent. In the second place, Dorothea's own relation with Will does throw some question on the fitness in the fact. The fact is, as we are bound to see here, that Casaubon has at least as much cause for jealousy as Dorothea. Our initial annoyance that Casaubon has once again spoiled Dorothea's spontaneity is qualified by an awareness that Dorothea and Will do partially deserve his suspicion.

Like most moments in George Eliot this one is explicitly saturated with consciousness. The constellations of awareness in this brief description compound rapidly to include Dorothea's awareness of Ladislaw, Dorothea's awareness of Casaubon's awareness of Ladislaw, Casaubon's awareness of Dorothea, Dorothea's awareness of a relation between Ladislaw and Mrs. Lydgate, Dorothea's awareness of analogies between herself and Mrs. Lydgate, and even the narrator's awareness of the obstacles to mutual awareness. This constellation of minds, furthermore, imported into the episode by Dorothea's reflections and by our comparative judgments on her thoughts, is dynamic and not at rest. The shifts of mental position create a sense of experience in process, contributing to the ambiguity of the event, its many-sided quality, its resistance to single interpretation, and its forward impulse towards resolution.

This multiplicity of viewpoints extends far beyond the particular cast of *Middlemarch*, even though that is quite large, to include crowds of anonymous spectators introduced in various metaphors: for example this passage describing some anonymous "others" in town who dislike Bulstrode's bending habit of listening along with the assumed superiority it implies. "If you are not proud of your cellar, there is no thrill of satisfaction in seeing your guest hold up his wine-glass to the light and look judicial. Such joys are reserved for conscious merit" (ch. 13, p. 91). Here is a constellation of awareness surrounding a glass of wine, itself a distillation from a long process: a medium for seeing the true quality of the uneasy host, and also an object in itself. The host, meanwhile, is looking at the observer, and the reader feels the presence of some relevant questions. Is there a connection between merit and observation? Is the conscious merit—the one

241

that flourishes under observation—really merit after all? One thinks of Rosamond's conscious perfections of the chapter preceding, and of Bulstrode himself. The narrator's observation about wine here is provoking and stylish; it is fun, it is at least half true. But quite apart from the complexities of judgment it introduces or develops in this brief way, the passage contributes a few more spectators to the general sum. Hundreds, probably even thousands, of viewpoints are introduced in this way by the style. Such gestures populate the novel with invisible extras and, like the various viewpoints imported by Dorothea into her scene, increase the pressure of consciousness on every moment. In this way George Eliot's novels explicitly show how the past-tense narration is a collective result. At the same time as the narrative medium is warped by individual presences, it is also wholly dependent on them.

By recognizing the close connection between time and consciousness and by binding the continuities of human experience to those of consciousness, George Eliot accepts the tenuousness of those continuities. If Lydgate and Rosamond really do each live in a world of which the other knows nothing, and if this kind of thing is unavoidable even in the best circumstances, then the possibility always exists that the continuous medium of experience will be disrupted, that its continuity will not be maintained because consensus finally is not possible. Not even the personalized narrator's presence heals this dangerous rift. It is rather in the management of the entire narrative perspective that the continuities of time and consciousness are maintained, persistently but precariously as one consensus after another is established and dissolved. These clusters of consciousness finally do all harmonize, or at least do not disagree; but we feel the resistance. Consensus is a collective trust, and individuals have the power to create lesions—those lapses of distinction that blur difference and so interfere with connections. Such lesions implicitly threaten the continuance of that common harmony.

The fragility of these crucial connections explains their importance in George Eliot's novels. When a character from one context—one household, or neighborhood, or mental world—

meets a character from another; when two minds overcome some gap of difference between them: these intersections are the moments of freedom and possibility in George Eliot's novels and also the moments of severest stress. When Dorothea visits Rosy and Farebrother visits Fred; when Adam Bede confronts Arthur Donnithorne and when Dinah visits Hetty in jail; when Romola confesses to Savonarola or confronts him; when Esther Lyon goes to Transome Court, or when Mordecai meets Deronda: these are the moments of transmission where individuals find openings from self-enclosed circuits into wider possibility.[15] Even the confrontation between one part of a personality and another is such a moment—for example, those endured by Gwendolen Harleth or Arthur Donnithorne. This creative moment in every case is associated with danger, difficulty, and conflict. It involves "the cry of soul to soul," a leap from the deck to a lifeboat, a risky venture into unknown territory carrying filaments of shared meaning.

Sequence and Difference

The separation between vantage-points in space is a clumsy metaphor for the temporal medium of narrative, and especially clumsy for the dynamics of time in George Eliot. Sequence is the great differentiator in her novels. There her temporal tides demonstrate the difficulty of mediating the differences created by linear time, and her management of narrative perspective demonstrates the way temporal continuity itself depends upon mediating consciousness.

A George Eliot novel characteristically makes temporal shifts too subtle for any linear diagram. Built into the tempo of *Adam Bede*, for example, is a distortion of natural rhythms by private histories. The more this happens, the more the common medium

---

[15] I owe this perception to Thomas Vargish. J. Hillis Miller's discussion of the "totalizing" metaphors in *Middlemarch* is suggestive, but I disagree with the formulation that they "cancel" each other's claims to validity; it is precisely the differences between them that makes possible their collaboration ("Optic and Semiotic in *Middlemarch*," in Jerome H. Buckley, ed., *The Worlds of Victorian Fiction* [Cambridge: Harvard University Press, 1975], p. 128).

243

gets disturbed. Hetty's crime is the result of an intricate series of failed communications and is then the cause of another series of dislocations. The novel begins in the golden sunshine of a natural, idyllic world and ends reduced by sorrow, spare, stripped of sensuous fullness. In the middle, during the period of greatest stress, separated characters wander apart fruitlessly searching for each other and unable to restore their common understandings. Although the novel resolves once again into the leisurely rhythms of marriage, birth, and death, after the immediate threats have passed, the losses are felt heavily. Linear time develops in response to a crisis in the heart of the community, a crisis that leaves a permanent mark. The deliberateness with which George Eliot develops this temporal dislocation demonstrates in the pattern of a whole work the intimacy between time and mutual consciousness.

The novel opens with a state of equipoise, a balance sustained partly by the attention to pairs: Arthur and Hetty, Seth and Dinah, the Hall and the Farm, the Bedes and the Poysers, Dinah's arrival and departure (Book First). But Adam's time is not Hetty's and the Hall's is not the Farm's, and these hairline fractures in temporal continuity, like the invisible differences of intention and meaning among the characters, eventually split under stress, opening dangerous, gaping holes in the connectedness of the Loamshire world. The idyllic world composed of balanced pairs is, after all, a double world, one divided by inevitable difference.

Book Second marks a reflective pause, introducing oblique perspectives on the scene, notably the narrator in Chapter 17 and at the end, Bartle Massey, another outsider. Despite these ominous deflections, however, Book Third brings the novel to its almost still center at the midsummer feast and birthday celebration: a doubly ritual event synchronizing the natural season with an important season in Arthur Donnithorne's life. This entire book takes place in a timeless, communal, extraordinary moment. It is a pause not deflective but centered; it celebrates the ordinary rhythm of a single community. The succeeding two books (fourth and fifth) contain the confrontations that blow apart the idyll. Adam fights Arthur, Arthur consequently leaves

244

Hetty, and the apparent calm is undermined by the "Hidden Dread."

The all-presupposing fact of Hetty's secret pregnancy exists for the reader in the gap between these two books. Although it is not named, this is the event around which all the rest of the action resolves. This reticence on George Eliot's part has little to do with prudery and everything to do with her belief that moral life is a process, not a point. The "natural" explanation is too easy, too careless of responsibility. The real explanations of Hetty's child murder and transportation and death are more subtle and complex than the natural explanations allow. The novel thus directs attention not to the simple located event but to the series of failed communications that produced it. Those are the substantial events, ones which, unlike Hetty's child "murder," could *not* have been altered by accident alone but only by the mutual effort of various characters.

The protracted period of crisis is conceived explicitly in terms of failed meetings. Hetty's journey in hope becomes a journey in despair. Adam departs from Loamshire on his "quest," just missing the "tidings" that reach Loamshire from outside it. Deflection follows deflection. Hetty disappears on her way to Dinah, but when Adam follows her there he finds Dinah has gone to Leeds. So far as Hetty is concerned Dinah in Leeds might as well be Dinah on the moon. Arthur, meanwhile, is nowhere: inaccessible even to the most urgent pursuit. A hopeful Adam on his "quest" is scarcely in the same world as the one where Hetty struggles with her hopeless terrors. The separateness of these paths, especially after the idyllic opening, suggests an unrecoverable fracture in the world, a threatening incapacity for the mutual communication that might reestablish these characters' common life.

At the end of Book Fifth time and space contract to a point of intensity as Hetty nears her place of execution: an intensity that is released with a vertiginous snap as Arthur rides in with the reprieve. All motion in the novel is deflected around single points that remain hidden—the moment Hetty's pregnancy begins, and the moment she delivers her child. These deflections reinforce the message that events are a process and not discrete.

245

This novel raises a general question about the relation between two utterly different times, and the possibility of transforming multiple times into a single Time, that is, a common medium sustained by a common understanding. Several commentators have noticed the dual time scheme associated with the contrast between Loamshire and Stonyshire.[16] Loamshire measures time by natural cycles. There, somehow, the consequences time brings (to Hetty in particular) run by unnoticed, so submerged are they by the clarity of foreground detail and by the aura of fanciful vision. Outside Loamshire, however, and especially in Hetty's desperate journey, the emphasis is reversed. "Time," writes Ian Adam, "in this world is not slow, with an emphasis on the recurrence of rural rhythms, but fast, recording changes and emphasizing sequence. . . . The reader . . . no longer perceives pictorial effects, those which come from the steady view of studied scene. . . . The style here is not for time recaptured, but for time running out."[17] The variety of conscious sequences appears to be at odds with any single, mutual awareness; and efforts by critics to reconstruct a single time scheme for the novel prove the impossibility of such reconstruction. Some parts remain unavailable. Only Hetty can tell her own story but, until near the end, she is able to contribute only a fragment. The final "meeting" between Adam and Dinah takes place only after some important casualties have disappeared from the scene; the final reconciliation takes place without Hetty. The terrible blank produced by that loss suggests how important a character Hetty is, how fully George Eliot recognizes her dispossession, and how seriously she takes Hetty's human claims to forbearance and sympathy.

As if to call attention to this pattern of expansion and con-

[16] For interesting treatments of the time-scheme in *Adam Bede* see Dorothy van Ghent's chapter on the novel in *The English Novel: Form and Function* (New York: Rinehart and Company, 1953); W. J. Harvey, "The Treatment of Time in *Adam Bede*," *Anglia*, 75 (1957), 429-40; Maurice Hussey, "Structure and Imagery in *Adam Bede*," *Nineteenth-Century Fiction*, 10 (1955), 115-29; and Adam, "Structure of Realisms." None of these considers the connection between time and consciousness, although Karl Kroeber suggests it in *Styles of Critical Structure* (Princeton: Princeton University Press, 1971), pp. 163-64.

[17] Adam, "Structure of Realisms," p. 142.

traction in time and space, Book Sixth (the last) recapitulates in miniature the temporal development of the preceding five books. The equipoise between the Bedes's cottage and Hall farm (chs. 49-50) gives way to a pause (chs. 51-52), only unlike the pause of Book Second this one is not oblique, and the development, like the cast, is more limited and more restrained. The next chapter (53) follows with a celebration, this time a Harvest, and in the next (ch. 54) the marriage of Dinah and Adam takes its modest place in a rapidly expanding temporal development, as the two-year gap between courtship and marriage quickly becomes nine years. The laborious time-keeping and strained attention of the crisis is succeeded by a collapse of time and an inattention to details. While the temporal development in *Adam Bede* comes to rest more decidedly than that of *Middlemarch*, the final pause scarcely obscures the central image of a community where mutual friendship fails.

Most interesting in terms of realism (perhaps most interesting psychologically as well) is the way nearly everybody just misses mutual understanding. Dinah does not understand Hetty's true plight, however much she may pity and warn her; how could she? Irwine neglects to act on his hunch about Arthur. Adam fails to see the actual Hetty through his ideal of her. The crucial moments are those meetings between separate, discrete individuals or, in Arthur's case, between discrete parts of one individual mind. Those are the moments of possibility where the saving continuities of consciousness might be sustained across the gaps that threaten them; they are the crucial interfaces to be negotiated if the inhabitants of Loamshire are to objectify a common world. But in *Adam Bede* few of the important, saving recognitions take place soon enough to preserve the consensus in its fullest flower; that flower, in fact, is associated with a delusive innocence belonging initially to a community unaware of history.

George Eliot consigns the continuities of human experience so thoroughly to a collection of minds, in fact, that she jeopardizes the temporal continuities supporting her realism. Her novels characteristically encourage readers to perform strenuous shifts of attention, zigzagging between minds, looping forward and backward in time. We are forced to be attentive and circumspect in coping with a differential system of relationships that requires heroic effort. In *Middlemarch*, perhaps the most finely textured example of her realism, the management of temporal sequence itself becomes a model of the difficulties and rewards of mediation. The questions of whether an event is the "same" event for different parties, or of whether a character is the "same" from one time to another, become urgent. By her management of the past tense George Eliot makes us feel in *Middlemarch* the power of individual consciousness to distort the medium of common experience by obsession or delay, and she makes us feel how intimately mutual consciousness is joined with the existence of common time.[18]

The most characteristic shift in George Eliot's medium is the loop that moves in two or three chapters from past, to past perfect, and back to past ("she went," "she had gone," "she went"). These fine-textured mnemonic transitions are sustained by the narrator acting as Nobody and they show how closely George Eliot can bind time and consciousness to the dynamics of form.[19] These mnemonic loops are especially evident in *Middlemarch*, and there a relatively condensed instance is the transition from Lydgate's courtship to Casaubon's marriage: a little shift with respect to space but a big one with respect to time. Framed by a narrated account of Lydgate's general intention to remain single and his

[18] See David Miller's acute analysis of how gossip substitutes for history in *Narrative and Its Discontents* (Princeton: Princeton University Press, 1981), pp. 123-24.

[19] See Barbara Hardy's fine discussion of the "three-part unit" in a single chapter, "The Surface of the Novel: Chapter 30," in Barbara Hardy, ed., *Middlemarch: Critical Approaches to the Novel* (New York: Oxford University Press, 1967), p. 169. This effect, like the personalized generalizations of the narrator, has often been treated as a mistake on George Eliot's part, even by sympathetic critics. In discussing these loops in time, for example, W. J. Harvey reprimands George Eliot for one of her chief effects, her "juggling with time," and especially for the "disconcerting switch into the historic present at climactic moments in the novel" (*The Art of George Eliot* [London: Chatto and Windus, 1961], p. 117). See Isobel Armstrong's more sympathetic discussion of the way these moments, with their "delicate, oracular dogmatism" and "curious equanimity," act to "slow down the novel in an almost processional way" ("Middlemarch: A Note on George Eliot's 'Wisdom,' " in Hardy, *Critical Approaches*, pp. 116-117).

pleased contemplation of growing success in the neighborhood, chapter 27 ends with this sentence.

> Only a few days later, when he had happened to overtake Rosamond on the Lowick Road and had got down from his horse to walk by her side until he had quite protected her from a passing drove, he had been stopped by a servant on horseback with a message calling him in to a house of some importance where Peacock had never attended; and it was the second instance of this kind.

The ultimate sentence initiates a new development. "The servant was Sir James Chettam's, and the house was Lowick Manor." The next chapter (28) begins by jumping backward in time to the point of Casaubon's return from Rome, and then, at the end (and "some weeks" later), the narrative grazes Lydgate and Rosamond again, this time from a vantage-point nearer to the group at Lowick. "So Mr. Lydgate was sent for and he came wonderfully soon, for the messenger, who was Sir James Chettam's man and knew Mr. Lydgate, met him leading his horse along the Lowick road and giving his arm to Miss Vincy" (p. 210). We return to the "same" point, separate times have been synchronized—but just barely. By the time we return to Lydgate on the road, several weeks have passed and it is no longer quite the "same" event. The "bare fact" has such different meanings for Lydgate, for Rosy, for Chettam's servant, and for the couple at Lowick, that its objective status is compromised. The transition has required some attention, and the landing is not so secure as to make us forget how tenuous is the filament of mnemonic recall, and how tenuous, even, is the consensus that gives continuity to time and objective identity to the event.

This transition is relatively easy to negotiate, but on a larger scale the narrative process poses more serious problems for the reader trying to hold things together. Book Seven ("Two Temptations"), for example, consists of two such past-perfect loops, each consisting of a three-chapter mnemonic development punctuated at the end by a single chapter dealing with a single temptation: Farebrother's in the first set, Bulstrode's in the second.

249

The first mnemonic loop (chs. 63-65) begins at Vincy's card party, one of those social occasions or intersections in the novel where the various private histories meet. We perceive Lydgate's irritability through Farebrother's sympathetic curiosity, which is shifted into a mediate position between Lydgate and the past-tense narrator. The narrative then moves backward in time to the preceding day when Rosamond had countermanded Lydgate's orders to Trumbull, written Uncle Godwin, and otherwise thwarted Lydgate's struggle for financial survival. The forward sequence in the novel is thus a reversion backwards in time, and one that deepens our understanding of Lydgate's behavior (though Farebrother is left to guess) as it draws our minds into one small act of recovery, complete in three short chapters.

But though it is small, this tiny mnemonic event becomes a virtual present so compelling that the subsequent shift back to Farebrother and the card party, only one short chapter and one short day later, seems like a tremendous step, and one we take with definite relief. After our experience of Rosamond's "torpedo contact," our arrival back, safe at Farebrother's mind, feels a bit like that moment of relief in *Paradise Lost* when Satan clambers up on the edge of chaos and sees afar "this pendant world." The clarity, the restored sense of perspective, is more than casually welcome. It is even something of a surprise to recover our footing again in the mind of Farebrother.

The promise of clarity and stability offered by Farebrother is immediately fulfilled in the following chapter (66) where he helps Fred to win the woman they both love. Leaving aside the issue of evaluating this apparently self-denying gesture (Farebrother at least thinks it is a self-confirming gesture), we can see in Farebrother's chapter a version of personal control and sympathy that stabilizes the narrative not only in moral terms but explicitly in temporal terms as well, putting an end to the tense unhappiness of the three chapters on Lydgate's marriage, and giving us some perspective on Lydgate—one at a middle distance.

The second mnemonic loop in Book Seven then immediately commences, this one concerning Bulstrode's troubles with Raffles (chs. 67-69). Again the three-chapter sequence begins and ends

250

in the same place (Bulstrode's office), and this time on the same day. This flashback, however, threatens even more vigorously than the preceding one to displace the temporal continuity, disrupting the sense of linear order and turning a past occurrence into an inescapably present one; in short, it mimics the violence and disorder of Bulstrode's condition. The flashback to Raffles' reappearance begins in the past perfect ("he had stood watching" and "had taken great care") but then slips into a simple past (Raffles "at this moment quailed"); and finally it shifts back into the past perfect again. The narrative literally doubles the viewpoint from which we look backward, disturbing any simple linear sense of time, and draws a distant moment by stages into a virtual present (one threatening step from the actual present) before distancing it again by shifting it back into the far past.

All this activity of the middle chapter functions like the chapter about Rosamond's torpedo contact, momentarily disturbing the relative distance between present and past. But this time the narrative does not recover its starting point so easily. We move into the personalized narrator's present (and our own): "Who can know how much of his most inward life is made up of the thoughts he believes other men to have about him, until that fabric of opinion is threatened with ruin?" (p. 504). Flashback and flashforward disturb linear development and maintain the disturbance until finally time and place are resolved again, back at Bulstrode's office. There the banker, having earlier refused Lydgate's appeal for money, now finds himself rejected in turn by Caleb Garth, who comes to announce Raffles' reappearance and his own resignation from Bulstrode's service.

This three-chapter loop in time, instead of giving us the flashback about Raffles in the distanced past (i.e., through someone's mind) forces the past into the virtual present and makes the exercise of recovering a vantage-point in time more strenuous. This time we do not proceed immediately to a final chapter of safe clarity, as we did with the chapter about Farebrother's temptation, but instead to the chapter where Bulstrode succumbs to temptation and effectively murders Raffles (ch. 70). What George Eliot compares in these two cases of temptation are not merely static instances but processes, each with similarities but each with different results that invite searching comparison. Each mnemonic loop distorts the reader's sense of temporal relationship and then reestablishes it, giving both a sense of depth to the individual situations and a sense of the precariousness of the vital continuities connecting person with person and past with present. The density of consciousness in the novel and its psychological depth depend mainly upon such mnemonic episodes that roll through the novel like temporal tides upon which the multiple consciousness of reader, narrator, and character alike must ride.

The final chapter of Book Seven (ch. 71) opens out to a social chorus, as word of Raffles' death spreads from Bambridge to Hawley, from Hawley to Toller, and from Toller to Mrs. Dollop to everybody. The gathering wave of public opinion includes Dorothea's resolution to aid Lydgate, and thus takes us in a new direction across a new boundary. Book Seven ends with a relaxation of tension, an expansion that opens up wider possibilities of rhythmic interchange between moments and between minds. The closely maintained relation between temporal position and mental position, the various degrees of magnitude in the shifts between one such position and another, give almost a breathing quality to the continuum of consciousness. There are many other such shifts—the one from Dorothea to Casaubon ("but why always Dorothea?") or the one where Dorothea is moved to the background of her own wedding party, in transition to Lydgate.

Even the often quoted passage in Book Seven recommending the scientific method of perpetual dilation and contraction is itself part of such a shift.

> Lydgate talked persistently when they were in his work-room, putting arguments for and against the probability of certain biological views; but he had none of those definite things to say or to show which give the way-marks of a patient uninterrupted pursuit, such as he used himself to insist on, saying that "there must be a systole and diastole in all inquiry," and that "a man's mind must be continually expanding and shrinking between the whole human horizon and the horizon of the

object glass." That evening he seemed to be talking widely and for the sake of resisting any personal bearing. . . . (P. 468.)

The statement in question itself appears in perspective, in quotes, qualified as a glimpse of the past state that Lydgate is gradually losing the capacity to recover.

The precariousness of consensus in George Eliot's novels throws a heavy burden on trust. "No soul is desolate," says the narrator in *Romola*, "as long as there is a human being for whom it can feel trust and reverence" (p. 379). All her novels deal with the politics of trust, that is, with those strategies for maintaining at least provisional agreement in a world characterized by misunderstanding and by clashes of will. The "covenant of reconciliation" envisioned by Mordecai in *Daniel Deronda* is one such strategy. Mordecai's Zionist vision for establishing a "visible community" is, he knows, "an illusion." " 'The history of our people's trust has been full of illusion,' " he says to Deronda. " '*So it might be with my trust, if you would make it an illusion. But you will not*' " (*Deronda*, pp. 596-97, 560). His vision requires an answering vision, in order to be confirmed, objectified, realized. But in attempting to ground an entire community and make it "visible," Mordecai's efforts are on the grand side. The politics of trust generally occupy George Eliot on a humbler scale.

Most often the harmonies of social life amount to little more than a negotiated settlement, just this side of blackmail, as in this dialogue between Rosamond Vincy and her brother Fred.

"I suppose you are not going out riding today?" said Rosamond, lingering a little after her mamma was gone.

"No; why?"

"Papa says I may have the chestnut to ride now."

"You can go with me to-morrow, if you like. Only I am going to Stone Court, remember."

"I want to ride so much, it is indifferent to me where we go." Rosamond really wished to go to Stone Court, of all other places.

"Oh, I say, Rosy," said Fred, as she was passing out of the

253

room, "if you are going to the piano, let me come and play some airs with you."

"Pray do not ask me this morning."

"Why not this morning?"

"Really, Fred, I wish you would leave off playing the flute. A man looks very silly playing the flute. And you play so out of tune."

"When next any one makes love to you, Miss Rosamond, I will tell him how obliging you are."

"Why should you expect me to oblige you by hearing you play the flute, any more than I should oblige you to oblige me by not playing it?"

"And why should you expect me to take you out riding?"

This question led to an adjustment, for Rosamond had set her mind on that particular ride.   (Ch. 11, p. 76.)

This passage, including its ironical musical metaphor, dramatizes a minimal sort of agreement: hardly consensus of a very stable or expansive sort, but a valuable negotiation of a difference nonetheless. Rosamond's concession, made against the grain for a desired end, is an epitome of the political bargaining that takes place in variations throughout the novel: Raffles' negotiations with Bulstrode, Featherstone's with Mary, and, immediately after this scene, Mr. Vincy's negotiations with Bulstrode for a letter exonerating Fred.

The harmonies between characters appear and dissolve, like the temporal patterns of the narration. They accomplish provisional consensus, but the resistance to more stable coalitions remains. Like Daniel Deronda's ideal of "separateness with communication" (*Deronda*, p. 792) George Eliot's moral and aesthetic ideal requires the most strenuous, heroic effort of consciousness. Perhaps the best that can be hoped for are provisional harmonies of the kind established, broken, and reestablished between Dorothea and Celia, as they disagree over the family jewels, over Casaubon, or over plans. "They quarrel and make up their quarrel, and then they quarrel again" says David Carroll, and his description suggests the tension always present in any consensus

254

of views, especially the temporal consensus, achieved in any of George Eliot's novels.[20]

George Eliot's narrative time cannot easily be grasped as a single, linear sequence. Her temporal developments involve considerable subordinating activity involving recollective loops that confuse the reader's sense of clock time and create an atmospheric world of consciousness dependent upon the motions of subjective minds. The density of the mental continuum she thus establishes, both by various constellations of consciousness and by the continuous zigzag of narrative between past and present, forces us to acknowledge the intimate connection between time and individual awareness and even to acknowledge the precariousness of any common consent sustained by this experience of time. George Eliot even qualifies the conventions of realism by calling attention to the fact that the invisible community of consent literally objectifies the world. Finally, though, she is committed to maintaining the system of common consent; she threatens its existence in order to demonstrate both its value and the need for eternal vigilance if this common medium is to survive.

The coordinates of common life in George Eliot explicitly rest on the human power of consent, and therefore on a changing, fluctuating support. "It is hard," she wrote to a friend, "to believe long together that anything is 'worth while' unless there is some eye to kindle with our own, some brief word uttered now and then to imply that what is infinitely precious to us is precious alike to another mind. I fancy that, to do without that guarantee, one must be rather insane—one must be a bad poet, or a spinner of impossible theories or an inventor of impossible machinery."[21]

---

[20] "*Middlemarch* and the Externality of Fact," in Ian Adam, ed., *This Particular Web: Essays on Middlemarch* (Toronto: University of Toronto Press, 1975), p. 77. See also Robert Kiely's fine discussion of "interrupted dialectics" in "The Limits of Dialogue in *Middlemarch*," in Buckley, *Worlds of Victorian Fiction*, esp. pp. 106-108, and Robert Caserio's treatment of threats to the significance of action in George Eliot, in *Plot, Story, and The Novel* (Princeton: Princeton University Press, 1979), especially pp. 105-106.

[21] *The George Eliot Letters*, ed. Gordon S. Haight, 9 vols. (New Haven: Yale University Press, 1954-1978), IV, 119.

Upon such slender meetings of mind the entire social network depends.

From beginning to end, George Eliot's narratives consist of the more or less inharmonious jostling among various minds. A certain amount has been said about the disappearance of community in her later novels, but that presupposes its more secure presence in her early ones. My discussion of *Adam Bede* makes clear how extensive even in that novel is the misunderstanding and distortion of common terms. Perhaps it is the explicitly political nature of the address to problems of community in *Daniel Deronda* that has invited the perception of change.[22] But however her treatment changes during the course of her career, George Eliot's attention to the real conflict of valid claims remains constant. Mutual resistance of the sort practiced among Mordecai and his friends at the Philosopher's Club is a form of mutual life. The fact that their community thrives on conflict is one symptom of its vitality, and a foremost symptom of weakness and disorder in George Eliot's characters is the inability to gain strength from such collisions. Mutual resistance benefits all sides and requires no resolution beyond the achieved harmony that results from mutual recognition.

[22] In Raymond Williams's view, "the real step that has been taken is the withdrawal from any full response to an existing society," leaving only the past and private sensibility ("The Knowable Community in George Eliot's Novels," *Novel*, 2, no. 3 [Spring 1969], p. 268); the "known community" has become "an uneasy contract, in language, with another interest and another sensibility" (p. 261). This seems to me merely another way of saying that George Eliot's last novel is most explicit about a theme deep in all her work, namely that the only real community is the invisible one of consciousness and shared culture. Avrom Fleishman deals in *Fiction and the Ways of Knowing* with the centrality of community as a problem in *Deronda* (Austin: University of Texas Press, 1978). George Eliot's treatment of quattrocento Florence in *Romola*, as Hugh Wittemeyer sees, is one more confirmation that "George Eliot would have had no sympathy with those who altered and finally broke the traditional Renaissance conventions of humanism and representational illusion" (*George Eliot and the Visual Arts* [New Haven: Yale University Press, 1979], p. 19).

The Example of Henry James

While realistic conventions richly demonstrate the power of consensus, the act of consensus itself stands in mid-air as an heroic act of faith. The more an author impresses upon readers the arbitrariness of that act, the more its power is compromised. The work of Henry James is illustrative because he still asserts the power of mutual agreement, though more provisionally than George Eliot. He remains in the tradition of realism, however, especially in comparison with two of his contemporaries, Joseph Conrad and Thomas Hardy, who both show in different ways how the unintelligible or irrational forces in human experience act to crowd and compromise the rationalizing power of consciousness.

Henry James strains the consensus of realism to the breaking-point. In his eminently civilized and social world the tensions between separate viewpoints become greater even than they do in George Eliot's. The conflict between different views in *Middlemarch* can be turned to creative uses, but in the novels I touch on here—*The Portrait of a Lady*, *The Ambassadors*, and *The Golden Bowl*—James increases the violence of such conflict, sometimes pressing the potential discord between different viewpoints into collision course. If it is true, as T. S. Eliot said, that "the real hero in any of James' stories is a social entity of which men and women are all constituents" (this holds as well for Jane Austen), it is also true that the various private understandings in his novels

257

threaten the continuities of the universal "human" society implied by realistic time.[1] Most readers will recognize the divisive strength of what Manfred Mackenzie calls "secret society in Henry James." For the American abroad, Europe is "an unofficial secret society," and so is marriage and "perhaps sexual relations in general."[2] There is a psychic territoriality in James. His novels all take place in the invisible world of consciousness, and there the continuities between one mind and another can seem nearly impossible to sustain.

Consensus is a matter of the greatest difficulty in James. He can show us what goes on inside a single mind interestingly, compellingly; but the exchange between minds, the meetings that establish a common discourse or a common medium of exchange, are centers of strain and difficulty. These moments, similar to the kind in George Eliot that are the growing points of the novels, generate in James's novels more acute stress. His scruples concerning both point of view and serial unfolding of truth tend to make difficult the synchronizations crucial to realism. He produces a plurality of viewpoints in a past-tense series, but he provides little mediation. No adjudication reconciles Strether's final view of Chad and Madame de Vionnet with his earlier ones, and even less adjudication seems possible between his point of view and theirs. The realist agreement, if it is possible, remains implicit and often unconfirmed by action. James's forms threaten to fall apart at every moment, syntactically stretched to the limit, as he portrays the immediacy of experience and the constant struggle for mental footholds and generalizations.

In the stylization of his language, most readers feel intensely the powerful dissociative currents of James. Though I do not want to take space for an extended analysis of his style, it should be plain to anyone who has attempted even the simplest of his novels how much continuity is a matter of style and consequently a matter of considerable precariousness. The sentences writhe and

---

[1] T. S. Eliot quoted in F. W. Dupee, ed., *The Question of Henry James* (New York: Henry Holt and Company, 1945), p. 100.

[2] Manfred Mackenzie, "Communities of Knowledge: Secret Society in Henry James," *ELH*, 39, no. 2 (June 1972), 147-68, esp. 152.

shift, turn their referents in unexpected directions, and lose sight of their beginnings before their endings appear. One chapter of *The Golden Bowl* (I, xiii) ends, "they moved together away." This locution does two contradictory things simultaneously, introducing two tiny movements that conflict rather than agree. Learning to follow long and often unpunctuated sequences of such language involves certain shifts of expectation concerning the referential function of language and its linear possibilities, shifts that often take readers some time to master. New readers especially find the first hundred pages hard going, after which something happens— something like learning to stay close to the moment—and the difficulty gives way.

The style not only suspends meaning during periods of syntactical accumulation, it hovers between meanings with some pivot word that disturbs the accumulation, the *enchaînement* of the syntax. Even where a choice between two meanings is finally made, the sustained alternative has, by its very existence, asserted a threat to resolution. The sentence, like other things in life, suddenly shows its capacity to be read two ways, and one must struggle to resolve an ambiguity that, because it has existed, continues to haunt or to enrich the sense of possibility. We work so hard for the resolution that achieving it seems a triumph over potential disorder and even breakdown. One example is this sentence from *The Golden Bowl* that begins innocently enough but by the end involves us in a difficulty, one compounded by the tiny word "of" in the last phrase.

> Fawns, as it had been for him, and as Maggie and Fanny Assingham had both been attested, was out of the world, whereas the scene actually about him, with the very sea a mere big booming medium for excursions and aquariums, affected him as so plump in the conscious centre that nothing could have been more complete for representing that pulse of life which they had come to unanimity at home on the subject of their advisedly not hereafter forgetting.[3]

[3] *The Golden Bowl* (Harmondsworth: Penguin Books, 1966), p. 170. All subsequent references will be to this edition and will be included parenthetically in the text.

259

In the last phrase we are, to use a Jamesian locution, "thrown" into some confusion by that word *of*. The word can refer in two directions (backward to "pulse of life" and forward to "not here-after forgetting"), and we have to sort it out.

At such moments our syntactical projections fail us with such suddenness that we experience a little shock of the sort that Maggie Verver worries about elsewhere, that shock of being "lost" without hope of recovery. It is this kind of action on the syn-tactical level, I think, that accounts for much of the pleasure of reading James and validates the vocabulary of violence—like being "lost"—that otherwise seems oddly out of place on the level of content. The mobility this syntactical action introduces into the past-tense narration gives an effect of arrest to the action of plot. What moves is consciousness guided by language; the action is in the language that flows around the figures, laps and withdraws, always busy, always seeking, like water finding its way into every crack and onto every level.

The experience of overall sequence resembles this experience of the sentence. Closely following the mind of a central character, *The Portrait of a Lady* and *The Ambassadors* follow the sense they make of experience until the point when, like a blow, the char-acter accidentally meets with an entirely different vision of what she or he had seen. When Isabel Archer and Lambert Strether look at things through others' eyes momentarily, the moment revolutionizes their entire consciousness. We go here a step be-yond Rosamond Vincy's or Gwendolen Harleth's revolution, the one of encounter with opposition that leaves their world in ruins. Here we have no self-conscious narrator providing a secure future for the event and a bridge of mediation between reader and text, but only the slender filament of the past tense and one that is twisted out of simple linear development by the language. The whole novel moves in each case to the moment that introduces questions, not answers, and that leaves each with more than a vague sense of the world somehow being cracked.

Isabel's revelations concerning Osmond, though they happen incrementally, require of her an adjustment that is not matter for compromise. James's interest is in the clash; he does not engage in dialectic, but instead characteristically divides into mutually exclusive pairs. *The Portrait of a Lady* attends to the process of education that brings Isabel to the point of questioning, and leaves her there. The one moment of mutual understanding that she does achieve occurs with Ralph Touchett when he is at the point of death. Characters like Ralph and Milly Theale for whom there is no more time, no inviting future, concentrate most intensely on the moment, and only there can Isabel find a mutual understanding.

Lambert Strether's pattern resembles Isabel's. Going to Europe to save Chad from the bad old world, he pursues his mission on the basis of certain assumptions. Suddenly, at one stroke, he discovers he has made a profound mistake. He comes up against a fact he had not accounted for, an indigestible piece of evidence that revolutionizes the entire structure of explanation making up his consciousness. When he and Madame de Vionnet sit down together, face to face, they do not do so in the same spirit that Emma met Frank Churchill at the end of Austen's novel but in a spirit of confrontation. Strether must undertake a massive effort of reconstruction. Even more than the earlier novel this one suggests the potential violence of meetings between minds and suggests that the results of experience are not significantly capable of being shared.

Dizzying leaps between minds and rapid, long-distance, destabilizing shifts between action and thought become a central preoccupation in these novels. Percy Lubbock makes this point elegantly, describing James's narrative treatment of Strether. "He sees, and we with him; but when he *talks* it is almost as though we were outside him and away from him altogether." The disembodiment of narrative consciousness familiar in realism remains the property of the central character whose mind we follow closely; the moment of truth involves a confrontation that nearly demolishes that consciousness by radically undermining its power. Things simply are not the way Isabel or Strether thought they were; and how they are remains in doubt. Comparing Strether's education with those in George Eliot, Jerome Thale comments that "Strether's outburst to Little Bilham surprises us because,

261

though we have seen most of the process that leads up to it, we have not understood the continuity, the meaning and direction of Strether's experience."[4] Both Lubbock and Thale capture the violence of the shift between consciousness and new experience that James constantly urges upon us. He makes us feel the tension involved in that process, and he attends far more to the tension of the process than to the stability of the result.

The Golden Bowl, the novel on which I will concentrate briefly, demonstrates fully and deliberately that the acknowledgment of a mutual gaze is not something to take for granted. James divides the novel between two points of view and into two books: Book First, The Prince; and Book Second, The Princess. He thus establishes two points of view that in the fully realistic novel would objectify the world by training two points of view on it. In realism their consensus sustains the objectivity of the world. But James uses the device differently. At the center of this novel is an object, the golden bowl, which becomes a token meaning radically different things to different people. Charlotte Stant intends it as a double pledge, confirming her secret relation to the Prince at the same time as she gives it as a wedding present to the Prince and Maggie Verver. To the Prince it is a flawed token. To Maggie it becomes a sign of betrayal. In realism the object's function is to collect various viewpoints into consensus, but in this novel the converging viewpoints destroy it. The mounting tension between Maggie and her husband, one capitalized by Charlotte Stant, Adam Verver, and the Assinghams, shatters the flawed central object. The more the whole matter of viewpoint and agreement receives attention, the more tentative and inharmonious is the result. The two central viewpoints are like vectors of energy that converge to smash this token of mutual life. It is a token with too many irreconcilable meanings.

In scrutinizing the process whereby a mind touches another mind, and in recognizing the difficulty of that achievement, James scrutinizes the central convention of his art and, though essen-

[4] Percy Lubbock, The Craft of Fiction (New York: Viking Press, 1957), p. 166; Jerome Thale, The Novels of George Eliot (New York: Columbia University Press, 1959), p. 141.

tially he does not abandon the premises of realism, takes a turn toward the self-reflexiveness of modern fiction. The whole action of *The Golden Bowl* concerns the single fulcrum shift that reorients an entire group and redraws the coordinates of the world. It is an action invisible to the eye, like that of planetary orbits, but one more monumental than more obvious actions, like Fanny Assingham smashing the bowl.

The difficulty of mutual gaze is a theme sounded through the novel in those moments of meeting or avoidance. This passage is typical of the way James suggests the tremendous effort of keeping up that mutual gaze.

> The measure of this, at least, had been given, that each would fight to the last for the protection, for the perversion, of any real anxiety. She had confessed, instantly, with her humbugging grin, not flinching by a hair, meeting his eyes as mildly as he met hers, she had confessed to her fancy that they might both, he and his son-in-law, have welcomed such an escapade, since they had both been so long so furiously domestic.
>
> (P. 359.)

The violence of the language for psychic stress belies the mildness of manner, producing a sense of strain and effort. "Only *see*, see that *I* see . . ." (p. 425), Maggie wants to say to the Prince at the first step in their crisis, but even at their final meeting—the one confirming their marriage, which is to say their mutual understanding—the sense of danger remains. The Prince says, " 'See?' I see nothing but *you*" (p. 547), and Maggie's triumph here has a power too great for her to sustain a mutual gaze. "And the truth of it had, with this force, after a moment, so strangely lighted his eyes that, as for pity and dread of them, she buried her own in his breast." Mutual gaze seems most possible when it belies what is behind the face, most intense and difficult when it is direct and mutual. James does not depart from the terms of realism in this, but he subjects them to more rigorous examination and uncovers the deep sources of strain in the convention.

One such source, the disembodiment of consciousness, becomes central to the technique of *The Golden Bowl*. Many of the

263

no actual dramatic expression at all. The silent conversation of consciousness appears in the "might have been" speeches—probably the majority of the speeches in the novel—in which someone thinks what they would like to say without actually saying it. "She wanted to say to him. . . . Only *see*, see that *I* see . . ." but she does not actually say it in the sense that she does not vocalize it to the Prince. This speech remains a resonance, a possibility ungrounded. So many of the speeches are confined in this way to a momentary and private reflection that it becomes difficult to locate oneself in time and space. All speeches are bracketed, ontologically in question.

Actual meetings, actual speeches are thus endlessly delayed in *The Golden Bowl.* Even the central confrontation is an event that takes over a hundred pages to become explicit. Left alone with Maggie and the broken bowl in chapter 34, the Prince learns that Maggie "knows" his secret. But when she confronts him, Maggie only initiates a process that will restore the understanding that has been broken between them. She tells him she has " 'ceased—' "

> "That you've ceased?" With her pause, in fact, she had fairly made him press her for it.
> "Why, to be as I was. *Not* to know." (P. 437.)

Maggie's magnificent move in this scene is to stop with the confrontation half complete, giving play to the lines of development and keeping the possibilities open. "I know nothing but what you tell me," says the equally cagey Prince.

> "Then I told you all I intended. Find out the rest—!"
> "Find it out—?" He waited.
> She stood before him a moment—it took that time to go on. Depth upon depth of her situation, as she met his face, surged and sank within her; but with the effect somehow, once more, that they rather lifted her than let her drop. She had her feet somewhere, through it all—it was her companion, absolutely, who was at sea. (P. 438.)

This confrontation has elemental qualities: it is associated with the difference between sea and land. At the same time Maggie maintains an exquisite equilibrium in their connection, like the full cup that repeatedly comes into the language of the novel to suggest the trembling brinkmanship played out at the level of consciousness.

Not until chapter 41 does the Prince tacitly acknowledge Maggie's discovery. He tells her that Charlotte does not know from him that Maggie knows and Maggie replies, "Am I to take from you then that you accept and recognize my knowledge?" (p. 534). This is not mere preciousness. The question is a real one in the Jamesian universe, and it amounts to an ontological question. Do you accept and recognize my knowledge? The fact that a choice exists opens an abyss around each private consciousness. He could choose not to recognize her knowledge, or meet her gaze. And that refusal would have ontological consequences for Maggie, as it does eventually for the weaker Charlotte Stant. To be left out of the mutual agreement is deeply threatening in James, and it is also quite possible. Left out of mutual understanding, Maggie could never live out her own fullest understanding and thus she could not fully *be* in her relation with the Prince and Charlotte.

The flawed bowl is not the only casualty in the novel. Charlotte Stant ends being completely excluded from the mutual understanding between Maggie and the Prince: perhaps the most subtle, tacit agreement in all fiction. Charlotte has proved herself by nature disqualified for participation. She begins the novel an initiate in a secret society that excludes Maggie, but Charlotte loses her place to Maggie without ever knowing how and why or even that she has done so. "The vision loomed" of Charlotte "having gropingly to go on, always not knowing and not knowing!" The effect of James's repeated insistence on knowing, like the effect for the Prince of Maggie's "repeated distinct 'know, know', on his nerves" (p. 436), stresses the importance of knowledge mutually held. In breaking the love affair, Maggie's business literally is "the business of cultivating continuity" (p. 354) and

265

getting others to live in it. "Her consistency" is her defense (p. 395), and in winning out over Charlotte she creates a world for others to live in, the Prince consciously and the weaker Charlotte unknowingly.

James turns his relentless gaze on the heart of realistic conventions when he suggests that personal identity depends on tacit agreements stretched like a fine tissue between individuals. This is the import of the climactic scene between Maggie and her father when she gets him to volunteer the action she most wants without openly eliciting it and in terms almost erotic: to "do it *all* for her" (p. 483). This feat preserves the separateness essential to communication in a way more explicit communication could never do.

> This was the moment, in the whole process of their mutual vigilance, in which it decidedly *most* hung by a hair that their thin wall might be pierced by the lightest wrong touch. It shook between them, this transparency, with their very breath; it was an exquisite tissue, but stretched on a frame, and would give way the next instant if either so much as breathed too hard. (P. 480.)

But they do not breathe too hard. The fragile boundary between Maggie and Adam Verver preserves their mutual integrity and so their mutual relationship. Stretched on its frame, the veil trembles and holds.

This vision of identity, one central to the convention of realism, is something the Prince has to learn. In undergoing his shift of allegiance the Prince learns more than just where his bread is buttered. He learns a different way to "*be.*" His early program for self-development ("It's always a question of doing the best for oneself one can—without injury to others," p. 67) turns out to be unworkable, corrupt in the worst hands and corrupting even in the best. In Chapter One he muses to himself,

> What should he do if he were to ask her frankly this afternoon what *was*, morally speaking, behind their veil? It would come to asking what they expected him to do. She would answer

him probably: "Oh, you know, it's what we expect you to *be!*" on which he would have no resource but to deny his knowledge. Would *that* break the spell, his saying he had no idea? What idea in fact could he have? He also took himself seriously—made a point of it; but it wasn't simply a question of fancy and pretension. His own estimate he saw ways, at one time and another, of dealing with; but theirs, sooner or later, say what they might, would put him to the practical proof.

(P. 43.)

The practical proof "would naturally be proportionate to the cluster of his attributes." This is a view of personality inconsistent with the Ververs', and with the realist enterprise. It is one that echoes Madame Merle's: "There's no such thing as an isolated man or woman; we're each of us made up of some cluster of appurtenances. What shall we call our 'self'? Where does it begin? where does it end? It overflows into everything that belongs to us—and then it flows back again. I know," she goes on, "a large part of myself is in the clothes I choose to wear. I've a great respect for *things!*" (*Portrait*, I, xix.)

This view is precisely the one that Maggie and her father—two Americans—resist at the crucial moment. Lest there be any mistake about relative importance, Adam's collected attributes are reviewed by Maggie a moment after the one in which they preserve the "exquisite tissue" between them. It is precisely his attributes that he refuses "to call her attention to. The 'successful', beneficent person, the beautiful, bountiful, original, dauntlessly wilful great citizen, the consummate collector and infallible high authority he had been and still was" (p. 484). This collection of appurtenances, while scarcely irrelevant, still does not make him what he is, though it helps to make him separate. The important thing for both Maggie and her father is the final exchange. " 'I believe in you more than anyone. . . . Than anyone at all.' She kept nothing of it back now, met his eyes over it . . . 'And that's the way, I think, you believe in me' " (p. 485). To be a personality rather than a cluster of appurtenances certainly cannot be taken for granted; it is something even the elegant Prince must learn, and something fragile, all-important, and dependent upon mutual recognitions like this between Maggie and her father. Without this exercise of being—not to *do*, as the Prince mused, but to *be*—one's doom is like Charlotte's (and Madame Merle's before her), "to arrange appearances." That is why Charlotte Stant's "punctuality of performance . . . was her weakness and her deep misfortune" (p. 61).

In this scrupulous attention to being, as distinct from doing, Henry James remains in the traditions I have been considering, but at the outer limit of possibility and the frontier of stress. The problem of consciousness as he treats it is so exquisite, in fact, that it can best be considered only apart from the ordinary constraints of physical existence. He deals in consciousness pared down to essentials. In *The Portrait of a Lady* he takes a young person who is intelligent, independent, and ambitious; he removes the ordinary obstacles to development, such as ignorance, poverty, or disinterest in shaping a future; and then he sees what she will do, given a "chance to develop" (p. 38). In *The Golden Bowl* he presents people free from the constraints of physical need. In James the drama has been pared down to the rub of mind on mind and to the vectors of invisible energy between them. Except in the most tenuous way, however, Charlotte Stant finally does not live in the same world as Maggie and the Prince; she has departed vanquished into another, and one utterly remote from Fawns. In *The Portrait of a Lady*, Madame Merle is vanquished in a similar fashion by Isabel.

James focuses attention on the tacit agreements essential to realistic conventions but without relinquishing them. The late nineteenth century, however, produced increasingly radical challenges to the idea of consensus and to the kinds of rationalization it entails, challenges evident in novels by two of James's contemporaries, Conrad and Hardy. Both consider human society in the context of nature, and they thus include in the temporal medium what is not human, what has no point of view. In such a context we see more of the ineffectuality of distance and deferral. Points of view taken together in sequence do not add up; the margin of "mystery"—a favored word of both novelists—is too great, and the individual consciousness too solitary to support strongly the consensus of realism. The social norm, where there is one, is the more Spartan consensus of solidarity and endurance, and the conception of individual power is more modest. In various ways Conrad and Hardy turn away from the conventions and values of realism toward the discontinuities and surfaces so evident in later more deliberately antirealistic fiction.

Conrad turns attention away from the rationalization of mysteries to the mystery of rationalization itself. He considers nature "purely spectacular," without ethical coloration, and he devotes considerable attention to this mindless brilliance in order to suggest the limits of rational enterprise. He characteristically sets his novels at some outpost of progress, and he tests human character at this margin of experience; here it reveals capacities for brutality undreamed of in the human city, where we "step delicately" between the butcher and the policeman. The jungle presents an unmediatable challenge to Kurtz in *Heart of Darkness*, with his ideas of progress made by "all Europe," or to Lord Jim's faith in an ideal of conduct derived from his parson father. The jungle contains a human heart of darkness, a horror of elemental brutality that drives Marlow out of his "conception of existence," but he crawls back into it as into a shell; "one must—don't you know?" (*Lord Jim*, ch. 33). Looked at from this margin, society and its arrangements appear mainly to be a refuge from the elements.

For Hardy, whatever force governs human affairs it is not human will or even any intelligible force but rather some "ingenious machinery of the Gods for reducing human possibilities of amelioration to a minimum" (*The Mayor of Casterbridge*, ch. 44). Experience does not turn to knowledge in Hardy, and the characters like Farfrae or Elizabeth-Jane who manage to rationalize their experience do so through ignorance or fear. Henchard, by contrast, fails to rationalize his experience, and this failure gives him stature. His past is a nemesis that he meets with a kind of heroic resistance. At the end, when he arrives at last on the same hilltop where he began, the distance he has come has produced no capital; it has merely made him a spectator in his own life,

269

and for Henchard that clearly is the beginning of the end. His power is rooted to place and is associated with physical power. In a world of corn-factors and glib mediation he is out of his element.

Time is cyclic in Hardy, not linear, and apparently inspired by outrageous forces. Memory is of little use against them. In *Tess of the D'Urbervilles*, the heroine's past is a curse that hounds her with a false name. Her brief season of happiness at the dairy with Angel lasts only so long as they remain ignorant of each other's "secret" and do not attempt "to pry into each other's history" (ch. 19). Perspective has a positively evil influence, being associated with the two men who objectify Tess: Angel from his "Andean altitude" and Alec watching her from a distance like a vulture hovering over her failing will. In the cases of Alec and Angel, "perspective" is merely the destructive power of false interpretations. When Angel finally arrives on his hilltop at the end, this perspective allows him to see an omen of death, the black flag announcing Tess's execution.

These shifts in value influence the form of Conrad's and Hardy's novels. They are full of discontinuities that disturb the clarity of rationalizing consciousness, even that of the past-tense narrator. Given Conrad's indictment of the abstracted and imperial consciousness in *Heart of Darkness*, it is not surprising to find that his narrator is somebody rather than Nobody. Conrad's personalized narrator, Marlow, enters the tales of Kurtz and Lord Jim shortly after they have begun, and eventually he takes over the past-tense narrative that initially included him. This interpolated teller also introduces an interpolated tale—that of Marlow and the friends who listen sometimes impatiently to his "inconclusive experiences" and who share the "bond of the sea." This interest repeatedly interrupts the ostensible story of Kurtz or of Jim, temporarily supplanting it. In general the narrated episodes in *Lord Jim* have tangential relations to one another, creating an effect of superimposition that confuses the sense of sequence and gives it an instability for which the sea is the familiar metaphor. The result is an emphasis on the present rather than the past, and on mystery not memory. Memory is even a liability, as Jim dem-

270

onstrates by his dogged, self-destructive, and perhaps heroic refusal to forget his weak moment, even though, as Marlow irritably
insists, he is the "only one who remembers." Whatever the rationalization behind his quixotic fidelity, it is not one that is
shareable. Its depths are "too dark," as Marlow says of Kurtz's
history, "too dark altogether." At the end of *Lord Jim* Marlow
hears, uncomprehending, of Jim's final triumphant glance; this
narrator does not open Jim's secret to discourse and is left with
only questions—"who knows?" Jim is consigned to a privacy in-
violable and complete.

Hardy's past-tense narrator maintains an aerial distance, but
it is one of ironic overview rather than of historical insight. From
this eminence all time and space are visible, and history is only
a "monotonous average" of pain (*Tess*, ch. 2). This narrator
introduces mythic or archetypal patterns that cut across the continuities of the past-tense narration. By comparing the operator
of a steam-thresher with "a creature from Tophet" serving a "Plu-
tonic master," or by invoking the gods or Roman gladiators and
Christian martyrs, the narrator moves rapidly between remote
points, distorting relative size and importance, creating disjunc-
tions, and collapsing historical sequence. The controlling consciousness has mobility, while the characters seem fixed in a
system that summons visionary rather than historical powers, an
effect evident in this description of Tess riding in her cart to
market: "The mute procession past her shoulders of trees and
hedges became attached to fantastic scenes outside reality, and
the occasional heave of the wind became the sigh of some immense sad soul, coterminous with the universe in space, and with
history in time" (ch. 4). Though Tess is supposedly moving, she
is really standing still while the breath of some dismal force moves
around her.

Hardy's descriptions—the opening passage of *The Mayor of
Casterbridge* is a well-known example—emphasize the discreteness
of details; things have an atmosphereless quality that suggests
emblematic value without actually producing it. Henchard's "brown
corduroy jacket," waistcoat with "white horn buttons," "straw
hat overlaid with black-glazed canvas," "measured, springless walk,"

271

"cynical indifference," and "interchanging fustian folds, now in the left leg, now in the right," have almost equal value, and that value is highly concrete—its discreteness in each case emphasized by selective attention to detail and an almost studious neglect of the relations between them. At other times Hardy creates disjunctiveness by compounding descriptive details to the point where they arrest attention and, with it, the sense of forward motion. The compounding horror of the dead and dying pheasants in *Tess* (ch. 41), for example, together with its emblematic significance for Tess's own fate, rivets attention by its violence and distorts the sense of continuity. Hardy emphasizes the qualitative differences between places and times in still other ways. When Tess crosses from the Vale of Blackmoor into the Vale of Froom, for example, Hardy tells us that each has a different atmosphere and set of characteristics. The streams of Blackmoor were "slow, silent, often turbid," while the "Froom waters were clear as the pure River of Life shown to the Evangelist, rapid as the shadow of a cloud." Froom Vale lacks "the intensely blue atmosphere" of Blackmoor "and its heavy soils and scents; the new air was clear bracing, ethereal. . . . There the water-flower was the lily; the crowfoot here" (ch. 16). The distances between places and times are not the quantitative distances of realism but more qualitative ones that resist its characteristic reductions.

Common experience in Conrad and Hardy is reduced to the common fate of mortality. Rationalizations may differ mysteriously and irreconcilably, but they all end in the same death. In Conrad solidarity is a residual form of consensus; in Hardy even this form seems tenuous. Although Marlow finally recognizes the arbitrariness of civilized ideals at the end of *Heart of Darkness*, he remains committed to them in a new spirit. Once he hated lies for their flavor of mortality, but in the jungle he learns something about truth that puts new value on artifice. When he lies to Kurtz's Intended for the sake of the "saving illusion," he accepts his mortality and thus his primary common bond, the bond of fellowship against the darkness. Kurtz's crime is not his ideas but his solitude, his belief in his power as a solitary agent. And even his crime, after his admission of it, seems secondary to the "pitiless and rapacious folly" of those pilgrims of progress who never sus-pect their need of illusion.

To return to Henry James, he imagines "the horror" differently from Conrad. The horror of the *Turn of the Screw* is that no consensus is possible. Contradictory explanations, equally bal-anced, appear to the mind in a linear sequence within which there is no secret that can be exposed to mediate them. Against this horror—the impossibility of any rationalization—not even solidarity may be adequate resistance; in any case, James does not settle for solidarity. He asserts the full powers of rationalizing consciousness in the face of what challenges or thwarts it and in the face of solipsism and solitude. At the same time, however, he does allow for unrecoverable differences of the kind that, like the differences between Charlotte Stant and Maggie Verver, make impossible any all-inclusive consensus. Common time, implied by the past tense, is reduced by James from the mnemonic loops of George Eliot to a smaller circuit, one that is often inseparable from the progression of James's language itself and keeps very close to the moment. James seems keenly aware that the temporal gap to be mediated in realism—the "necessary absence," which Richardson finds fundamental for initiating a correspondence—may actually be an insurmountable obstacle; and that the idea of mediation itself is a fiction that merely conceals the fact that no bonds can exist. In *The Golden Bowl* the Prince would have only to say, "I do not accept your knowledge," to bring down the mutual understanding that the entire novel works to establish. He does not, but the fact that this possibility hovers continually in the novel makes the moments of mutual understanding as powerful as they are tenuous.

INDEX

LIBRARY OF CONGRESS CATALOGING IN PUBLICATION DATA

Ermarth, Elizabeth, 1939-
  Realism and consensus in the English novel.

  Includes index.
  1. English fiction—History and criticism.
  2. Realism in literature. I. Title. II. Title:
Consensus in the English novel.
PR830.R4E75   1983   823'.009'12   82-61360
ISBN 0-691-06560-8